Martha Skelton

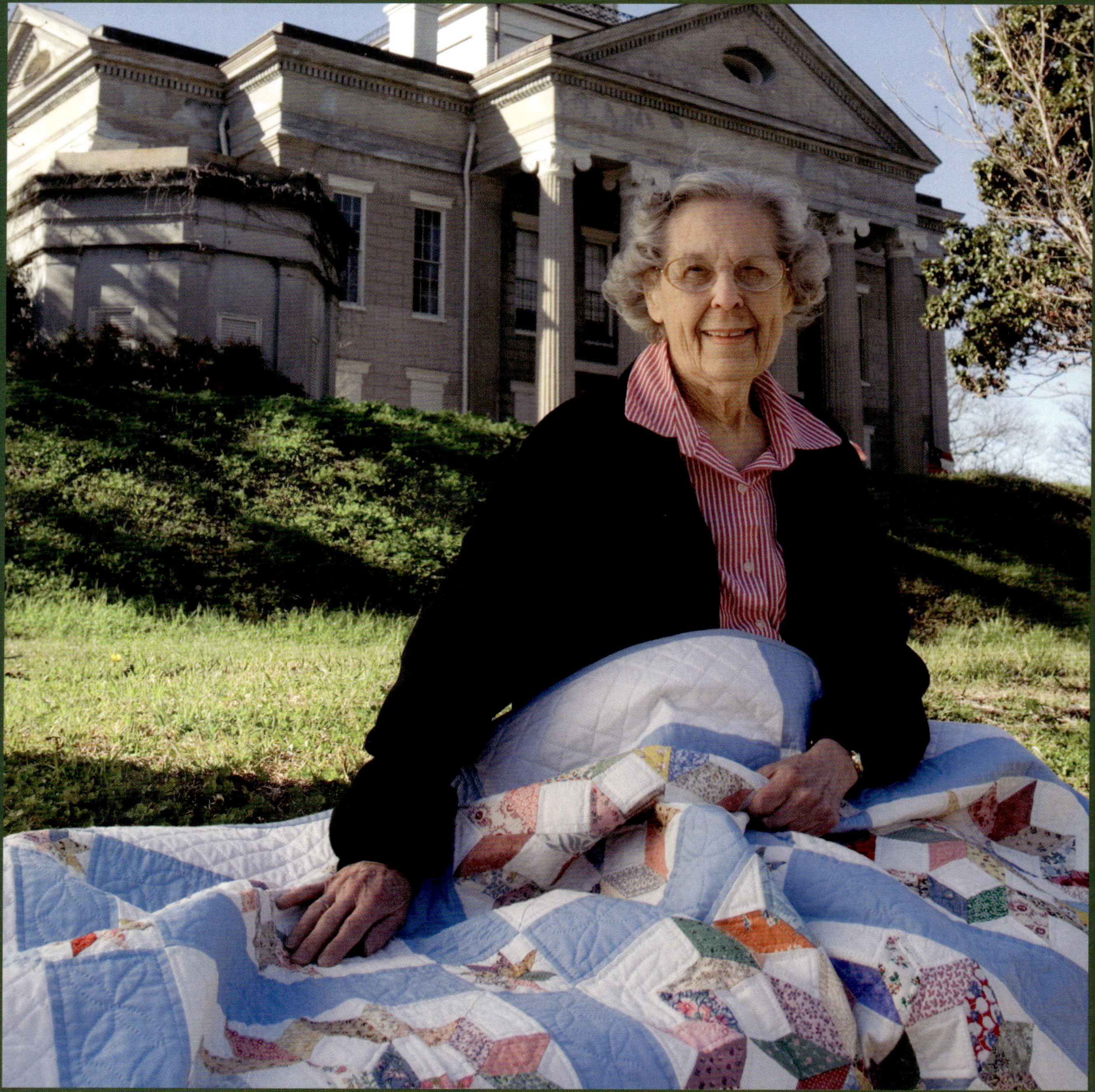

Martha Skelton

Master Quilter of Mississippi

Mary Elizabeth Johnson

Photographs by J. D. Schwalm

UNIVERSITY PRESS OF MISSISSIPPI, JACKSON,
WITH THE MISSISSIPPI QUILT ASSOCIATION

www.upress.state.ms.us

The University Press of Mississippi is a member
of the Association of American University Presses.

Manufactured in China

First printing 2008

Library of Congress Cataloging-in-Publication Data

Huff, Mary Elizabeth Johnson, 1944–
Martha Skelton : master quilter of Mississippi / Mary Elizabeth Johnson.
p. cm.
Includes bibliographical references and index.
ISBN 978-1-934110-81-2 (cloth : alk. paper) 1. Skelton, Martha, 1919–
2. Quiltmakers—Mississippi—Biography. I. Mississippi Quilt Association. II.
Title.
NK9198.S57H84 2008
746.46092—dc22
[B]
2007043539

British Library Cataloging-in-Publication Data available

Unless credited otherwise, photographs of quilts are by J. D. Schwalm,
and family photographs are courtesy of Martha Skelton.

Page ii: Martha Skelton on the lawn of the Old Courthouse Museum in Vicksburg
showing her new quilt "Dutch Rose" in spring 2007.
Page x: Martha's delicate hands busily quilting at her frame on the "Star of Bethlehem."
Page xiv: "Coxcombs and Tulips." *See page 133.*

CONTENTS

CONTENTS

FOREWORD

by Walt Grayson

Mama had a rag bag. In it were all sorts and sizes and colors and textures of scraps of cloth of every description. Every once in a while I'd sift through it to find a particular piece of material I could use as a tent for my plastic soldiers or as a sail for a toy boat. And every time Mama would catch me rummaging through her rag bag she'd tell me to stop, that those weren't toys. She was saving all those odd pieces to make a quilt.

That was the first time in my life I ever associated a finished quilt with the raw materials that they are made from. For all I knew, you went to the store and bought quilts like you bought sheets and spreads. But Mama explained that there wasn't a store-bought quilt in our house. Grandmother had made most of them. Some aunts made the others. And every one had a story behind it, either in the material used or in the occasion on which it was commissioned.

Furthermore, one of the quilts we were using as winter cover on one of the beds at our house had been made by Grandmother especially for me. She had made a special quilt for all the grandkids. And when I grew up and got married, I could take that quilt with me. Mama showed me which one.

Then Mama pulled out a few pieces of material from her rag bag and told where each one came from; dresses from years ago, children's clothes, one of Daddy's favorite old shirts that had grown too frayed to wear any longer. Each rag was a memory that would someday be collected and quilted together and put to use again, to cover us as we dreamed.

Mama never got around to making that quilt. And I am sure the rag bag got discarded when we were cleaning out Mama's house after she passed away. But with her collection of scraps and some of the finished quilts made by Grandmother and others, she introduced me to a concept of "family" that I may not have as fully understood any other way. How that although we are different people, cut from different bolts of material, somehow we all belong together, and are stitched together into a single unit when taken as a completed whole.

And whether Grandmother consciously intended to subtly illustrate our family unity by making and giving all of us grandkids our own quilt, I don't know for sure. But it sure worked. I feel knitted to my cousins and brothers and sisters more tightly than I've noticed other people feel in other families. Some of that closeness has to do with the way we were raised, taught to honor our family and cherish it and each individual in it. But I think that all of us getting a quilt from Grandmother helped that feeling of unity we share and have shared down through the years to this day.

To read *Martha Skelton: Master Quilter of Mississippi*, I feel as if I have discovered Mama's rag bag all over again, only to a much greater depth. To discover the love people have for quilting, and the discipline and hours and patience that go into each quilt has added a fresh, new level to my appreciation for quilting beyond the level I already knew—family ties and ties to old times and simply keeping warm under a quilt on a cold winter night.

Martha Skelton takes that same basic foundation and builds art on it. Quilts with specific pattern names and specific ways of being put together, or patterns she makes up herself, from the colors and shapes of autumn leaves in her yard to free-handed quilts made to commemorate a specific occasion. Such makes a one-of-a-kind quilt to match the unique event it memorializes.

I am not a quilter by any stretch of the imagination, but I am the recipient of the almost magical wonders a hand-made quilt conveys from its maker to the one it is made for. Love is top on that list of benefits. Because no one would go through all of the painstaking trouble to make you a quilt if they didn't love you.

But understanding little about quilting beyond that, I am fascinated with this book. How a quilter comes to be a quilter piques my interest in history and family lore and my curiosity about how someone ends up doing what they do in life, given all the options, especially when they have achieved master status as Martha has.

And then there are the chapters about the insider's views of quilting. This is fascinating to me because Grandmother quilted. Now I can appreciate better how she did it. And marvel that she ever had time to do it at all. And I learn more about how this craft, that started as a necessity, has evolved to the level of art, propelled by those people who are its extremely gifted, fine-eyed, steady-handed, patient, and dedicated practitioners.

I am ashamed to admit that the quilt Grandmother made to commemorate my coming into the world all those decades ago has deteriorated into little more than the status of a large rag itself, after several moves over a career and unconscious neglect. This in no way reflects my feelings for my roots, but sort of does actually illustrate what can happen in life if you ever get distracted and concentrate too long on passing things that end up not mattering, as we all do during the middle years.

So was I ever surprised when, within the last year while visiting the last surviving aunt on Mama's side of the family, she opened a big sack and pulled out a fresh, new quilt. She explained this was the last one Grandmother was working on and had only finished the facing and it had sat at the top of a closet for over forty years, unfinished. But recently, my aunt pulled it out and got someone to tack on the backing and gave it to me.

Grandmother's last quilt.

I'd rather have that quilt than a pot of gold. Now, I'm trying to think of who I am going to pass it along to. It's more than just pieces of cloth stitched together. It's a part of life and part of my family. And things like old quilts handed down keep us all snug on cold nights, and keep us snugly in our place as a part of the pattern of family.

Martha Skelton creates for us to see with our eyes in the material world the fine art that is a quilt, which we already feel in the spirit world of imagination, and sacrifice and family love.

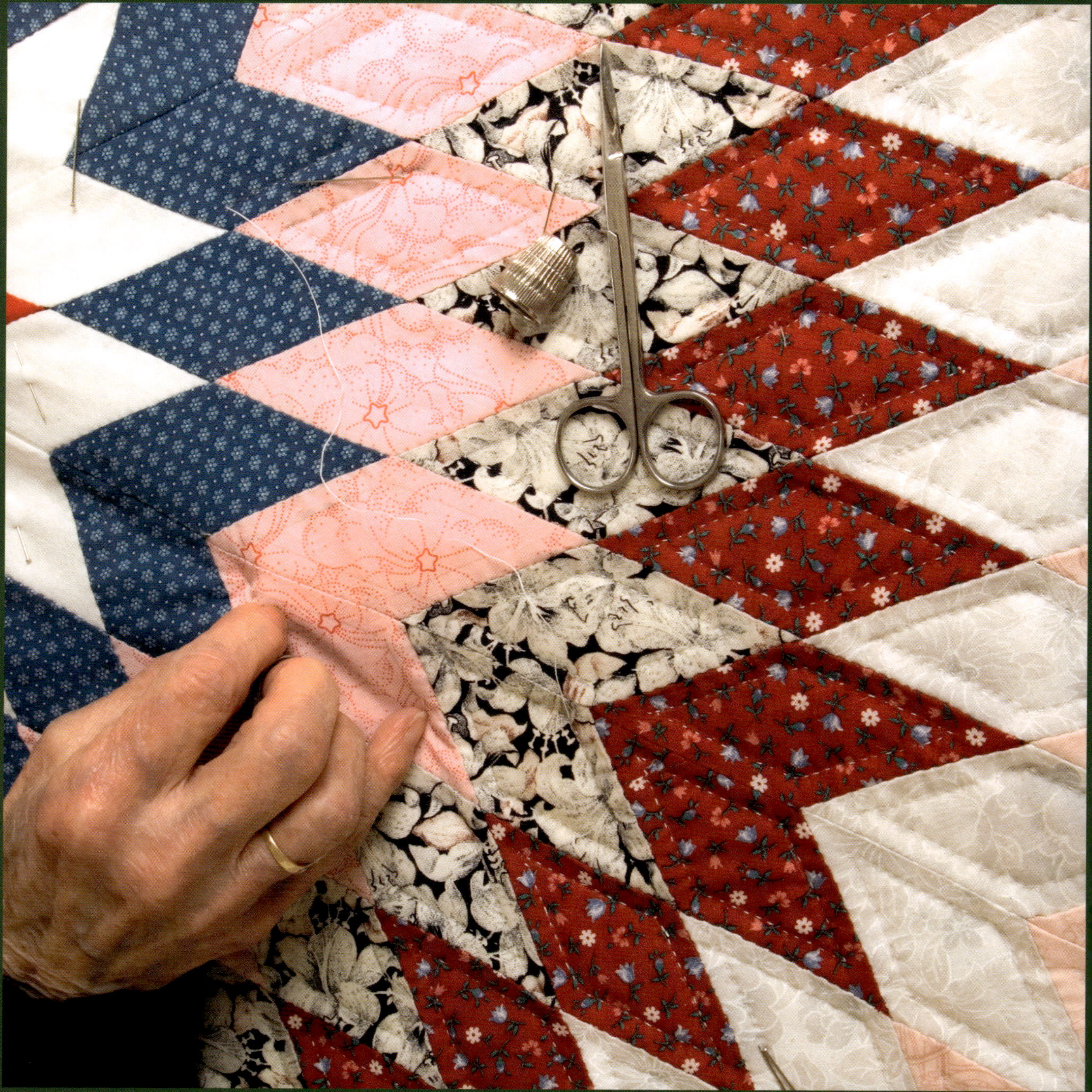

PREFACE

If the United States had a congressional program like the one in Japan that appoints working artists as national living treasures, Martha Skelton would undoubtedly be an American treasure for quilting. For almost sixty years, Martha has challenged herself to continually improve her many quilting skills and, similar to those Japanese artists, has attained a level of mastery unmatched by other traditional quilters.

Her personal body of work includes approximately 225 quilts at this writing, and most of them are full-size quilts, not wall hangings or small pieces. (And this number does not include quilts she has quietly given away.) At her current rate of production, she will probably add another three to five quilts each year to that number. However, it is not the accumulation of a large number of finished quilts that excites her: it is the *process*. With each quilt, she sets a different goal for herself and has a different experience from any with a previous quilt.

Martha Skelton loves all the techniques that comprise the discipline of quilting. They include pattern and fabric selection, drawing the design, pattern drafting, and the stitching involved with appliqué, reverse appliqué, piecing, raised work, embroidery, and quilting. She even enjoys the final step that many quilters find tedious: binding the quilt. "I'm really happy when I get to the binding, because that means this quilt is finished and I can start another one," she says.

Martha Skelton represents a perfect blend of the quilter of old—the traditionalist who believed that "you should do nice work," as her grandmother insisted—and the twenty-first-century quilter who feels free to add, subtract, blend, and experiment with designs to suit her own eye and the needlework skills she wants to employ at the time. The old and the new have found perfect repose in Martha Skelton's attitude toward her work and in her execution of it.

More, though, than an artist of remarkable talent and skill, Martha is an emissary, one could even say missionary or diplomat, for the art she practices. While it would be extraordinary in itself to have produced a body of work the size of hers, perhaps more astonishing is the number of people she has taught. Beginning in 1973, Martha began giving quilting lessons in a local Vicksburg department store, now defunct. Soon she was also teaching home demonstration agents, who shared their quilting lessons with homemakers at group meetings in their homes; many agents went on to train other teachers in the techniques Martha shared. And those two examples are only the beginning of the teaching she has done. Over the years she has led countless workshops for quilt guilds and organizations and has sought out opportunities to take the story of quilting to children of all ages.

It is impossible to accurately tabulate the number of people she has touched in those nearly forty years. Her correspondence confirms that the figure is high, indeed, and that those students are devoted to her for her depth of knowledge, countless hours of experience, and patience in instructing others in her finely honed skills.

In recounting the history of a woman whose life has been so filled with quilts, the obvious course is to let the quilts do the talking. That is pretty much the direction I have taken, and that is why the quilts are arranged essentially chronologically. Occasionally, a quilt or two will be pulled into the text to illustrate a recounting of an event, or a certain point, but for the most part, the earliest quilts are in the front of the book and the most recent ones are in the back, with those in the middle appearing in the order they were made. Every quilt shown in this book was made by Martha Skelton.

The text is informed by my study of Martha's work, my twenty-five-year personal acquaintance with her, access to the voluminous scrapbooks of memorabilia she and her daughter have archived throughout the years, and, most of all, by a series of seven in-depth interviews conducted in Martha's home in Vicksburg between August and November 2006, by Barbara Cashman and Cay Jones, and transcribed by Nancy Harber. In the interest of integration and continuity of material, some direct quotations are a blend of remarks taken from several different parts of the transcription, and I did some routine editing to eliminate repetitions and for clarity. However, I have made every effort to ensure that Martha's meaning is never obscured or mistaken.

Unless otherwise noted, the quilts were made in Vicksburg, Mississippi, and are of cotton fabrics. All the quilt photographs were taken with his usual excellent attention to detail by J. D. Schwalm, unless otherwise noted. He even persuaded Martha to pose for some shots in her home and at landmarks around Vicksburg. Historic photographs are from Martha's personal collection.

Martha Skelton's enormous following in Mississippi guarantees that all who read this account of her life will feel personally invested in seeing that she has been represented in the manner due her. It is the earnest hope of all who conducted the interviews, gathered the data, checked the details, documented and photographed the quilts, and wrote the text and produced the book that we have presented the subject in a manner that does her justice and makes her happy. (*Proud* is not a word one uses, even obliquely, in speaking of Martha!)

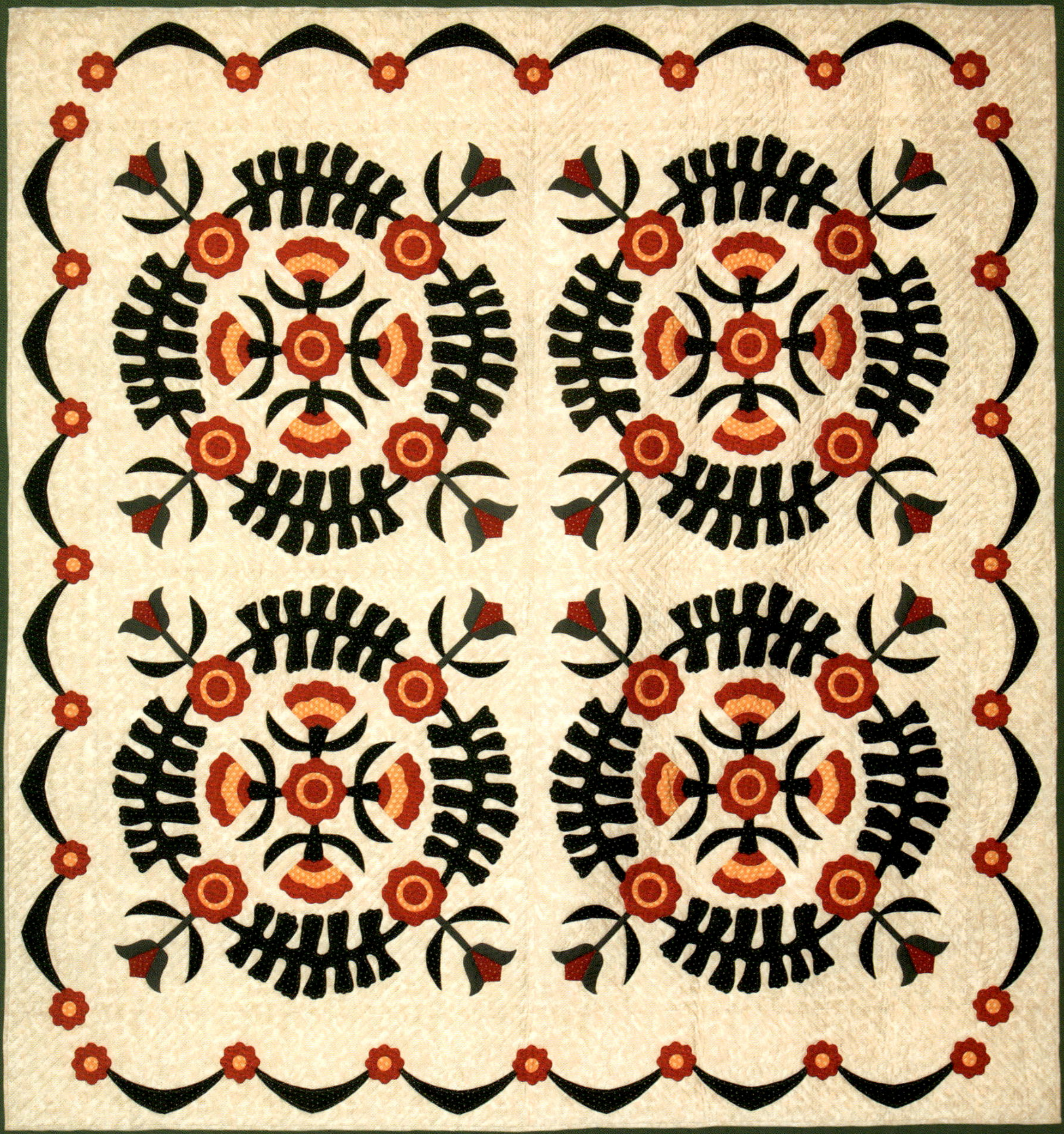

The Early Years: Martha Growing Up

Martha Skelton comes from a long line of people who work extremely hard, cherish their independence, enjoy the company of other folks, know the value of service to the community, like the outdoors, and revere their families. She is a current embodiment of all those values.

William Henry Harrison Butcher, who would become Martha's father, was born in Montana, even though his parents made their home in West Virginia, because Martha's grandfather always wanted to see, as Martha says, "the other side of the mountain."[1] The grandfather had been a participant in the original Gold Rush of the late 1840s, and his itch for adventure resulted in his moving the family around continuously. As a grown man, William Henry also moved around a lot, but his mobility was a result of his career in the oil fields, first in West Virginia, then in Texas and Oklahoma. Unlike his father, he suffered no wanderlust and saw to it that his family stayed relatively settled, once he got them moved from West Virginia to the Midwest.

"Oil field towns in Oklahoma were not really places to raise families," Martha explains. Consequently, when her father's job as a master driller called for relocation, the family would settle in a "normal" town near the "oil patch," and her father would commute daily to his job; or, if he was required to stay on-site for a longer period, he spent more of the resulting compensatory downtime at home rather than traveling between home and the oil field.[2]

Despite the fact that he wasn't physically in the house all the time, there was no sense of separation between father and family. "When we were living in Carthage, Missouri (in the early 1920s), Dad was still working in Oklahoma, but he was coming back and forth a whole lot. None of my family ever seemed to think anything about getting in the car and going someplace, although most people didn't feel nearly so free to get on the road whenever they felt like it. Because he came home whenever he could, we felt close to Dad and he felt close to us. Dad also was a good letter writer."[3]

Martha remembers her father with great affection: "It was easy for him to talk to people. I am a little bit like him in that regard. He was comfortable with people and so he visited with them, and he had a pretty good sense of humor. He was always doing something funny. He was a kind person. I don't suppose that my father ever really corrected me all my life. Dad just expected things of you, and you did them.

"He really liked to grow things. We always had an orchard, wherever we lived, and Dad did the pruning and those kinds of hands-on things. When we lived near Norman, there were black walnut seedlings on the place, and he had them grafted with English walnut buds. The resulting nuts had the great flavor of black walnuts, with shells that were easy to remove like English walnuts. We also had pecan and all kinds of fruit trees—apricot, plums, and cherries—most of which Dad planted."[4]

Martha's parents met when her father (who was probably in his late teens or early twenties) was working in Roane and Wetzel counties in West Virginia as a logger. Martha's mother, Katie Virginia Guthrie, lived with her parents, four sisters (Ettie, Ethel, Pearl, and Hattie), and two brothers (Walter and Harold) on a farm near New Martinsville. Not only did Martha's grandfather Guthrie work the rather large farm, he was also a surveyor and furniture maker. "He seemed to be skilled with his hands in everything he tried," Martha recalls.[5] Grandmother Guthrie, Sarah, was very concerned that all the children get as much education as possible. "She was good with children and was always teaching a child to read, or spell, or sew, no matter what else she was doing. I think that came through in seeing how all her daughters were also good with their children."[6]

Martha's mother had rheumatic fever as a child, leaving her with a weak heart. Nonetheless, she lived life to the fullest and spent lots of time outdoors, where she learned the names of wildflowers and which mushrooms were edible. Katie Virginia became an excellent cook and was especially adept with candy. She honed her sewing and needlework talents, gaining skill as a seamstress who made all her clothes. "She was somebody who was always interested in what was going on around her," remembers her daughter fondly. "She was a friendly person and got along with her neighbors. Everybody liked her."[7]

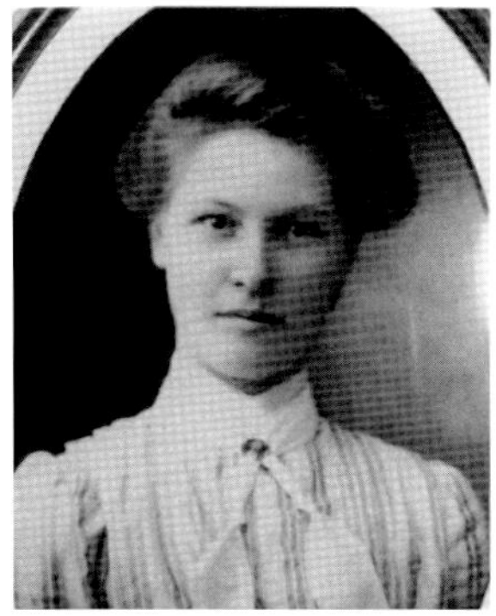

Martha Skelton's mother, Katie Virginia Butcher, about the time of her marriage to Martha's father.

Perhaps the most telling trait Martha associates with her mother is that she endured with grace the chronic bad health resulting from her childhood illness. "I think that's so important—that people not complain. I got a lot of that from my mother. She never said, 'I can't do that; I don't feel good.' She did it anyway. I attribute a lot of my doing the way I do to how my mother was. She was very independent and accustomed to answering for herself. I think that's a good attribute, too. She always said you might as well laugh as cry. She thought you could make something good out of anything that happened. You didn't have to feel like it was the end of the world."[8]

It is little wonder that William Henry Butcher was attracted to such a person—upbeat, well loved, multi-talented, and, as her photographs illustrate, quite pretty. Although Martha never talked to her mother about how or when her parents met, she figures it must have been when Katie Virginia was in her late teens, shortly after she finished summer normal school, which qualified her as a teacher. "I never asked a lot of questions when I was young, because I thought, like everyone, that I'd have my family forever. However, I could always see that Mother and Dad were devoted to each other; it was obvious."[9]

As an adult, Martha questioned her Aunt Pearl for details about her parents' wedding. Aunt Pearl responded with memories of her own role in it, which had

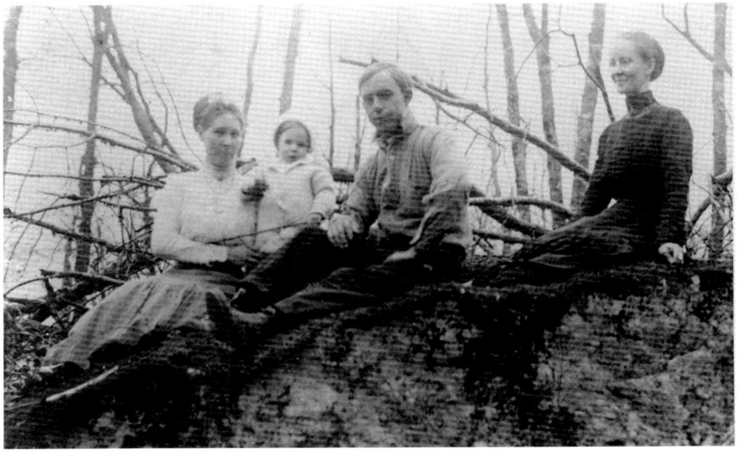

Taken in West Virginia in 1911 or 1912, this photograph shows Martha's mother, Katie Virginia (Guthrie) Butcher; Harold Emory Butcher ("Little Harold"); Martha father, William Harrison Butcher and Elsie Bell Guthrie ("Aunt Etti Martha's "second mother").

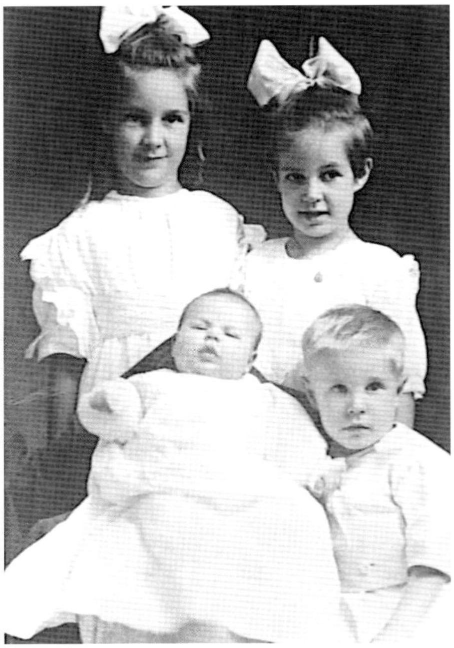

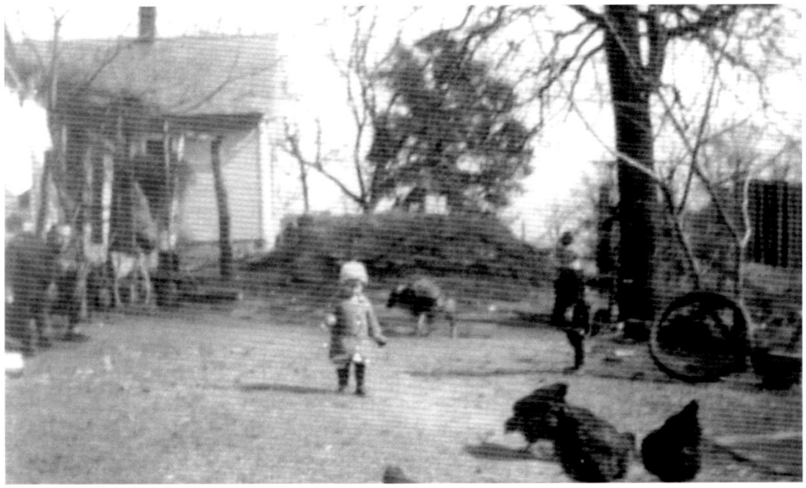

(left) Martha as an infant, lower left, with (counterclockwise from Martha's left) her brother, Walter William, and older sisters, Garnett and Virginia. Two sisters, Sarah Rose and Betty Jo, joined the family later.

(above) Martha (far right) watches as her father (seated at extreme left) encourages Sarah Rose to toddle about in the backyard of their home in Ripley, Oklahoma, in 1923.

to do with her getting a ride into a nearby town to shop for her sister's wedding outfit. She bought a beautiful traveling suit with a very full skirt—seventeen or more gores—and a matching hat trimmed with violets. However, when the shopping was finished, much to her dismay, none of the family showed up to give her a ride home. She ended up walking the entire seven miles back to the family farm, carrying the bride's new wedding finery with her.

William Henry and Katie Virginia set up housekeeping in Spencer, West Virginia, but he had begun working in the oil fields, first in West Virginia and Pennsylvania, then in Texas and Oklahoma. He was commuting out west during the years that his first four children were born. There were two daughters, Virginia and Garnett, and a son, Walter, then Martha (whose middle name is Hope), born on July 22, 1919. (The other son, Harold, died at nineteen months and is still referred to as "Little Harold" within the family.) Father didn't get to meet his third daughter until she was nearly three months old, which might have been the reason that, three months later, he moved Katie Virginia and the four children to Oklahoma City. Over the next several years, the family moved around a bit—to Sapulpa and Ripley, Oklahoma, then Carthage, Missouri—before finally settling in Norman, Oklahoma, when Martha was nine years old. As time passed, two more daughters, Sarah Rose and Betty Jo, were born.

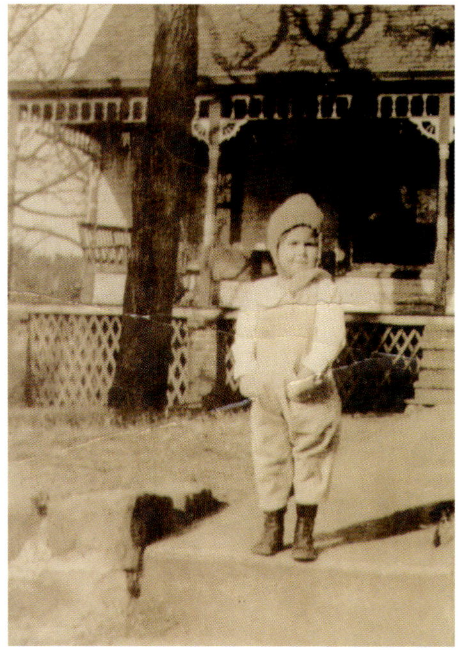

Martha, at age four, wearing her brother's overalls, poses in front of the Butchers' Sapulpa home.

In the years between 1920 and 1928, three of Martha's maternal aunts also moved to Oklahoma: Hattie and Ethel, who took their husbands along; and Pearl, who left hers, a man much older than she, behind in West Virginia. ("I think she was ready to let Uncle Raymond go, you know, even though he was a good-looking man, raised horses, and had a beautiful place. She came to Oklahoma and taught school," muses Martha today.[10]) Uncle Walter frequently visited from West Virginia, bringing Grandmother Guthrie out for six-month-long visits, until he decided to marry and settle himself in Texas at the ripe old age of thirty.

Happy though the family was that so many of them were living in the new state of Oklahoma (established in 1907), they had tough times to live through, and many of the family, including Martha's dad, were out of work for long periods. The stock market crashed in 1929, and the Great Depression swiftly followed. "There wasn't any work. You cannot imagine," Martha says, still horrified at the deprivation visited on the nation. "I saw the bread lines in Oklahoma City, and they were just like those photographs you see in books—long lines of people standing, waiting to get something to eat. It was hard on everybody. Nobody had anything."[11]

William Henry and Katie Virginia Butcher took a look at their brood of six children and realized that, with so many to educate, they would never be able to afford to send them all away to college, whenever that time came. "They always tried their best to give us what they could of what they thought people needed. Always they wanted us to have more than they had. Dad always said every generation should do better than the one before it. They talked about it and began to look around for a college town to which to move. Because we were living in Carthage, Missouri, at the time, they checked out the University of Missouri at Columbia. Then they went and looked at the University of Oklahoma in Norman and decided they liked it better because it would be closer to where Dad would be working. There was drilling going on in Oklahoma City, at Purcell and Stroud, all around Norman. There would be plenty of work and Dad could live at home," Martha remembers.[12] The Butchers settled near the University of Oklahoma campus, and Martha was able to attend high school on the U.O. campus.

Another bonus of their move to Norman was that it kept them within visiting distance of Katie Virginia's sisters. One of them, Elsie Bell ("Aunt Ettie"), lived with the family in Norman, sharing a large bedroom with Martha and her two younger sisters. Katie Virginia and Ettie, Martha recalls, "were not only sisters, but good friends. They got along so well together. I don't ever remember hearing a cross word between them. They worked together—if they got ready to make a pie, one made the crust and the other made the filling. It didn't matter what they were doing, they went along together."[13] They and the other sisters also drove their own cars during a time when few people, least of all women, were driving. "Mother and Aunt Ethel used to meet about halfway between Pawhuska and Norman and swap off kids or give Grandmother to one or the other."[14]

It was during this time—in 1932—that Mr. Butcher took a job as a driller in Angola, a country on the southwestern coast of Africa. It offered him an opportunity to earn a good living for his family when there was no work to be had in the oil business in the States. A similar assignment in Israel followed. During his time away, he continued his habit of writing long and frequent letters home, keeping the family ties closely bound.

Martha adds, "Mother was a person who was self-sufficient and didn't have to have anybody to do things for her. For example, if she needed to go to the bank, she just went to the bank; she didn't wait for Dad to be home from the oil fields. She was ahead of her time. She let us have pets—there's a picture somewhere of Sarah Rose and me together, each of us holding a baby duck. I can remember Mother going to town to the library and getting as many books as they would let her check out. The library was there, and the church was there, and you went to both. It was all part of our growing up."[15]

Evenings in the wintertime were often spent gathered in the one heated room of the house, the kitchen/dining area. Martha's mother would tend to the hand sewing—darning and mending, perhaps making buttonholes by hand. The children would do their homework, and Aunt Ettie would read aloud from the books Martha's mother had checked out from the library. "Mother didn't have the breath, as she said, to read out loud for a long time. So Aunt Ettie would read. She read Zane Grey and Gene Stratton Porter and all the rest who were popular at that time. That way, Mother and Aunt Ettie both enjoyed the books, and we could listen if we wanted to."[16]

Those family evenings nurtured Martha's interest in needlework of all kinds—embroidery, crochet, knitting, and, always, the sewing of garments and household accessories such as curtains. Quilting was a natural part of the needlework that took place in the Butcher home. Not only did Martha's mother quilt, but so did

Aunts Ettie, Ethel, Pearl, and Hattie. Martha still has a quilt that was made by Aunt Ettie before her mother was married (pre-1915, possibly much earlier)—it was in red, white, green, and "cheddar," in a design of appliquéd cherries.[17] However, most of the quilts her mother and the aunts turned out were "used up," as Martha puts it. She recalls that most of them were pieced, as was the "Ocean Waves" that her paternal grandmother, Margaret Jane Boggs Butcher, put together for Martha around 1920 or 1925.

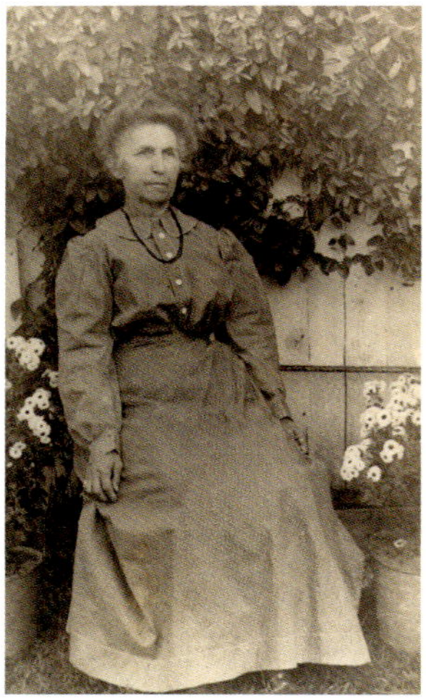

Margaret Jane Boggs Butcher, Martha Skelton's paternal grandmother, around 1910. Clearly, someone in the family was quite a gardener, a passion that was passed down to Martha, who has always been an avid outdoorswoman and gardener.

Martha was a very young sophomore at the University of Oklahoma—she had begun elementary school at five, then later graduated high school in three years—when Katie Virginia Guthrie Butcher died quietly and unexpectedly at the age of forty-nine in December of 1936. "I was getting breakfast together; Aunt Ettie and I were in the kitchen. . . . Dad was working away. Mother was sleeping just off the kitchen. I said to her, 'Mother, I'm fixing grapefruit today. Do you want half?' She didn't answer me. I went to see why and called to Aunt Ettie and said, 'Aunt Ettie, Mother is gone.' She came into the bedroom and kept saying, 'It can't be; it just can't be.' The doctor, who had paid a house call the night before, later said it had been a heart attack."[18]

This left Martha and Aunt Ettie to keep the family going. Although Martha's two older sisters, Virginia and Garnett, were both on their own and teaching in country schools,[19] Martha's brother Walter was still at home, attending college at the University of Oklahoma, and her sisters Betty Jo and Sarah Rose were young teenagers. Martha's dad sent money home every month, and Martha paid the bills while Aunt Ettie "kept them all straight" and did much of the housekeeping.[20] Martha recorded her expenditures in a monthly report to her father. "You did an awful good job of keeping up with the money," he told her. "You saved more than I ever expected you to."[21]

One should not get the idea that Martha's teenage years were gloomy; although she grieved for her mother, she went ahead with the activities of any normal seventeen-year-old. One of the things she did was join her girlfriends in making items for her "hope chest," which was, to those who may never have heard of one, an

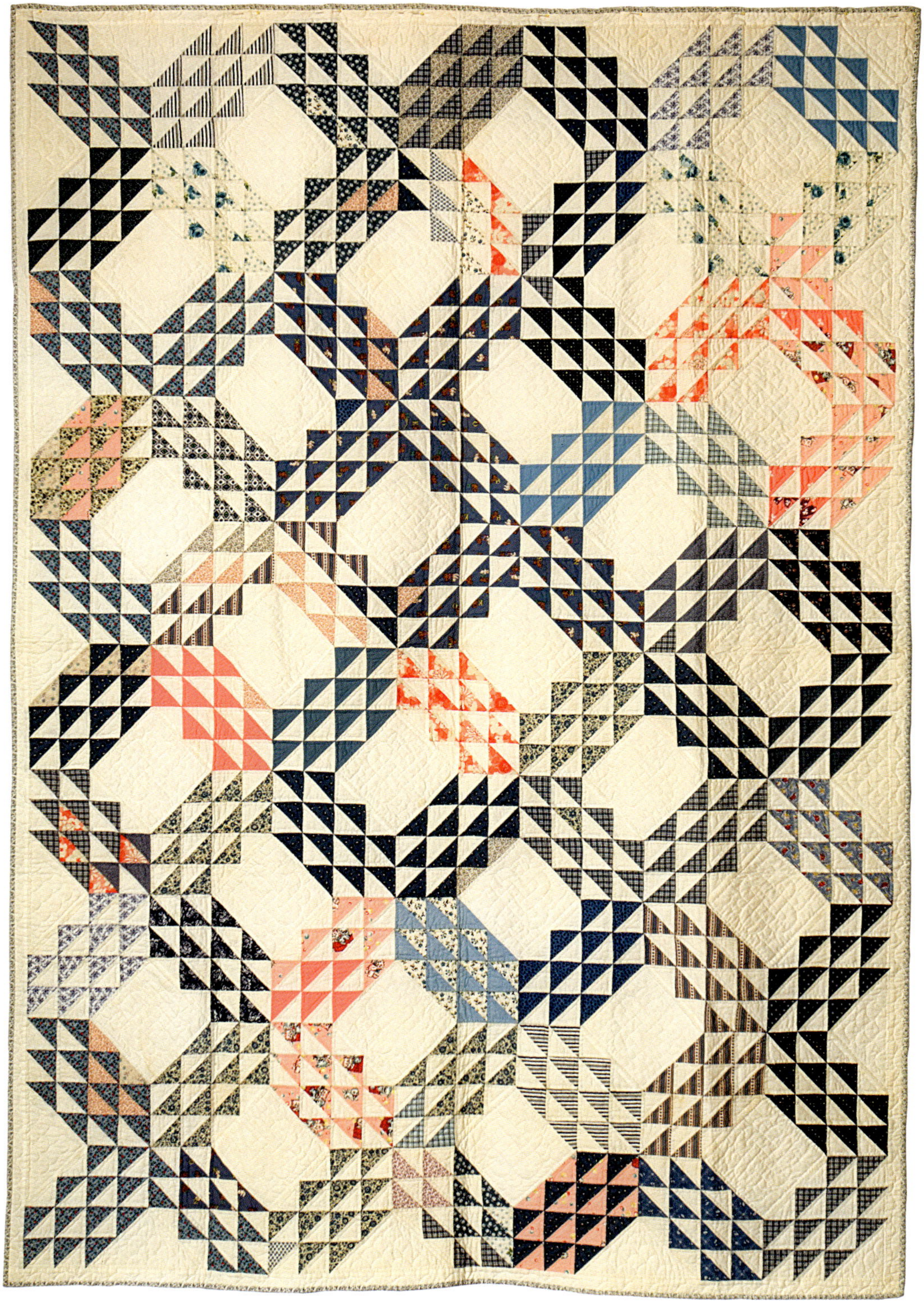

Quilt #121. "Ocean Waves" made before 1995; it is 64 inches wide by 90 inches long. A photograph of this quilt was published in *American Quilter*, winter 1995, to accompany an article Martha was asked by the magazine's editor to write about herself. The pattern came from *Lady's Circle Patchwork Quilts*, July 1989, and it duplicated the quilt top given to Martha's mother by Martha's grandmother, Margaret Jane Boggs Butcher, when Martha was a baby. Martha quilted that top in the 1940s and eventually "used the quilt up." She tried to make this replication "feel like Grandmother Butcher." Collection of the maker.

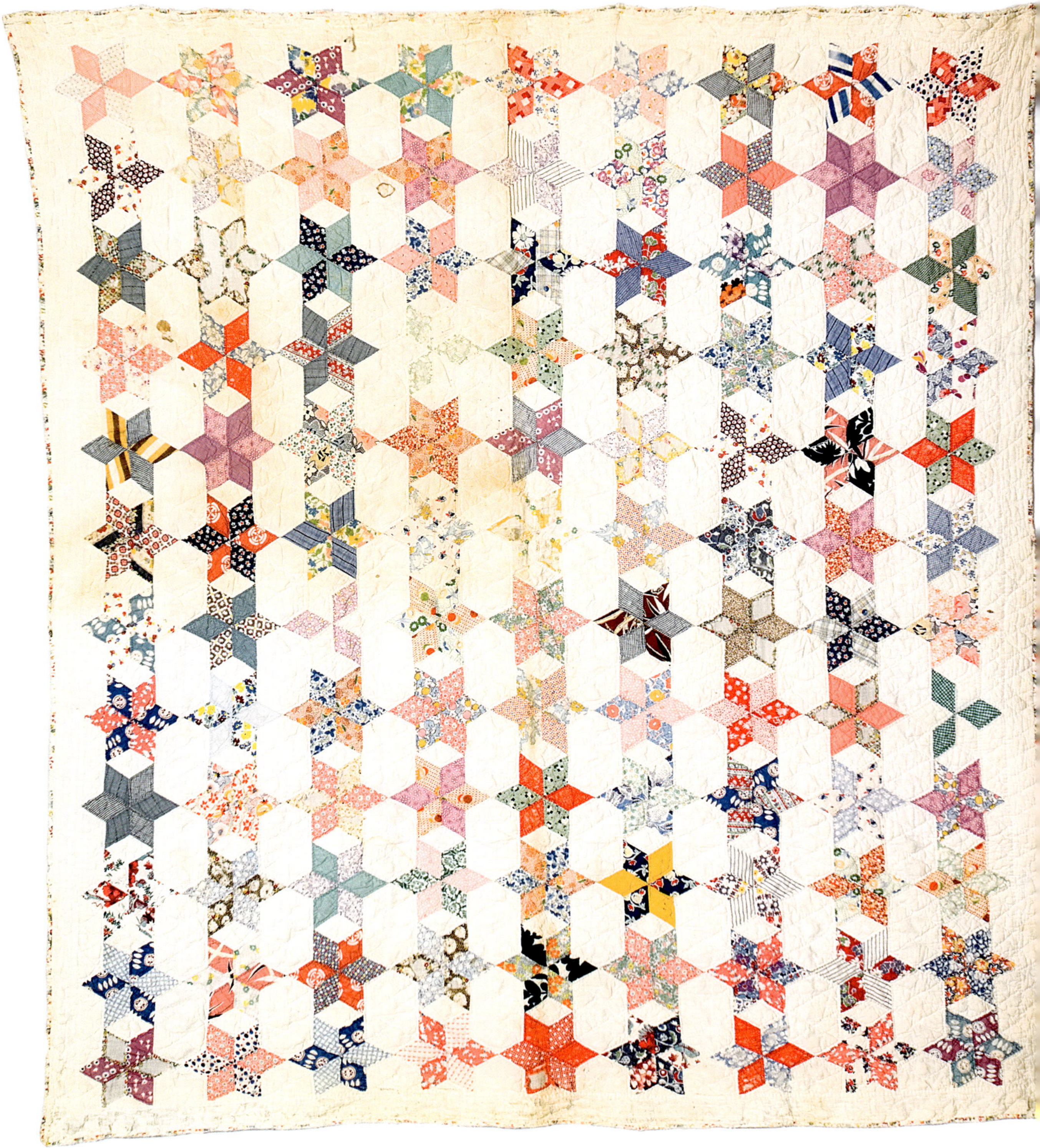

actual chest, usually made of cedar, in which young women stored up handmade and embroidered table and bed linens they hoped to use as brides. Martha pieced her first quilt top in the winter of 1934–35 for her hope chest. It was a little six-pointed star, with each star containing two fabrics selected from cotton scraps left over from homemade family clothing. Martha figured out for herself how to set the stars together, and later her Aunt Ethel made the same design; the two of them enjoyed sharing quilting ideas for many years.[22]

A "Small Wedding Ring" was the second quilt Martha pieced. Although it follows the design of the "Double Wedding Ring," the smaller size of the pieced rings inspired its name. "Everybody was making this quilt when I was seventeen or eighteen," Martha says. "Friends exchanged fabrics to obtain a greater variety. The only fabric I purchased was the white percale to set it together."[23]

Martha's choice of patterns for her first two quilts demonstrated great confidence in her sewing abilities, because neither is particularly easy to put together. Her self-assurance was in no small way the result of the constant help and advice available to her from all the women on both sides of her family. "I don't remember a time when I couldn't find someone to help me if I wanted to do something, no matter what it was," Martha says about her mother and aunts.[24]

Martha's mother was working on an "Improved Nine Patch" when she died. In this design, the four corner squares have been stretched out into elongated points, and the sides of the blocks are curved slightly inward. Although she had pieced all the blocks, Katie Virginia was missing the elongated oval pattern piece that fit between the blocks to join them one to another. Martha recalls that Aunt Ettie said to her, "You can have these blocks Katie was working on. You're the only one of the girls who would finish the quilt."[25] Martha was pleased with the compliment and glad to have the blocks. Accepting that the missing pattern piece was permanently lost, she trimmed the blocks down to a normal "Nine Patch" and set them together into a quilt that she loved and eventually used up. (When Martha was in her late thirties, she finally obtained a whole pattern for "Improved Nine Patch," through one of her aunts in Oklahoma, and made the quilt in memory of her mother.[26])

Quilt #29. "Star" made in Norman, Oklahoma, pieced in 1934 and 1935, and quilted in 1940. It is 70 inches wide by 75 inches long. Martha's first quilt shows signs of wear from many years of use. Collection of Ann Skelton Deemer, Westwego, Louisiana.

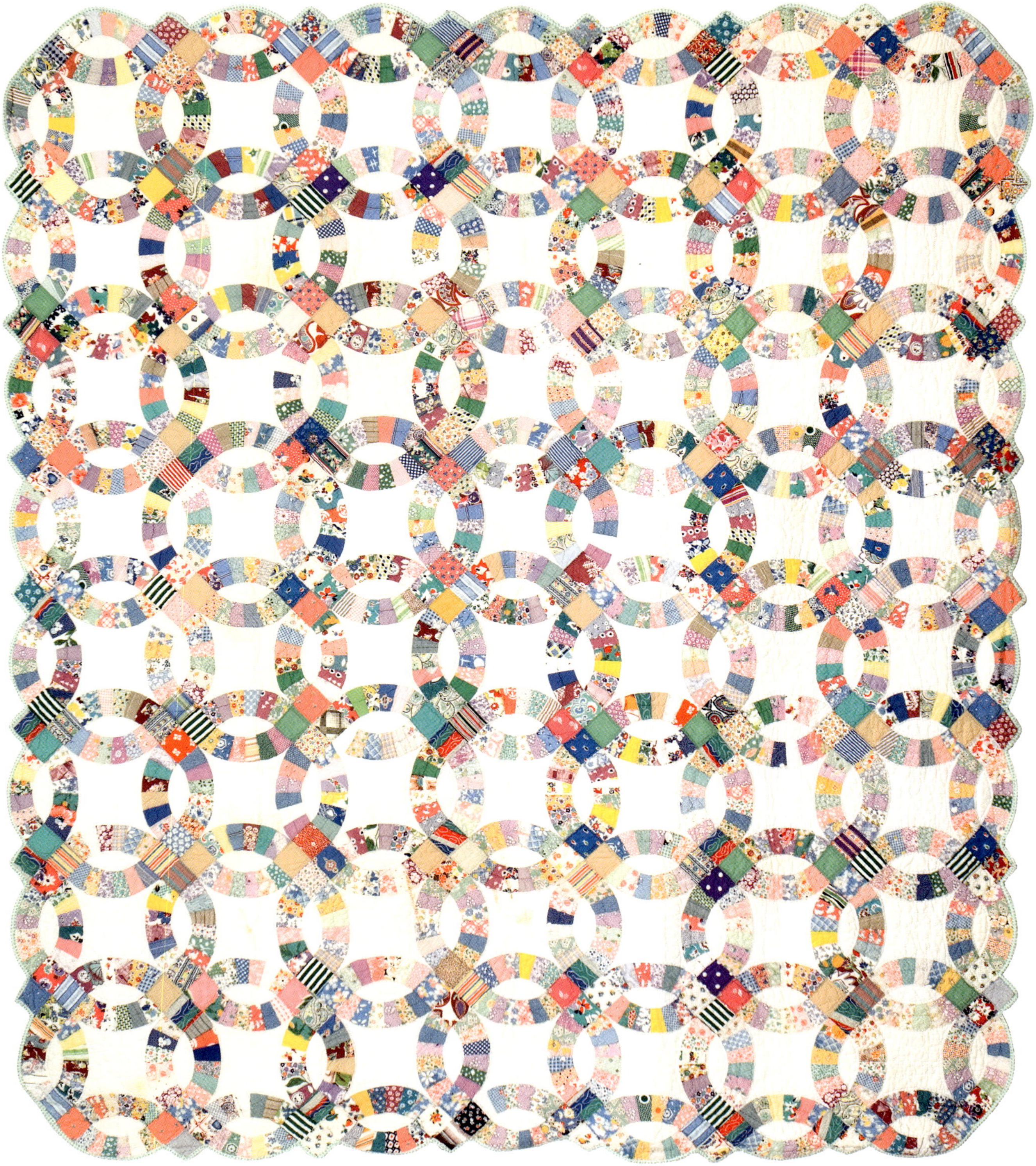

Reminiscing about the needlecraft activities of her family, Martha said, "Finishing my mother's quilt made me realize two things: that I was always going to have help from my family and that I was going to be doing the quilting. Now my older sister, Virginia, I suppose she probably made two or three quilts. She was a beautiful needleworker, but she was always doing something else, so she wasn't interested in making many quilts. My next older sister, Garnett, made several, but she ended up doing more quilting or repairing someone else's quilts than she did starting one from scratch and going all the way through. My younger sister, Sarah Rose, made a few quilts. She would have liked to have made more, but she taught home economics all the time, and she was a lot busier than some of the rest of us. My baby sister, Betty Jo, made a few quilts but not very many because she was more interested in doing needlepoint and that sort of thing than in quilting. I really took to quilting, so that's one of the reasons, I think, that it stayed with me—I had been encouraged."[27]

Although her life proceeded in a fairly normal fashion after her mother's death, it is certainly true that Martha had much more responsibility thrust on her at an early age than do most young women. Undoubtedly, that contributed to the development of her rock-solid center, which is built on deeply held religious beliefs, a conviction of the worth of challenging work, a fierce love of and loyalty to family, an enduring joy in interacting with others, and a quiet devotion and appreciation of the natural world.

Quilt #1. "Small Wedding Ring" made in Norman, Oklahoma, pieced in 1937, and quilted in early 1940s. It is 74 inches wide by 83 inches long. The second quilt Martha made was a popular design among her friends. Collection of Ann Skelton Deemer, Westwego, Louisiana.

Love, Marriage, and Family

Martha's quilting friends are often fascinated, and perhaps somewhat perplexed, to learn that she is a geologist. However, as Martha points out, every successful adult she knew as a young person was associated with either oil or mining—those were the big industries in Oklahoma—and the University of Oklahoma (OU) was geared to providing scholars in areas that would support them. A 1939 graduate, Martha majored in micropaleontology, learning how to make slides from slices of the earth's strata and studying them for prehistoric flora and fauna. "After you determined what period of time you were working with, you figured in other indicators we had been trained to recognize, and you were able to determine the chances of finding oil in that particular soil. That was what suited me," she says.[1]

What came to suit her even more was the new librarian at the School of Geology. It was Martha's senior year at OU, and she was working in the geology library. When her boss left for another job, he recommended his friend, Alan Skelton, as his replacement. Soon after settling in as library director and as Martha's new boss, Alan persuaded her to pursue a graduate degree in library science (which she would attain in the spring of 1940). Both could see that jobs in geology had become scarce as the country grew increasingly nervous about being drawn into the war in Europe (World War II).

The romance started out slowly. "Alan and I worked together well; I got along with him fine, and we had no problems. I always had boyfriends, some more serious than others. I hadn't met anybody that I was ready to settle down with," says Martha, adding, "Of course, Aunt Ettie wasn't real anxious for me to get married; she thought I ought to wait awhile. I was only nineteen when I finished university."[2]

A year slipped by as Martha and Alan fell into the habit of taking regular coffee breaks together, always with a third party—usually faculty from the school of geology. Then, to Martha's surprise, Alan invited her to have Thanksgiving dinner with his mother at her home. It soon became apparent that Alan was serious about Martha; by Christmas, she found that she returned his affection. They married between semesters, on January 26, 1940, in a simple ceremony in the preacher's study. Martha bought a new dress, coat, and hat in navy blue for her wedding and subsequent honeymoon weekend in Tulsa. An uncomplicated and modest celebration seemed to be appropriate for the temper of the time: post-Depression, pre–World War II.

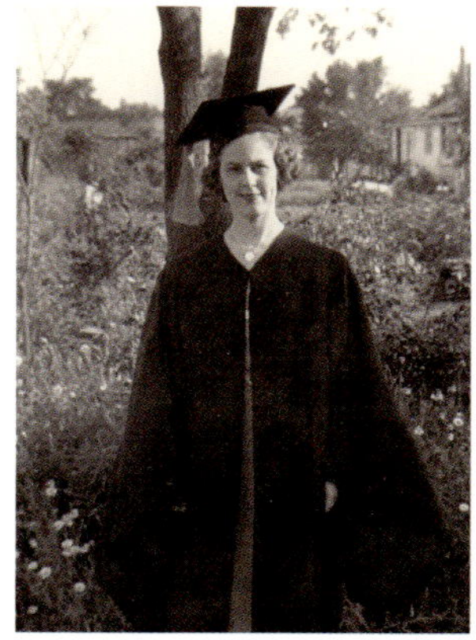

Martha Hope Butcher at her graduation from the University of Oklahoma in 1939; she was nineteen years old.

School started again for Martha on the Monday after her honeymoon weekend in Tulsa. The newlyweds lived with the groom's mother in her home, only four blocks from the university. They had no car and walked back and forth to campus. They were very happy living with Mrs. Skelton (Josephine Carter Skelton, nicknamed "Doll"), a good cook who made her own bread, enjoyed the utmost goodwill of her neighbors, and was skilled in all kinds of needlework, including quilting. She made a lovely "Double Wedding Ring" quilt top as a Christmas gift for Martha and Alan the first year they were married. (Martha quilted it in the 1950s.)[3]

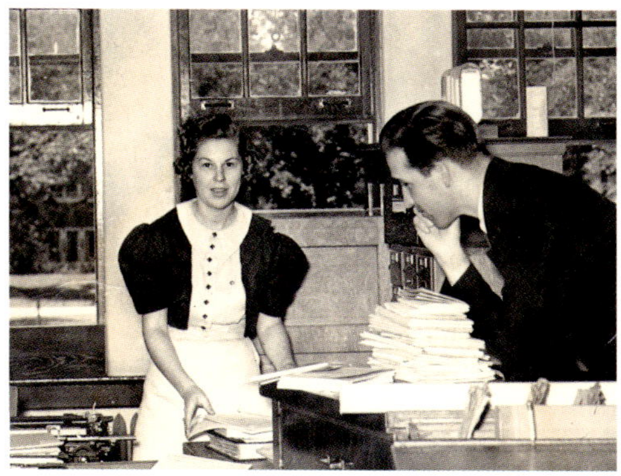

Martha, with an unidentified admirer, worked in the library at the School of Geology at Oklahoma University in Norman after graduation from college.

"She was very good to me. She really wanted us with her, and I felt very comfortable there. It also spared me from having to worry about meals or anything like that. I was finishing up my Master of Library Sciences degree during the day and working at the library at night, so time was at a premium. Mrs. Skelton also made it possible for me to check on things at home with my younger sister and keep an eye on that household. It worked out very nicely for me," Martha remembers appreciatively. "I never felt like, when I got married, that I had to leave my sisters and Aunt Ettie behind. I think that's real important. It was for me."[4]

At the end of the spring semester of 1940, Martha had completed her second degree from OU. She worked the following summer in the library on campus, glad to have a job because it was so difficult for a married woman to find work. Times were still hard, and the general feeling was that men needed all available jobs to support their families. She and Alan had by that time moved into an apartment, where they stayed for about a year. After that they rented a small house, and, finally, a couple of years after their marriage, they bought a little brick house near downtown Norman.

It was after they had settled into the little brick house that Ella, the much older sister of Martha's father, came to visit in Norman. Aunt Ella stayed six weeks, ostensibly with Martha's dad, but she spent nearly all the days with Martha, who wasn't working at the time. "We enjoyed it; I talked with her and asked her questions about sewing and that kind of thing," says Martha of the relationship she patterned, either consciously or subconsciously, on those she enjoyed with her maternal aunts.[5]

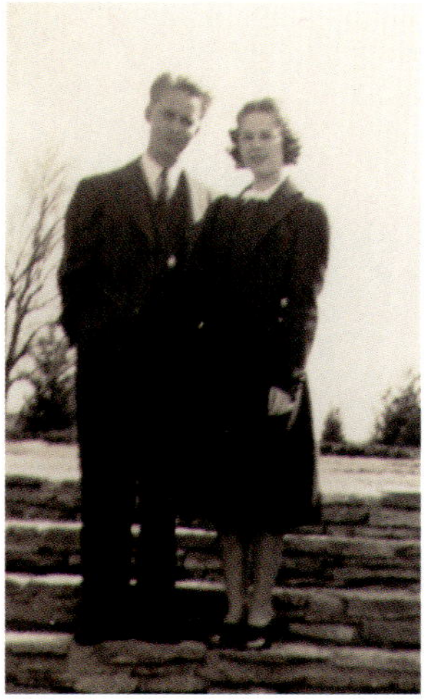

Newlyweds Alan and Martha Skelton pose in the spring of 1940 at the Sunken Gardens at Oklahoma University.

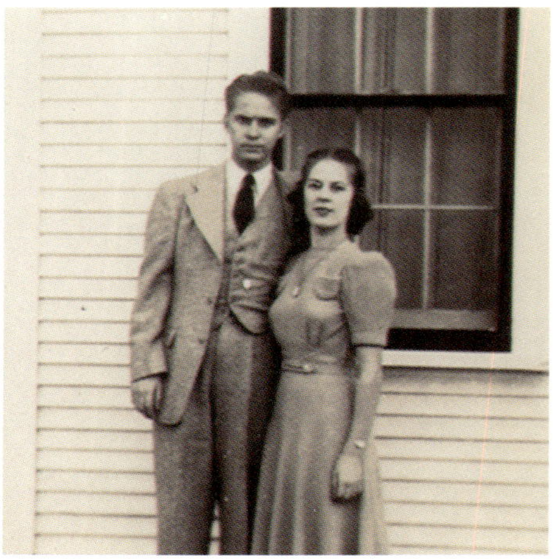

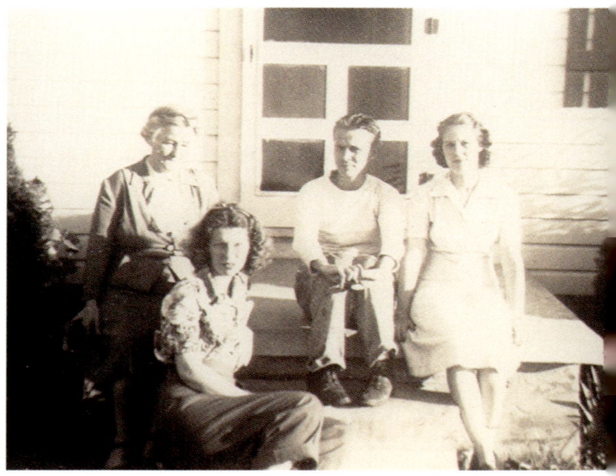

Right: Alan and Martha moved to a furnished apartment after living with "Doll" Skelton, Alan's mother, for about six months. This photo was taken ten months after they married, at Thanksgiving, 1940.

Far right: Within a couple of years of their marriage, the young couple found a house to rent and could, to their delight, finally furnish their home with their own things.

Because Alan often went back to work in the evenings, he and Martha developed a little routine in which she went along with him, carrying a needlework project with her to help her pass the time. "He'd say to me, 'Get your sewing and come with me,' and I'd put it in a little box. Sometimes I would help him with his library work, but most of the time I just went along for company and carried my needlework with me," Martha remembers. She was doing "a little bit of piecing" (on the "Small Wedding Ring" she had begun for her hope chest), as well as "all sorts of embroidery," plus crochet and a bit of knitting.[6]

When they had been married for a little more than two years, Alan and Martha decided it was time to begin the family each was eager to have. They also felt the pressure of world war coming closer, and all young married couples realized that the men could be called away at any time. Alan had tried to volunteer for both the army and the navy, but was turned down by both because of his high blood pressure. "This really bothered him, because he thought he was supposed to go; he didn't want to stay at home," Martha remembers, giving voice to the patriotism felt by the majority of young American men at the time.[7]

When Martha learned that a baby was on the way, they bought a larger house, and Alan agreed to wait until after the child was born to try again to volunteer for military service. Because the war had drawn the majority of young doctors into the medical corps, the only ones left in Norman were quite elderly, so the Skeltons decided that a young woman newly out of medical school would attend Martha. On February 2, 1943, Martha "had a long, hard delivery, and I can remember as I sort of came to, I could hear the nurses talking, saying they were afraid this was going to happen, and the poor mother was going. I knew then the baby was dead. I think what happened was that the doctor gave me so much to ease the pain that it killed the baby. I never saw her. My family said she was a beautiful little girl, and they couldn't see anything wrong with her except that she didn't live."[8]

Several weeks after leaving the hospital, when Martha had physically recovered, Aunt Ettie invited her to come visit and cut quilt pieces, perhaps with the unstated purpose of temporarily distracting Martha from her loss. Aunt and niece decided they would each make a "Pinwheel" quilt and dug happily into the family scrap bag, discovering a treasure of wonderful cotton prints. At the end of the day, Martha put her stash of right-angle triangles into a tin candy box and took them home. Her life would become so busy that it would be many years before the quilt was finished.[9]

Sometime also in 1943, Martha put together a simple "Nine Patch" woolen quilt that she filled with a cotton batting, lined with a flannel backing, and tied.[10] It is unusual only in that it was not used up—it remains in excellent condition in Martha's collection. This was not the only utility piece Martha stitched up quickly. Such quilts were to be used for bedcovers, as protection when she wanted to play with her babies on the lawn, or as pallets at naptime. Although it is easily possible that in 1943 Martha made more quilts than the "Arkansas Snowflake" and the woolen "Nine Patch," there is no record of them.

Later in 1943, Alan was offered a job with a trade association headquartered in Tulsa. After thinking it over and deciding it was a good opportunity for his advancement, the couple sold the house in Norman and moved. Alan liked the new job, which involved a good bit of travel, and Martha enjoyed her work in the Tulsa Public Library. They settled right in to Tulsa, making new friends and enjoying visits from different family members.

In late March of 1945, Martha discovered that she was again expecting a child, and she gave up her job to stay at home. While she waited for the baby's arrival, she cross-stitched a stamped panel from Woolworth's (a chain of variety stores) featuring two teddy bears with umbrellas floating in the clouds above a little village. She finished the panel into a baby quilt that she tied with blue thread. Ann Hope was born on December 28, 1945, and Aunt Ethel, who lived about forty-five miles from Tulsa, came to help out when Martha brought the baby home. Martha's dad came frequently, sometimes staying a few days, as did other uncles and aunts.

Despite their happiness in and contentment with Tulsa, the young couple was intrigued by a job offer Alan received in 1947 from the Army Corps of Engineers in Vicksburg. The Corps was looking for a librarian, and the job sounded like a chal-

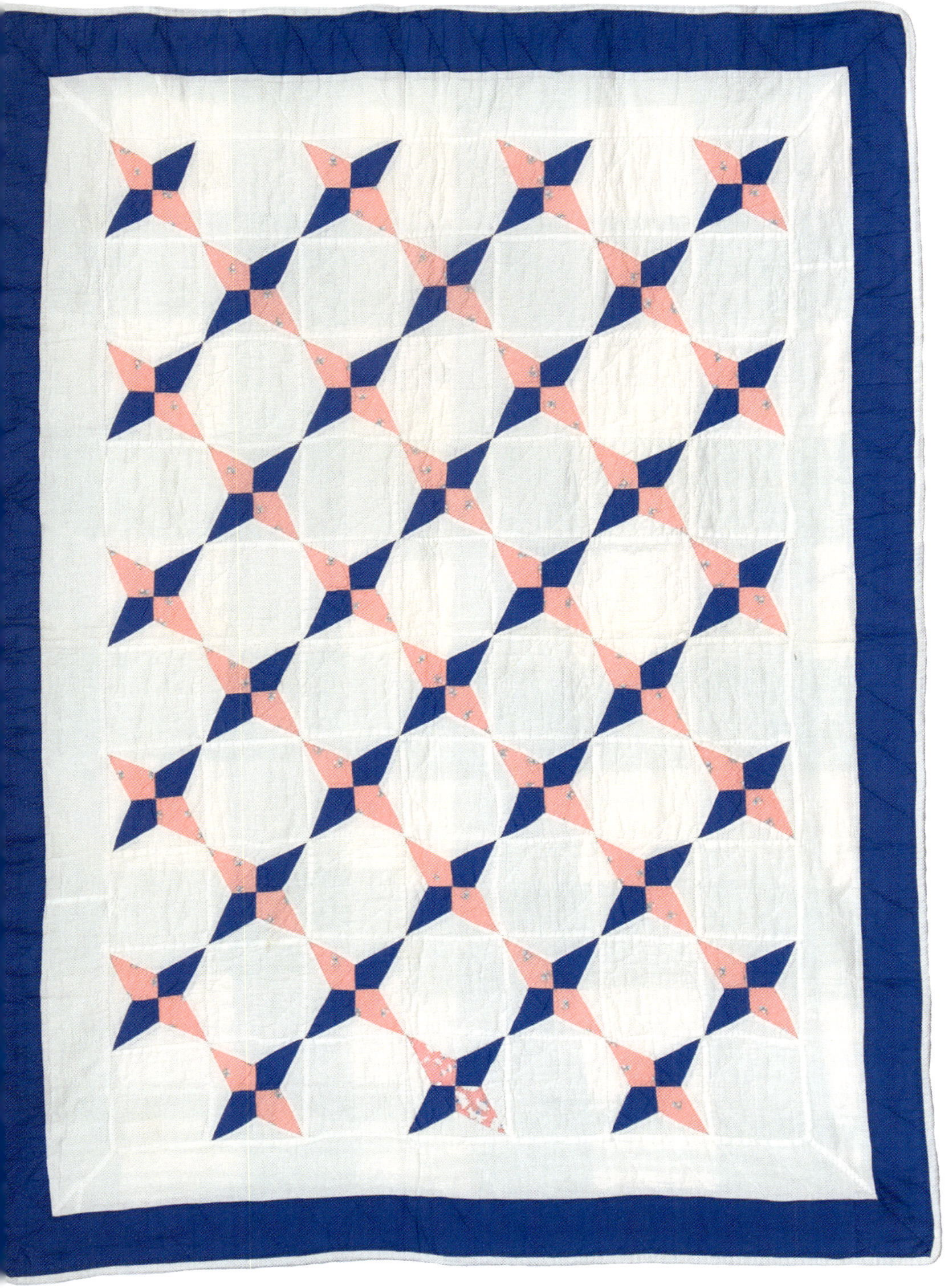

Quilt #8. "Arkansas Snowflake" made in Norman, Oklahoma, in late 1942 and early 1943; it is 35 inches wide by 46 inches long. Here is Martha's sanguine description of a quilt that had the potential to bring her only sad feelings: "This pink, blue, and white baby quilt was made when we were expecting our first child. Our daughter did not survive the difficult delivery. However, the quilt was happily used by our next daughter, our son, and our two grandchildren; plus, through the years, it has covered many small visitors to our home." Collection of Ann Skelton Deemer, Westwego, Louisiana.

lenge to Alan, which was something he liked. It also appeared to be another step up for Alan's career, although Martha didn't really know what to think about moving to Mississippi. "My sister had lived in Mississippi with her soldier husband a few months during World War II, and she didn't have a very positive opinion of the state," Martha said. "A lot of people thought it was old and 'backwards,' as opposed to Oklahoma, which was a new state, with an active and enthusiastic population. One thing I really loved about Oklahoma was living on the prairie, where the wind blew every day. I liked that south wind, and I still miss it.

"The climate of Mississippi is so different. There are lots of days here with no wind, nothing, stirring. However, much about the state has become wonderful to me—the longer I've lived here, the more I've liked it. I was fortunate when I came to Vicksburg that I immediately joined a lot of groups and became acquainted with lots of people really fast. We went to the First Presbyterian Church. I belonged to the American Association of University Women and two or three garden clubs. It's so important when you move to a new town to make friends with people who are not tied to your husband's job. I knew a lot of people connected with the [Corps of Engineers] station, but I also enjoyed people whose husbands did different things and had different interests."[11]

A son, Gordon, soon joined the family. He was born on October 31, 1949, when Ann Hope was almost four years old. Martha's life was very busy with tending to her infant son, shuttling Ann

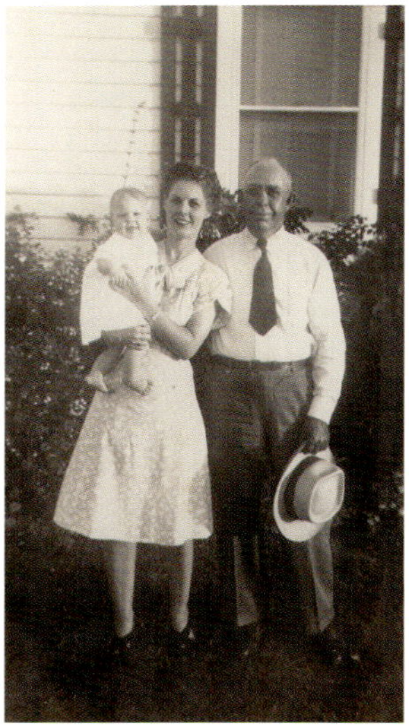

A proud grandfather, William Harrison Butcher, beams as his daughter, Martha, holds his granddaughter, Ann Hope, in Tulsa in 1946.

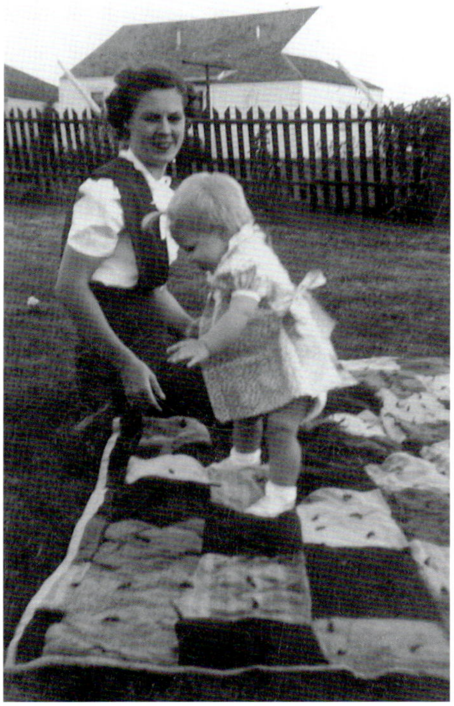

Right: Ann tests her balance at nearly one year of age, on October 27, 1946, in Tulsa. Note the quilt on which mother and daughter are playing, undoubtedly made by Martha to be used just as shown—as a utility piece.

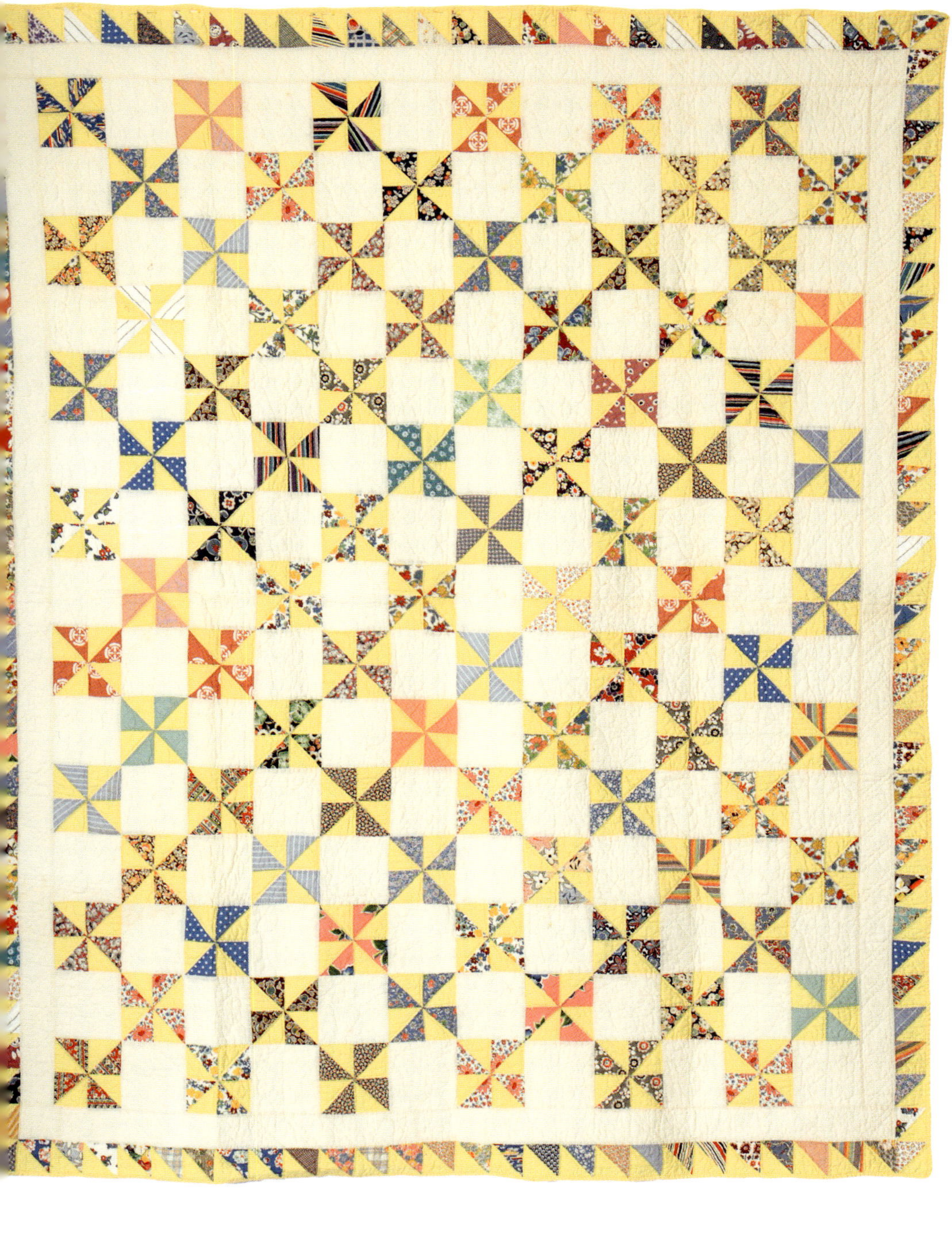

Quilt #131. "Pinwheel" cut in Norman, Oklahoma, in 1943, pieced in Vicksburg in 1948, and quilted in Vicksburg in 1957 and 1958. It is 73.5 inches wide by 86.25 inches long. Lots of tiny triangles in 1930s prints lay in a metal box for years before Martha decided to pair them with a yellow percale to make pinwheel blocks. After she had all the pinwheel blocks she needed, there were triangles left over. "[Because] I couldn't bear to not use all the triangles cut so long ago, I pieced the remaining ones into the border," said Martha. Collection of the maker.

to kindergarten, and keeping up with her gardening and church work. Alan and Martha had been part of a group that formed a new Presbyterian church (Westminster) not far from their home, and she was immediately recruited to be in charge of the primary Sunday School. She also taught a church "circle," or women's group, regularly, for "years and years."[12] Meantime, she "was always making something. That's part of my life—sewing is. Of course, I made all of Ann's clothes and my own clothes. I did any sewing that needed to be done for the household."[13] She also, in 1949, made a doll quilt for Ann—just a little "One Patch" with no batting,[14] but that is the only quilt on record (besides the "Pinwheel" she pieced) from that extraordinarily active time in Martha's life as a young wife and mother.

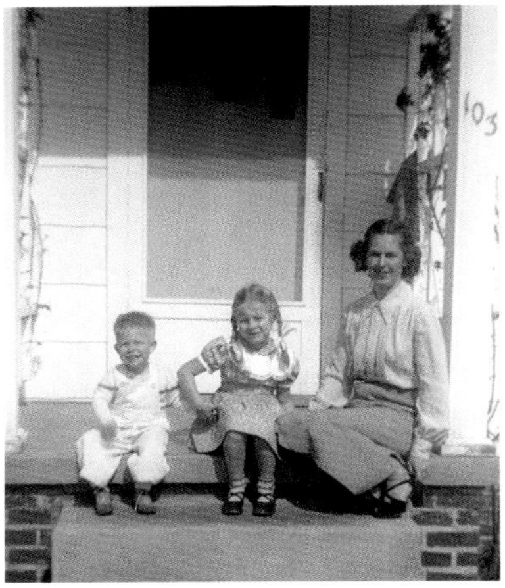

Gordon, about one year old, sits on the front steps of their home in Vicksburg with his sister, Ann, who is nearly five, and his mother, Martha, at thirty-one; the year is 1950.

When Ann got to be about six years old, Martha was asked to start a Brownie Scout troop for girls of Ann's age. Some thirty years later, in a letter dated April 4, 1980, one of the Brownies Martha had led recalled Martha's influence on her.

> I remember one particular Brownie Scout meeting in her (Martha's) living room. Each Brownie had a cigar box of fabric scraps and a needle and thread. And, she stood there and taught us the running stitch. It amazed me. I know what a traditionalist she is when it comes to quilting, so I use that same running stitch to sew my crosses (a patchwork pattern she uses in gifts) together. I can positively never knot off a thread without thinking of her. That knotting off was part of the same lesson. My running stitch hasn't improved much, but I think I have. Her Christian influence is in part responsible for that. Her Christian love like a thread runs through the fabric of my growing-up years.[15]

Thus Martha passed along the practice that had served her so well for so long, that of keeping a portable box of needlework on hand at all times. The work with the Brownie Scouts served as the beginning of her service as quilting teacher, an activity that not only would bring happiness to hundreds, if not thousands, of people, but would be one of the great joys and satisfactions of Martha's life. The teaching and sharing of her own work started slowly, however, because of the demands of motherhood. Martha continued to work with the Brownie Scouts for several years, occasionally agreeing to demonstrate quilting at Girl Scout meetings or at Pioneer Days at school.

Much to Martha's delight, her daughter Ann "really liked to sew. I showed her when she was young how to do embroidery and cross stitch and that kind of thing. We bought her an old treadle sewing machine when she was nine or ten years old. I thought she could start with that and then move on to electric later, and so she did. Her school friends would come over and they would sew and sew. They made doll clothes and aprons and whatever else they could think of. Ann still has that sewing machine today!"[16]

Ann and Gordon were always interested in whatever their mother was doing, including her stitching. Martha points out that one can carry on a conversation when one is sewing, especially if it is handwork rather than machine work, although it is possible with both. "If you've got a child who really wants to tell you something but doesn't want to look you straight in the eye when they do it, you will find that they'll talk to you if you are watching something else, like your sewing. It doesn't matter how young or old they are—they will talk more easily to you, ask you questions, or tell you something that happened at school. They want you to know, but don't know how to tell you. The children often came to me when I was sewing, because I always listened to them."[17] One can imagine that Gordon was particularly interested in watching his mother piece a "Bow Tie" for him in 1956, a design she chose because it is so appropriate for little boys. She used scraps from her sewing and quilted it in 1962.[18]

As the children got older and as Martha began to be invited to show her quilts and participate in events such as the Mississippi-Louisiana Fair in Vicksburg, they enjoyed seeing their mother in the public eye. "The children would go along; they were both really proud of my quilts. They really were (and are); that's a good feeling."[19]

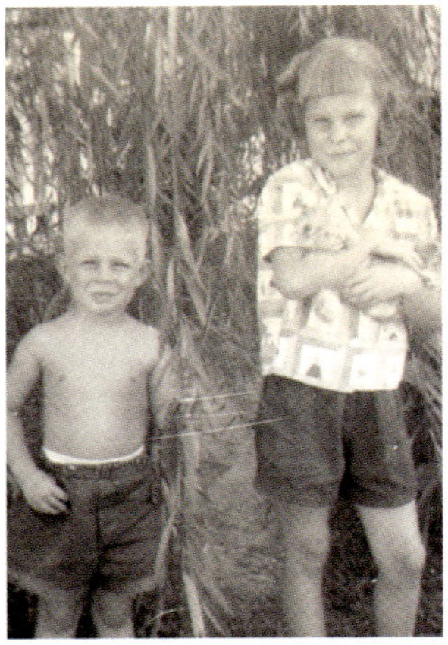

Gordon, at three, and Ann, at seven, with a new kitten, were always interested in whatever their mother was doing; they found they could talk to her about anything they wanted while she was sewing.

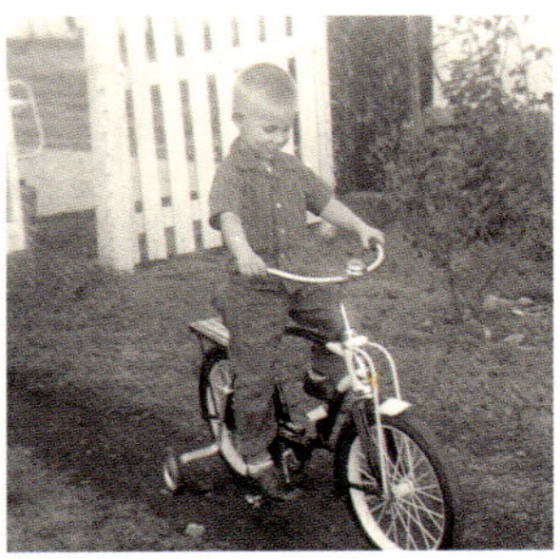

Gordon proudly shows off his brand-new bicycle, complete with training wheels, that he received on his fifth birthday. By this age, he and his sister could accompany Martha as she demonstrated quilting at county fairs and other such events.

Alan was always extremely encouraging and supportive of his wife's quilting. He made it possible for Martha to go to quilting events and would sometimes go with her if the outing was a one-day affair, especially if he could be of help. He supported her avocation in other ways as well. "At Christmas he always gave me material for a quilt. He would wrap each fabric in a different package, making a fun thing of it. He was always interested in what I was making, and it's always been a part of our time together—the fact that I did needlework and could go someplace with him and wait a while if necessary. I carried my sewing, so I was never bored."[20]

In 1959, Martha went back to work, starting at the junior high school, then moving to the library at the senior high. Her own children were old enough for her to have a little independence, she felt, and also, she had help in the home two or three days a week. Martha loved her job because she found that she really enjoyed working with teenagers. She also began making many more quilts, piecing them in the winter and quilting them in the summer. She could take her piecing to work with her in a box and work on it as she had time; in the summer she had time to put the quilt top into the frame and finish it. Of the ten or so quilts Martha made in the late 1950s and early 1960s, included are "Endless Chain,"[21] "Broken Dishes,"[22] a double star design Martha named "Mississippi Stars,"[23] two "Maple Leaf" quilts,[24] and "Wild Geese Flying,"[25] as well as the ones in the accompanying photographs.

Martha worked at the high school library for twelve or thirteen years, during which time she used her earnings to purchase a tract of land outside Vicksburg that the family calls "the Farm." "Alan and I had the philosophy that the family wasn't supposed to spend the second paycheck; we agreed that it was to go to something special, something we could see. It would have been all right to use it for college or something, but with the first money I earned, we bought the farm. It was the best thing I've ever spent my money on; it was wonderful, just wonderful. I love all the trees and walking the trails through them. For a while we had cows out there, and Ann named each of them, although you're not supposed to name your livestock. Gordon loved it and still does. We once put a little travel trailer out there so that

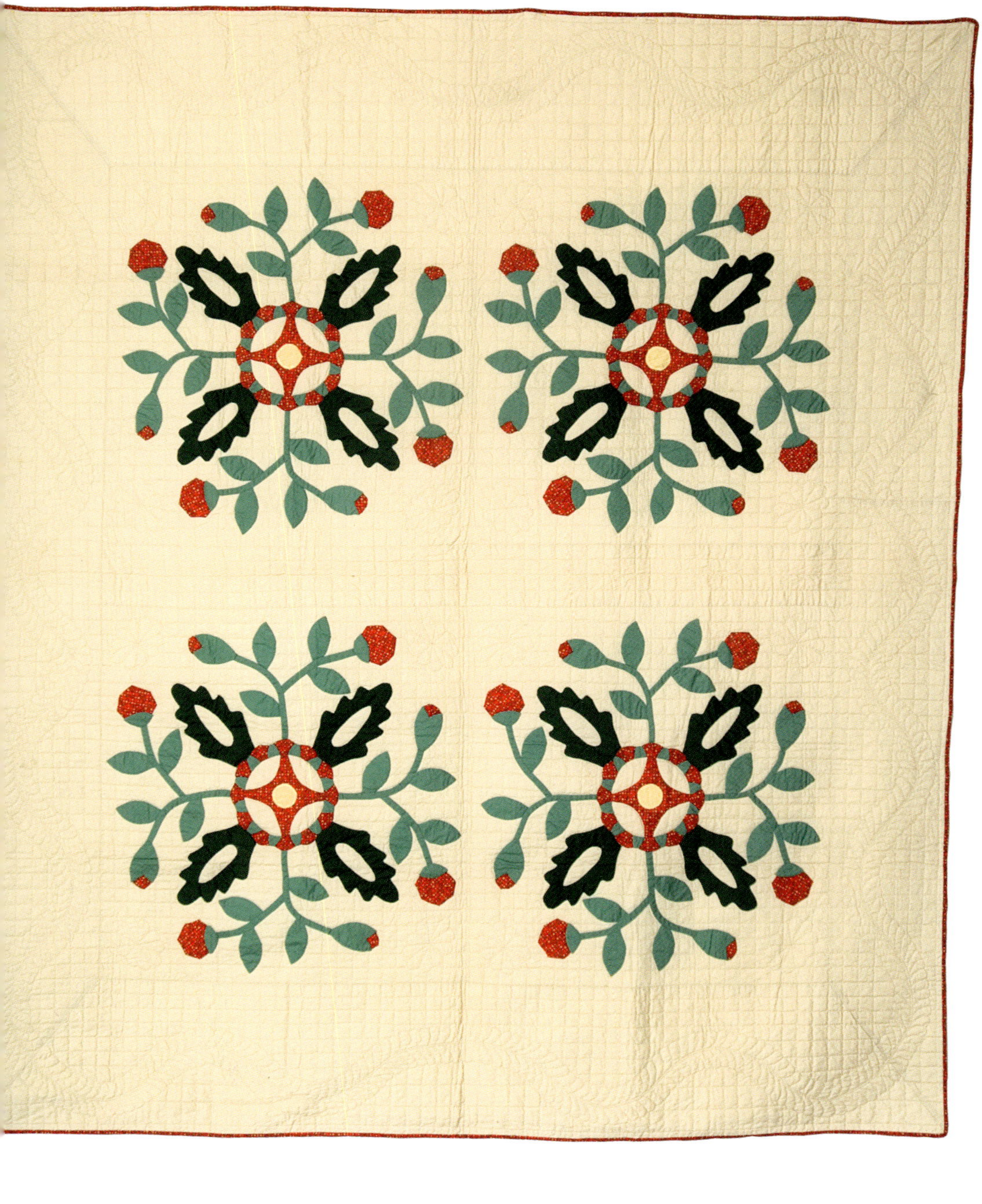

Quilt #13. "Rose of Sharon" made in 1963; it is 86.5 inches wide by 75 inches long. During a visit to the Fayetteville, Arkansas, area in the late 1950s or early '60s, the Skelton family drove past a house displaying quilts for sale; one of this design was among the offerings. Alan stopped the car, and Martha visited for quite a while with the quilt maker, Mrs. Bruce Brashears, wife of a retired University of Alabama professor. The two shared their love of quilting, and, when Martha expressed interest in buying a pattern for this quilt, Mrs. Brashears insisted on giving her personal copy of the pattern to Martha because she didn't plan to make another quilt of this design. Collection of the maker.

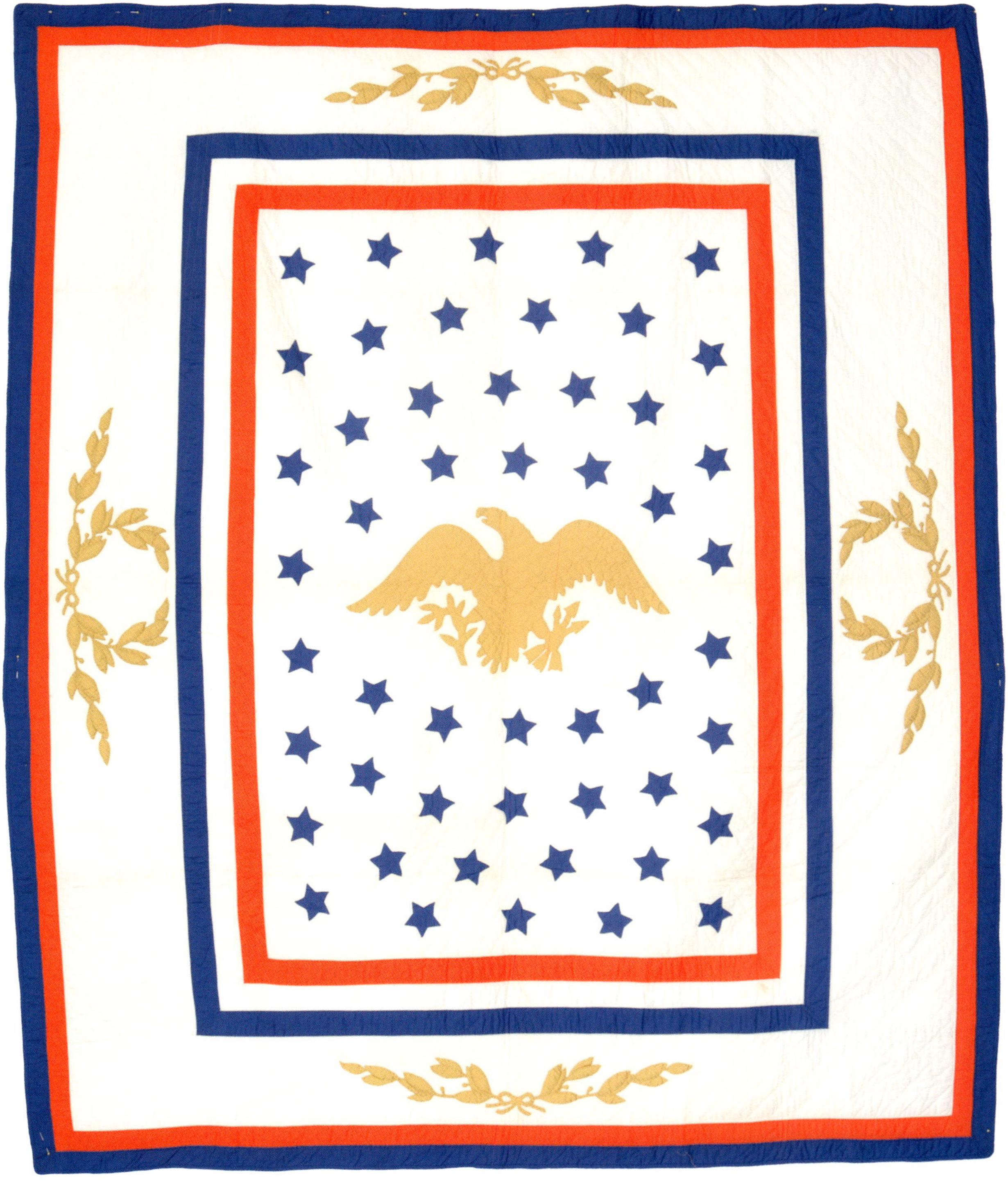

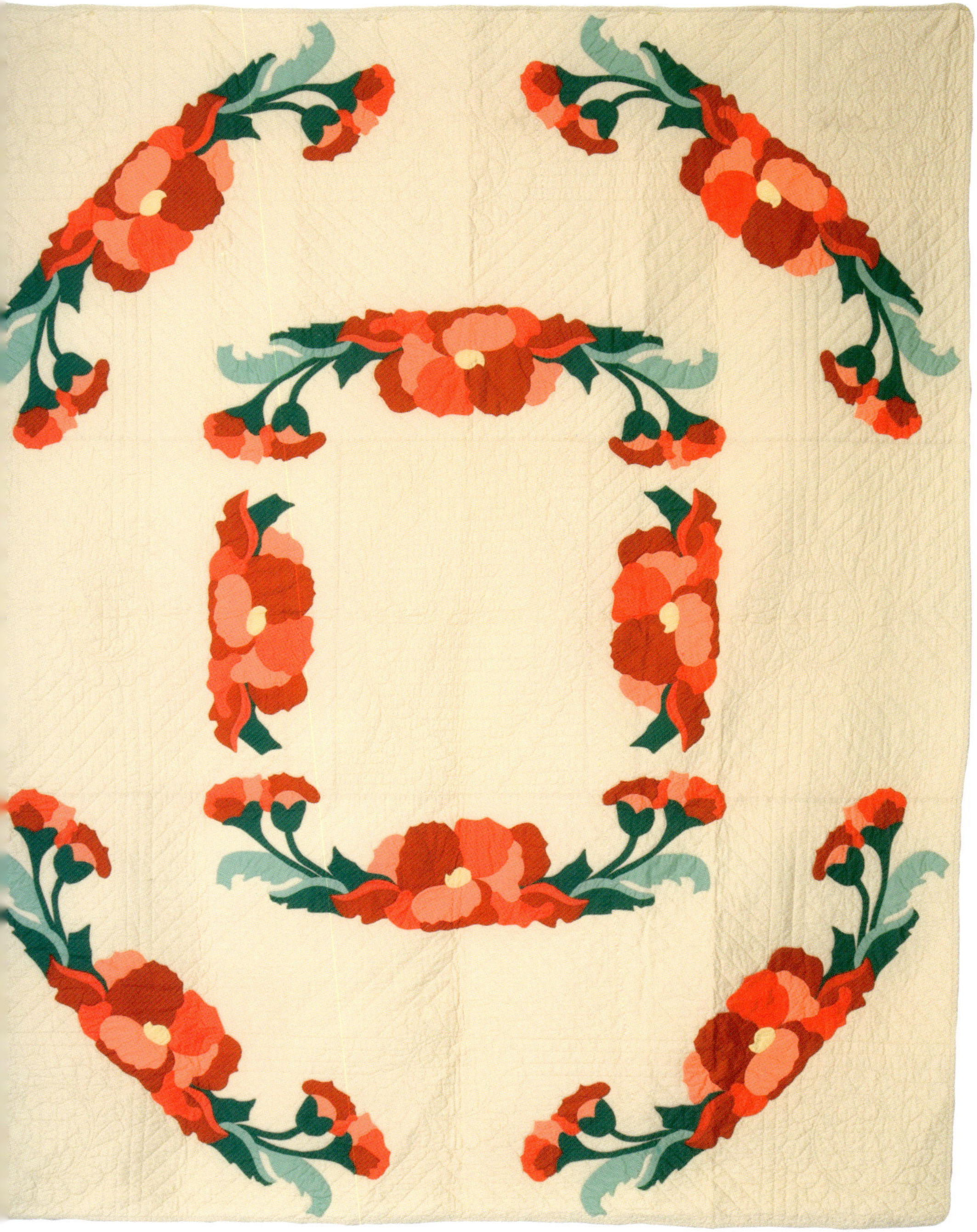

Quilt #46 (preceding page). "Eagle and Stars" made in 1964; it is 75.5 inches wide by 89.25 inches long. Gordon was an avid coin collector, so Martha adapted designs from silver dollars shown in his books for the olive branches and ribbons. The eagle is a traditional design to which Martha added details, and the stars represent each of the 50 states. The quilt was exhibited at the Mississippi State Fair in 1967. Collection of Gordon Skelton, Madison, Mississippi.

Quilt #51. "Poppy Wreath" made in 1965; it is 75 inches wide by 89 inches long. Although she followed exactly the suggestions in the directions for making this Mountain Mist pattern, Martha realized that she "doesn't like being restricted to a pattern for every detail of a quilt. It is lots more fun to improvise quilting to fit spaces." Collection of the maker.

Quilt #15. "Snow White Turtle Dove" made in 1972; it is 79.5 inches wide by 97.25 inches long. A literal interpretation of a soft-drink ditty allowed Martha to express her yearning for peace. The apple blossoms and the turtledoves have extra stuffing under the appliqué to make them a bit three-dimensional, and there are honey bees embroidered around the blossoms. Collection of the maker.

Alan and I could go for the weekend, get him completely away from work, and just be the two of us together. I still treasure it [the Farm]."[26]

During the years that Martha worked at the library, Ann Hope graduated from the University of Southern Mississippi, married, and had a son of her own (Marc Alan, born in 1970), to be followed by a daughter (Jennifer, born in 1976). On one of her visits to Vicksburg (from her own home in Mobile), Ann spotted a quilt top Martha had just finished and expressed her deep desire to have the finished quilt. Martha told her that she didn't know when she'd be able to get around to quilting it, so if Ann wanted it any time soon, she was just going to have to quilt it herself. "I wasn't being ugly. I just couldn't get to it," Martha says. "But I also knew that if she learned then, then she'll be able to quilt for herself from that time forward. When Ann responded that she had no quilting frame, her father told her that if that was all she needed, he could fix that. Sure enough, we got her set up with her own quilting frame, then helped her pin the layers of the quilt together. She took them home, quilted that first quilt, and hasn't stopped quilting since. She has made a fine quilter and I'm really proud of her. I think she does beautiful work, and this is the story of how she got started."[27]

In 1971, Gordon was in Vietnam with the army but was coming home in October for a month; Martha decided it was a good time to stop working at the library. Although there were many reasons for her retiring at that particular time, chief among them was that she wanted to be available to spend as much of that month as possible with her son before the army claimed him for his third and final year of service. "He and I had always done a lot of things together; we were pretty good buddies, and I felt like I needed to be home."[28] Gordon made it home from Vietnam whole in mind and body, served his final year for the army in Abilene, eventually earned bachelor's and master's degrees in political science, married, and settled in Jackson, Mississippi. Martha was grateful and relieved that Gordon was not injured in Vietnam, but the war haunted her, and she longed for the conflict to be over. A song in a soft-drink company's television advertising inspired a special quilt:

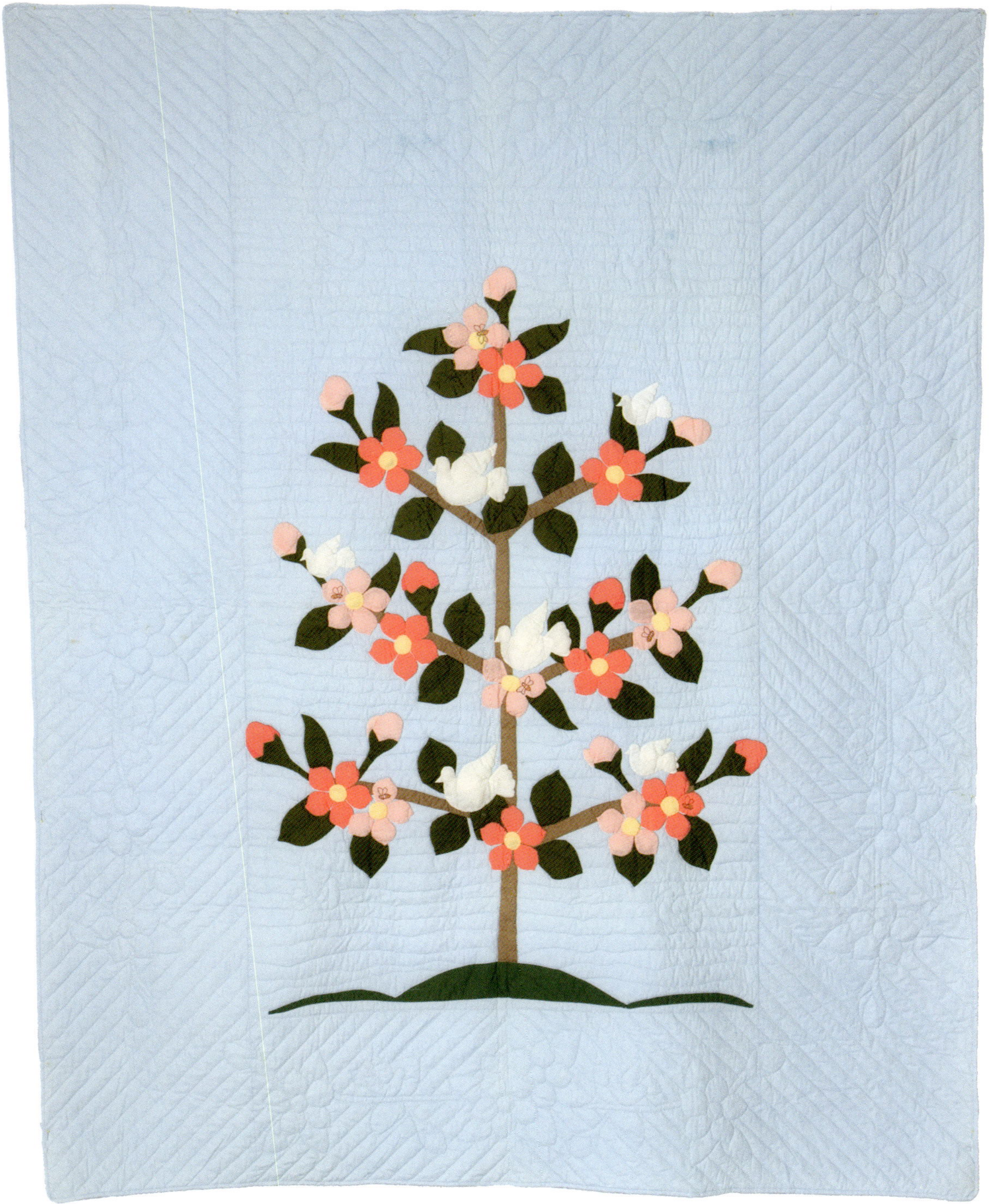

I'd like to build the world a home
And furnish it with love,
Grow apple trees and honey bees,
And snow-white turtledoves.

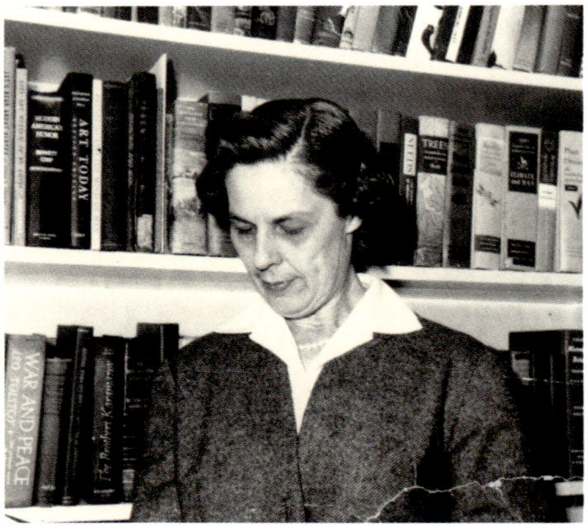

Martha at fifty-two, about the time she decided to retire from library work in 1971.

Of course, Alan was delighted when Martha retired because he had always wanted her to be free to travel with him, especially when his work took him out of Vicksburg. Besides sharing a love of gardening—Alan had beautiful roses—he and Martha enjoyed the farm and its trees and bird watching. Alan loved the outdoors and spent as much time as he could outside. Martha continued making quilts, completing at least twenty before 1975 and another fifteen or so between 1975 and 1980 (see lists at end of chapter). The arrival of the first grandchild, Marc Alan, Ann's son, was a joyous occasion for the Skeltons, and Martha made him a little appliquéd medallion quilt in the "Sunbonnet Sue and Overall Sam" design.[29] In late 1975, in anticipation of the arrival of Ann's second child, Martha made the new baby a special appliquéd quilt in an original interpretation of the "Wynken, Blynken, and Nod" poem by Eugene Fields.[30]

Alan and Martha had reached a point of happy satisfaction in their life. Their children were settled in their own homes, and there were two healthy grandchildren to enjoy. Alan had solved many of the challenges that had attracted him to the Corps of Engineers, but there was always something new to accomplish. Martha was retired from the daily grind and having a wonderful time with her quilting. Now that she had more free time, she was beginning to explore the interesting new opportunities that began to open up, with surprising frequency, as a result of her unfailing (though almost solitary) interest and proficiency in the age-old home art. On January 25, 1974, Alan wrote to his daughter, then living in Mobile, with the

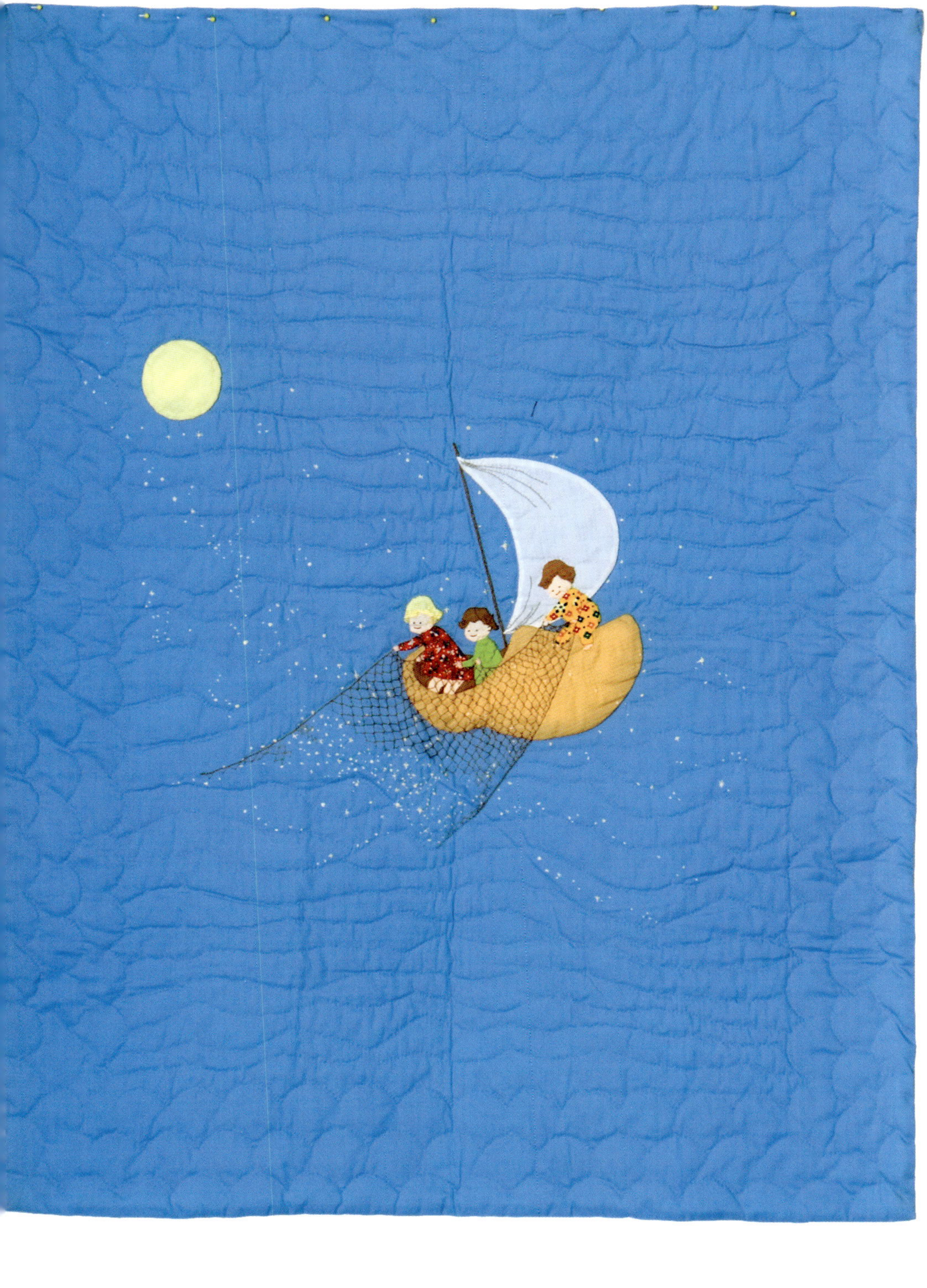

Quilt #6. "Fishermen Three" (aka "Wynken, Blynken, and Nod") made in 1975; it is 32.25 inches wide by 42 inches long. Martha studied the illustrations accompanying this well-known poem in a number of different children's books to find inspiration for her appliquéd and quilted interpretation. The little boy in pajamas is meant to represent her grandson, Marc Alan. The wooden shoe is padded to "make it round and plump as a wooden shoe should be." Collection of the granddaughter for whom it was made, Jennifer Ann Fentress, Baton Rouge, Louisiana.

purpose of reporting on Martha's accomplishments, but the letter also affords us a glimpse of the closeness and love that was core to the family:

> Dear Ann:
>
> The outreach of Mother's activities has touched the lives of many people! Evidence is enclosed including an item about Marc Alan which was enclosed with a picture the [Mississippi Park] Commission sent to Martha.
>
> Martha is so modest I know she will never send all the clippings, so I'm doing so.
>
> We are working on our trailer—new tires—new trailer coupler—new trailer hitches—one for each car. Now we are painting the trailer—undercoat of rust resistant paint—then we will paint it same color.
>
> Regards to Marc & Marc Alan, Pumpkin and Baby Kitten Kat.
>
> Love, Daddy

Although it would appear that little else was required for their perfect contentment, a wonderful honor and surprise was about to be bestowed on Martha. A letter arrived from the Smithsonian Institution inviting her to participate in the Mississippi presentation at the Eighth Annual Festival of American Folklife (now the American Folklife Festival) to be held July 3 through July 7, 1974, on the National Mall in Washington, D.C. The letter explained the methodology used to select participants:

> Throughout the year, experienced folklorists have been gathering information about the locales, peoples, customs, and life styles of the state of Mississippi. Through careful field research, we have identified those individuals who demonstrate the rich cultural traditions of our state. After meeting hundreds of musicians, cooks and skilled craftsmen, we selected approximately one hundred and twenty-five people who we feel represent the proud heritage of Mississippi. The decisions were difficult to make, but we will have succeeded if individuals like you come to Washington and share your unique experience with your countrymen from around the nation and the world.[31]

The invitation was followed within days by letters of congratulation from Governor Bill Waller and U.S. congressman from Mississippi Thad Cochran and from the U.S. Senate with senators James O. Eastland and John C. Stennis signing as well as congressmen Jamie Whitten, David Bowen, G. V. Montgomery, Trent Lott, and Thad Cochran. Not the kind of letters one generally expects in their morning mail! Martha was thrilled.

"They were looking for people who had made things and done things with their hands for a long time. It was really wonderful when they asked me if I would come," she remembered, still with a note of excitement in her voice. "They said you could get up to Washington one of two ways: they would give you a stipend and you could arrange your own transportation, or you could go on the chartered flight they were setting up. I chose the chartered flight.

"It was set up on the big open space of the Mall, with the prettiest little green and white tents. They had people cooking the foods of their area; they had people demonstrating all the different things that make up the flavor of the area that you're in. They had net makers from the coast, an oil well, and a saw mill. They had my quilting frames set up for me. They had picked them up ahead of time, along with a quilt that was all ready to go into the frames, and when I got there it was all ready for me. They had a different tent where they had hung two of my quilts, along with some pictures of me. They really had it set up so that people got a sense of what the state was like."[32]

Sarah Rose, Martha's sister, traveled to the Festival; she was the only one of Martha's family that could attend. In an interesting quirk of fate, Sarah Rose turned out to be the quilter who represented Oklahoma a few years later, when it was her state's turn to be featured. Fortunately, Martha, her older sister Garnett, and Ann Hope were all able to get to Washington to see Sarah Rose.

About the same time, the nation's upcoming bicentennial celebration was stirring up a great deal of interest in all the time-honored crafts, including, of course, quilting. Magazines had begun publishing articles and conducting contests as early as late 1974 and throughout 1975, in preparation for complete coverage of

Quilt #12. "Bicentennial Quilt" made in 1976; it is 73 inches wide by 92 inches long. In the newspaper clipping about this quilt, Martha is quoted as saying that she thought she might give it to her grandson, who, "at 5½ years old, is quite taken with the Bicentennial." The border contains 50 appliquéd stars, and the quilt has been exhibited at the Department of Agriculture's Agriculture and Forestry Museum in Jackson. Collection of the Old Capitol Museum, Jackson, Mississippi.

traditional crafts in 1976. Martha's quilting activities were affected by the national interest in 1776, just as were those of many other quilters across the nation (most of whom worked by themselves, with little knowledge of other people who were doing the same thing). Several articles about Martha's quilts appeared in the *Vicksburg Evening Post* in 1976, one in May, another in July, and a final one in November. In addition to the "Bicentennial Quilt," Martha designed and made the top for another "Bicentennial Quilt" that was quilted during the State Fair in Jackson in 1976. Seventy-two quilters worked on the Fair's "Bicentennial Quilt" through the "Quilting Bee," which had been organized by Martha.[33]

The Fair quilt consisted of a central red appliquéd "76" through which thirteen blue stars, representing the original colonies, were interspersed. Embroidered details included olive branches, symbolizing peace, as well as autographs of the president and vice president of the United States, the U.S. senators and representatives from Mississippi, and ten elected state officials and the Fair manager. Fifty stars are incorporated into the outer border. It is part of the permanent collection of the Department of Agriculture's Agriculture and Forestry Museum in Jackson, the state capital.

A decade filled with unexpected surprises, great accomplishments, and lots of familial love and harmony came to a sad end. The year 1979 had barely gotten started when Martha's happiness was shattered by Alan's sudden death of a heart attack at sixty-six, on January 26. There was no warning, and, just as with her mother, Martha was only a room away. The only difference in the two occasions was that this time she was alone—there was no Aunt Ettie. "I've had lots of people to die, and I've been standing by somebody when they got sick and died, but what happened to me with Alan was so hard because it had been a really nice day. It was a Friday, and Alan had spent the whole day checking on all of the thirty-three people who worked for him, speaking to everyone, telling jokes. His people really liked him," Martha said. "When he came home, he said he didn't feel so good, but it wasn't anything he could put his finger on. Bedtime came and he was in the back; I told him I'd lock up and check the house and be right along. I was in the front of

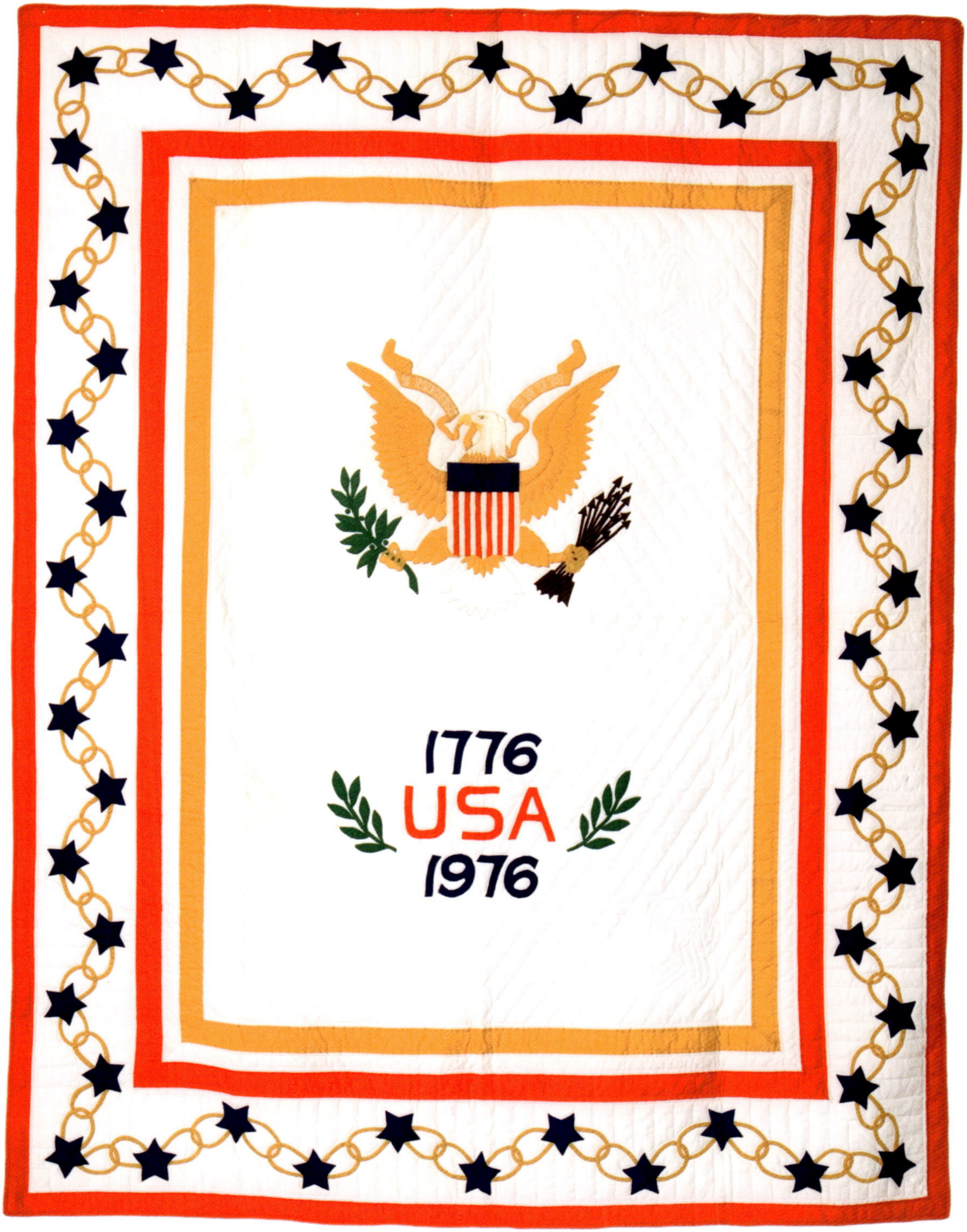
1776
USA
1976

Quilt #67. "Blue Clematis" made in the mid-1970s; it is 86 inches wide by 76 inches long. A pattern for the appliquéd flower block caught Martha's eye, and she decided to make a quilt. It was featured in *A Garden of Quilts* by this author in 1981 and was exhibited at the City of Mobile Museum in 1984. Collection of the maker. Photograph by Brian Loden.

Quilt #26 (following page). "Stamp Basket" made in 1978; it is 70 inches wide by 85.5 inches long. The issuance by the U.S. Post Office of a stamp that honored quilting was of great significance to what had been an almost-lost art. Martha's quilt repeats the design of the stamp, which is of four baskets with handles toward the center, six times to make a central medallion. Five borders complete the design. Collection of the maker.

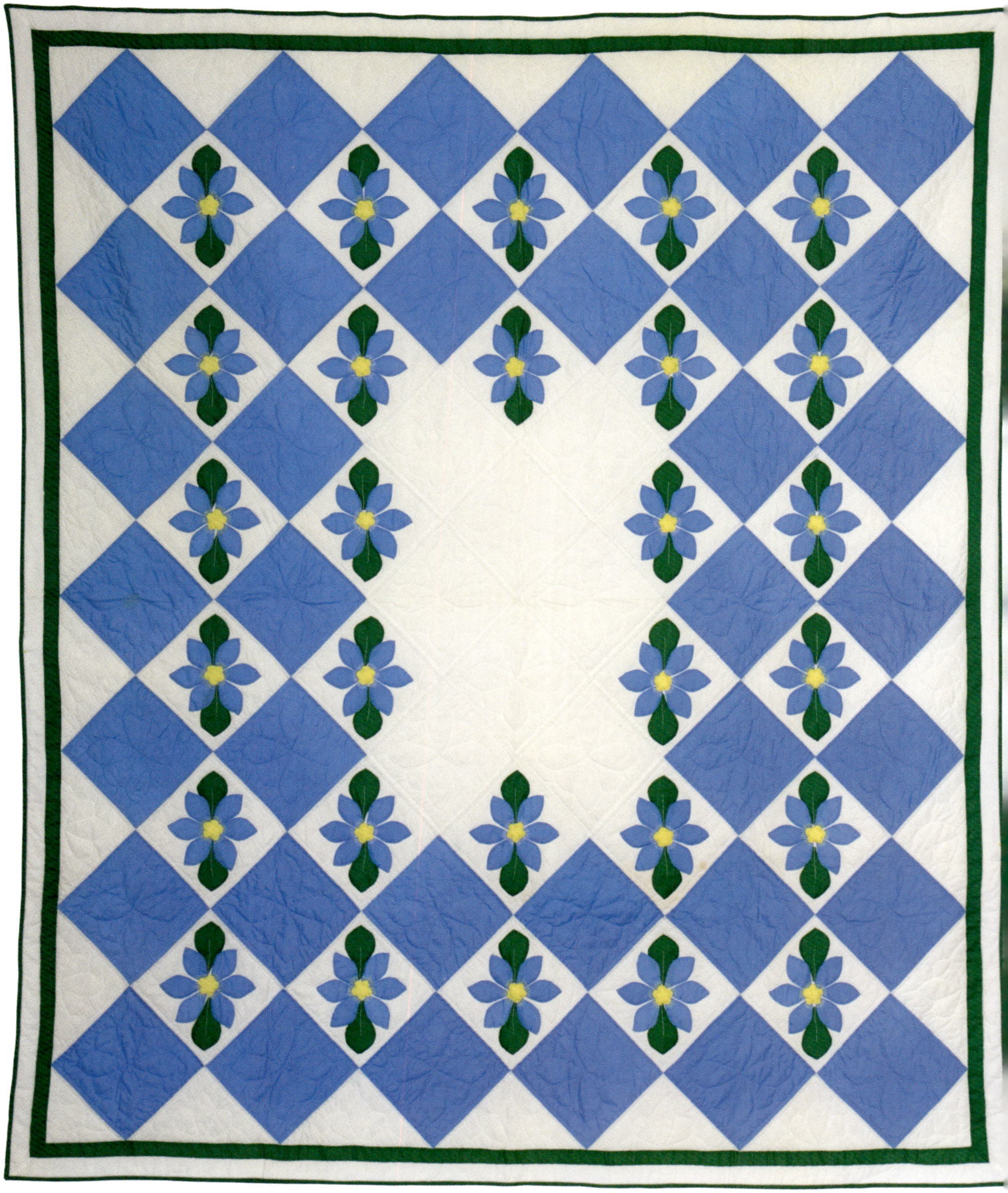

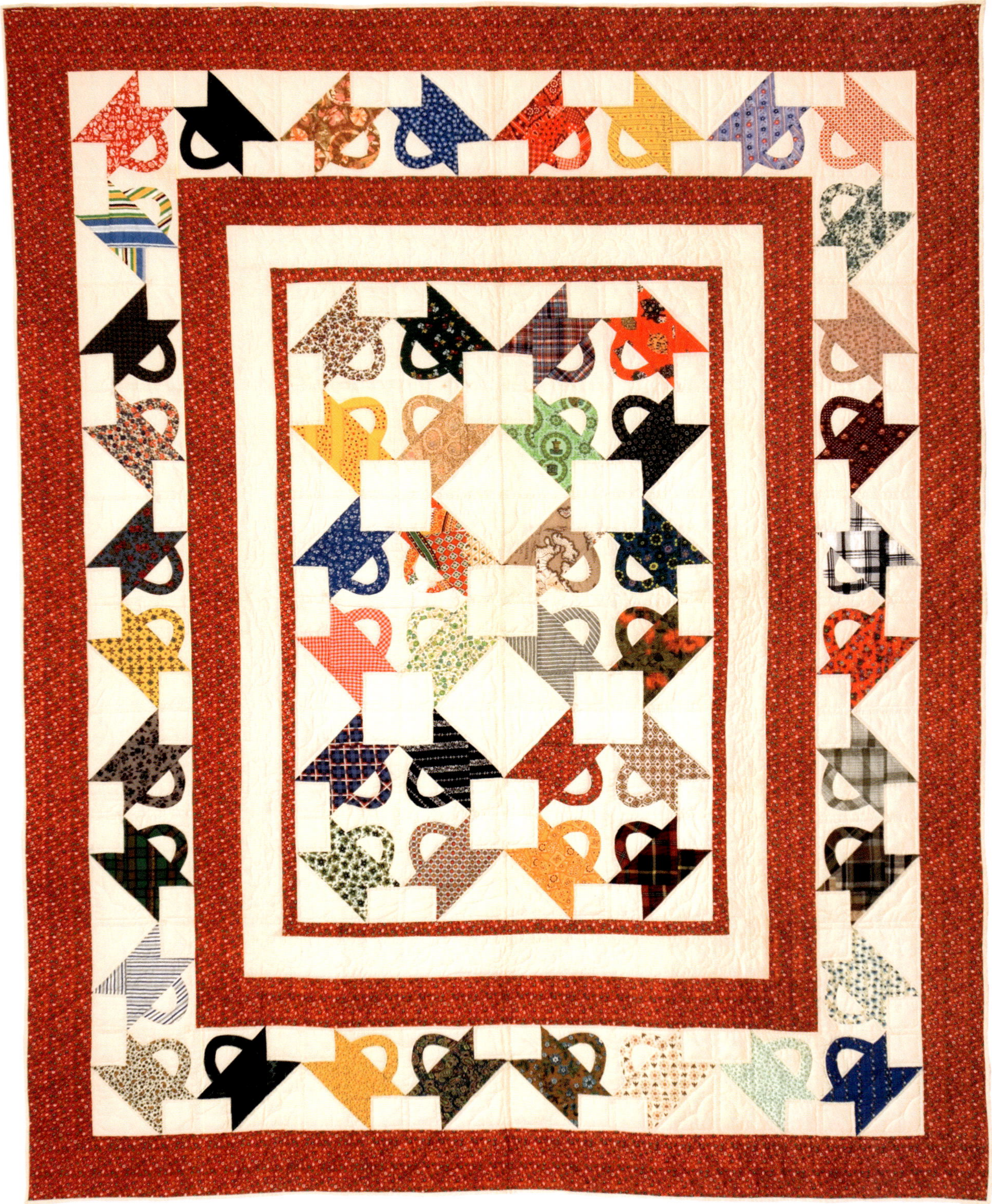

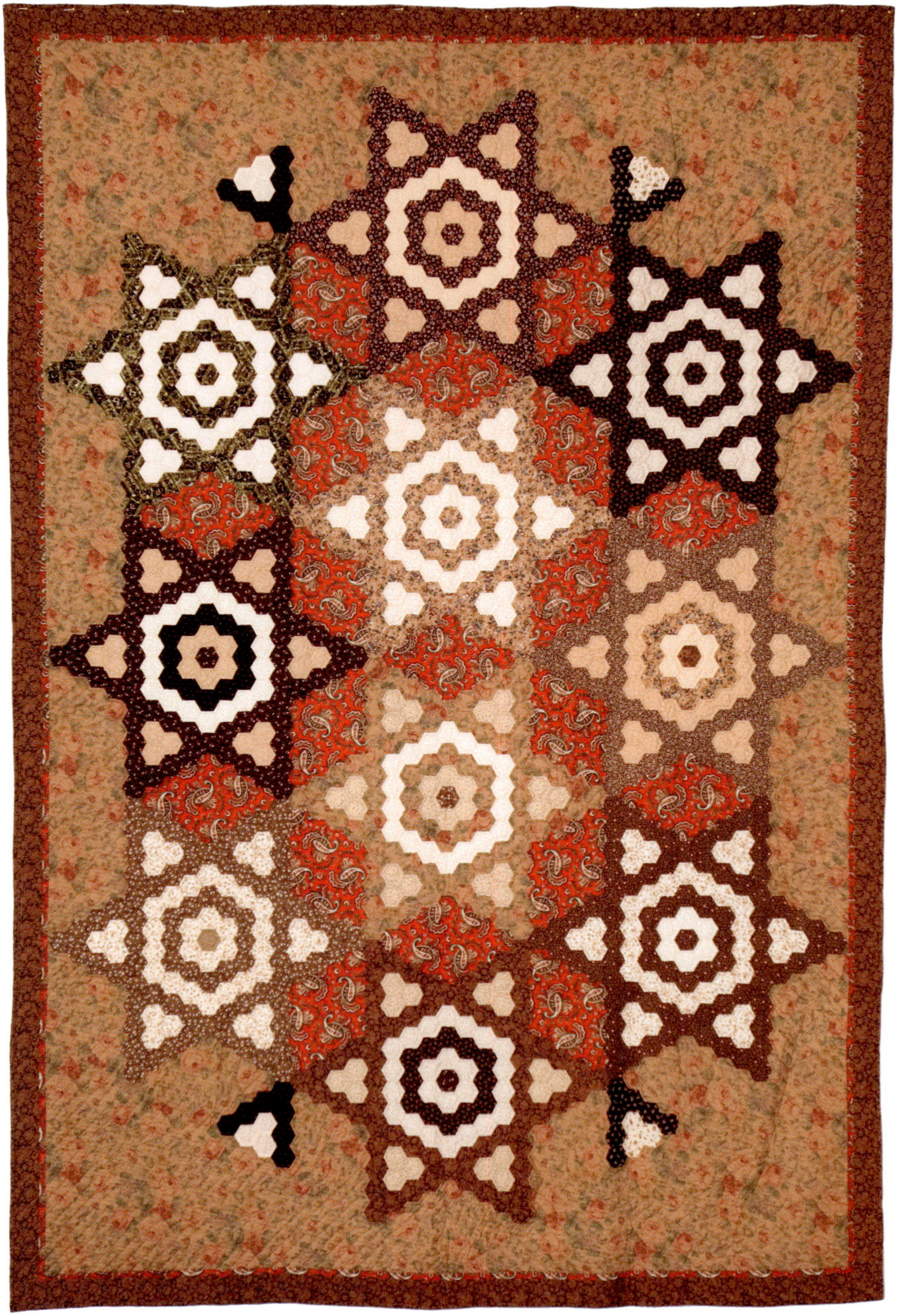

the house and I heard him make some kind of noise. When I got to the bedroom, he was lying across the bed and he was gone. I knew that immediately."[34]

At 10:30 in the evening, Martha drove herself to the hospital behind the ambulance, but when all the necessary things were taken care of, the concerned hospital staff would not allow her to drive herself back home. By the time her neighbors, called to the hospital, got her home, the house was filled with people. Gordon, who was living in Jackson with his wife, Sandy, came right over, and Ann came the next day. Ann stayed with her mother as long as she could, but she had young children at home who needed her. Martha's sister Garnett came and stayed a week; a cousin, Aunt Ethel's daughter, also came for a week. "So that's how I got through the very first part of it," Martha remembers. "But I think the main thing that got me through was that I knew I didn't have anything to regret. I had a great deal of faith that the Lord would take care of me and He only asks you to get through one day. I got through that day, and then the next day, and He got me through the next day. So, that's how I got through—a day at a time."[35]

Quilt #39. "Hexagon Star" made in late 1970s and early 1980s; it is 67.25 inches wide by 98 inches long. A quilt hanging in a booth at Quilt Festival in Houston spurred the idea for this unique piece; rarely does Martha use a printed background. This one is lavished with feathered plumes in the quilting. Collection of the maker.

Her quilts and her quilting friends also helped. Because it was Martha's habit to always have a project going, she didn't have to start something new to occupy herself. "I had always found that if I kept my hands busy and myself busy, I could work through a lot of things, so that's really what I did. As soon as the weather got a little better, I went outside and worked in the yard. Did lots and lots of yard work. Then I would come back inside and sew. I soon got back to going to the Cotton Patchers [quilt guild]. I didn't stay out long; I mean I didn't stay at home and not get out with people because for me that would have been a mistake. When I went back to the Cotton Patchers, they all understood that it was not always easy for me. That's what it takes—you have to have friends. You have to have your church. My preacher was real good—he was a wonderful man."[36]

Within a year or so, Martha was able, with the Cotton Patchers' help, to go ahead with a showing of her quilts that had been planned for an earlier date at the Vicksburg Library. "It was fun because it gave me a chance to see my quilts all in one group. Some of them were really important to me, such as one I had made for Alan, so that added to the pleasure of the exhibit."[37] Martha was living up to her mother's credo that she had heard so often in the first years of her life: "You might as well laugh as cry. You can make something good out of anything that happens. You don't have to feel like it is the end of the world."

Quilt #125. "'A,' the Alan Quilt" made in 1978 and 1979; it is 64.5 inches wide by 76 inches long. This is the second of two quilts Martha made for Alan. When *Quilter's Newsletter Magazine* announced a competition for quilt designs based on a letter of the alphabet, Martha chose "A" for her entry to honor Alan. She is grateful that she finished the quilt before he passed away, on January 26, 1979. Collection of the maker.

Additional Quilts Made between 1970 and 1980

"Sunbonnet Sue and Overall Sam," 1970
"Duck Paddle," 1970[38]
"Attic Windows," 1970[39]
"54-40 or Fight/Sunburst," pieced in 1970, quilted in 1999[40]
"Boston Commons," 1971[41]
"Golden Dreams," 1972[42]
"Butterflies and Flowers," 1973[43]
"Rose of Sharon," 1973[44]
"Mississippi Spring," 1973[45]
"Brown and Gold Medallion," 1974[46]
"Tumbling Block variation," 1974[47]
"Lancaster Rose and Tulip Ring," 1975[48]
"Class Sampler," early 1970s[49]
"Centennial Lily," early 1970s[50]
"Drunkard's Path" ("Rob Peter to Pay Paul"), early 1970s[51]
"Ohio Star," early 1970s[52]
"Cosmos," early 1970s[53]
"Yellow Rose Sampler," early 1970s[54]
"Trip Around the World," early 1970s[55]
"Star of Bethlehem" ("Lone Star"), 1970s[56]
"Rolling Star," 1975[57]
"Strippie Quilt," 1970s[58]
"Robin" wall hanging, 1970s[59]

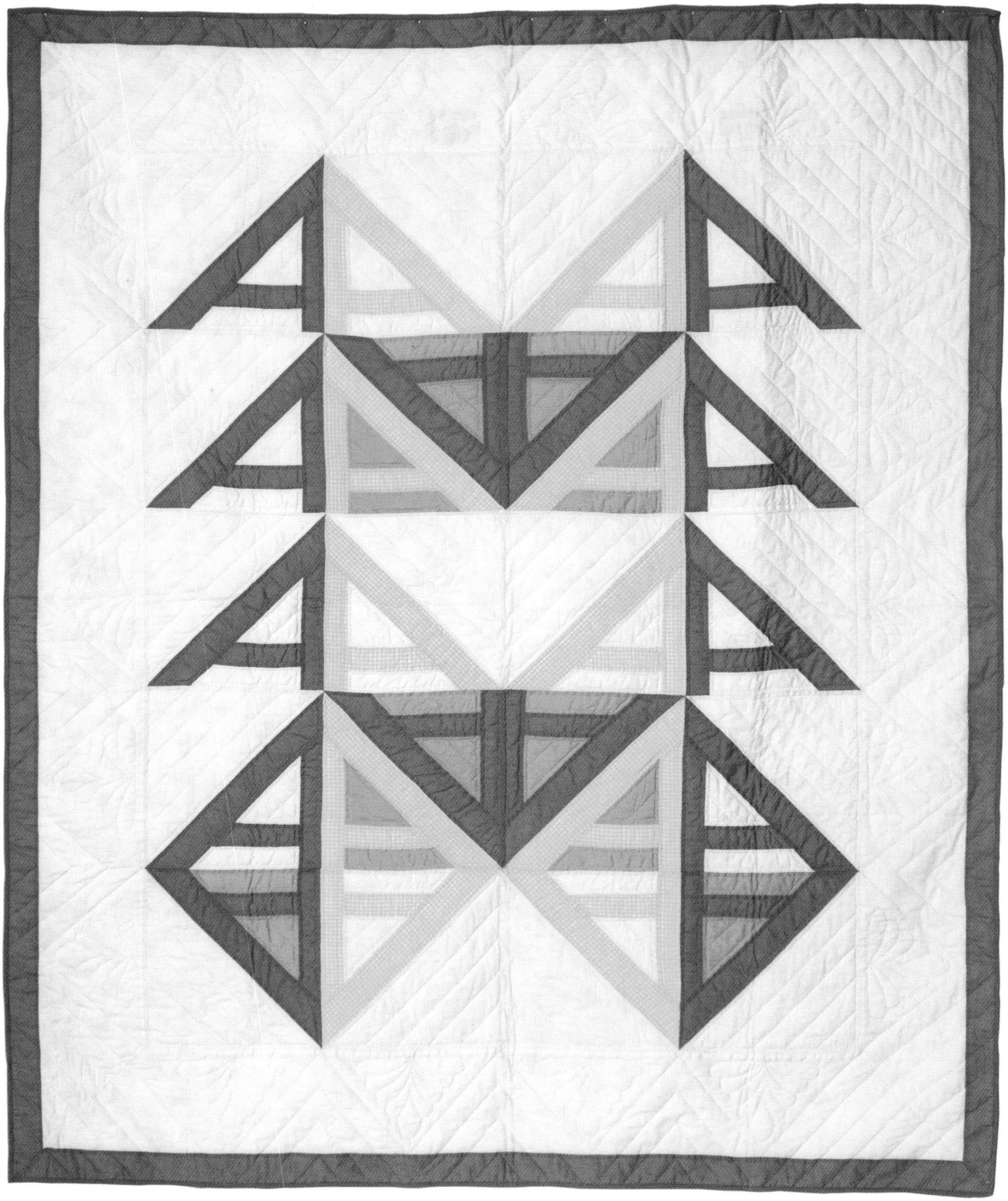

"Caesar's Crown," 1970s[60]
"Cathedral Windows," 1970s[61]
"Green Medallion Quilt," mid-1970s[62]
"Lily," 1977[63]
"Bride's Album Quilt," 1975–1980[64]

Martha in the 1980s: Teaching, Exhibiting, Competing

Martha's beginning as a teacher took place at the Valley Department Store in downtown Vicksburg. One day in the early 1970s, she was in the Valley shopping for fabric and began chatting with a clerk about what she was going to do with her purchase. They soon got around to the subject of quilting, and by the time the conversation was over, Martha had agreed to take some of her quilts down to the store for an exhibit. Because the fabric department was on the balcony, the steam pipes that ran across the ceiling of the first floor were at eye level and easy to reach, so Martha and the clerk simply draped the quilts over them. The effect from the first floor must have been spectacular, because store traffic immediately shot up, and management promptly invited Martha to teach regular classes at the store. She agreed with enthusiasm. "I was really into it," she says.[1]

Regular advertising in the *Vicksburg Evening Post* placed by the store supported the initial show and subsequent classes. Following is the text from an ad as it appeared on Thursday, September 6, 1973, accompanied by a line drawing of a bed with the sheets invitingly turned down over a quilt.

> Come and Learn Quilting. . . . Mrs. Alan Skelton will be on the Balcony, Friday, Sept. 7th demonstrating quilting, answering your questions, and displaying some of her beautiful quilts. Mrs. Skelton has taught a workshop for the Stitchery

> Guild in Jackson. She has won blue ribbons for her traditional and original designs at the State Fair. She has done demonstrations to various groups in the state and some television demonstrations.
>
> *You are cordially invited to come in and meet Mrs. Alan Skelton.*
>
> If you have an old or unusual quilt you would like to display, Contact Miss Tillie Harp, [telephone number].

Martha set up a schedule of three classes, each of which lasted from 1:00 to 4:00 p.m. The charge was a total of five dollars for the three sessions, and although there was no rule that the fabric must be purchased at the Valley, there was an emphasis on using good materials. The classes met on the balcony, and all the stitching was by hand because the quarters were too cramped to set up sewing machines. On the first day, each student—the class was limited to twelve—learned how to make templates, choose fabrics, and cut a small "Four Patch," which they hand-quilted before they left class. They were encouraged to turn their first day's work into a pincushion. As they learned advanced piecing and appliqué in the following two sessions, they turned their class work into pillow tops.

Vicksburg's first quilt guild, Cotton Patchers, was an outgrowth of the classes at the Valley. "I don't know how many people took classes at the Valley, but there was an awful lot of them. We always had a lot of new ones who would come from a good little ways away because they knew the classes were going on," Martha says.[2] She and her students formed the guild in order to keep in touch with one another after their classes had finished and to promote this "new" interest in quilting, about which little was widely known. They met every other Thursday from 1:00 to 4:00 in one of the member's homes. Many of them had decided that this quilting thing could be pretty exciting because, by this time, Martha was doing a little traveling for public appearances with her quilts, including a spot on television now and then. This is from the *Vicksburg Evening Post*, Wednesday, July 25, 1973:

> **Quilts, Pillows on TV Program By Mrs. Skelton**
>
> Quilts and pillows made by Mrs. Alan Skelton will be shown when she is interviewed on "Lyn's Notebook," a television program on WAPT Channel 16, Jackson, scheduled for 10:00 a.m. Thursday, July 26.

This same show will be seen in the Tupelo area one week later.

Both her original designs and traditional quilts will be featured. Mrs. Skelton has participated as a quilter in the Artisans in Action division of the Mississippi Arts Festival in 1972 and 1973. She has conducted workshops in quilting in Jackson and Vicksburg, and is a member of the Jackson Stitchery Guild.

Within three weeks, the *Clarion-Ledger* of Jackson was reporting this:

Exhibit Scheduled at Roosevelt Park

MENDENHALL—A colorful collection of quilted pillows by Mrs. Alan Skelton will be on display at Roosevelt State Park lodge Saturday, August 11 from 11:00 a.m. to 4:00 p.m., reports Larry Broadhead, State Park commissioner.

Mrs. Skelton, who recently displayed her stitchery craft at the Mississippi Arts Festival, is a member of the Jackson Stitchery Guild.

When asked about her stitchery work, Mrs. Skelton said, "I became interested in quilting about ten years ago. It is a time-consuming craft because of the great amount of needlework required to make a quilt. Usually it takes about two months to complete a quilt for a double bed."

"The quilting exhibit at Roosevelt Park lodge," stated Commissioner Broadhead, "is one of several craft exhibits being displayed in our state parks. We are pleased that Mrs. Skelton will be able to demonstrate her *unusual craft* [author's emphasis] at Roosevelt Park."

Quilts with dazzling patterns, some with traditional designs, others with creations of Mrs. Skelton's own, will be on exhibit for park guests' enjoyment. Dacron® quilted pillows, machine washable, will also be available for purchase.

A follow-up thank-you letter to Martha from the Mississippi Park Commission stated, "Your stitchery display was a great success as evidenced by the large number of park guests who came by to see your quilting."[3] This was not, however, Martha's first public appearance for the Mississippi Park Commission; that had been several years earlier on the Natchez Trace, just past Kosciusko. Alan had gone with her and helped her set up her quilt frame on sawhorses outdoors, where she demonstrated quilting and visited with folks. "We had a wonderful day; we had a good crowd. We were just out on the Trace doing this. People came and talked and visited. That was

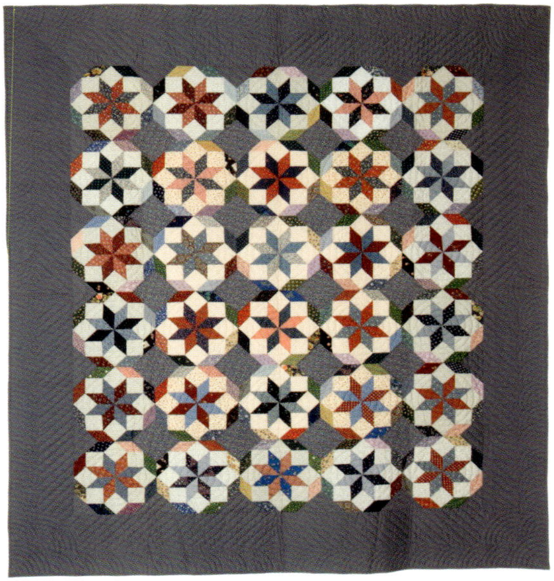

Quilt #40. "Rolling Star" made in 1975; it is 76.5 inches wide by 89 inches long. Students repeatedly asked Martha for a star pattern made in large blocks, and after a great deal of searching through her pattern stash, she found this one. She likes the secondary patterns that emerge when the blocks are set together. It was exhibited at the Mobile Museum of Fine Art, October 1984. Collection of the maker.

one of the first things I did. Once you ever do something like that, someone down the way will say, 'Come and do it here.' So when I could, I would go."[4]

Several years later, in September of 1979, the Mississippi Park Commission would again make use of Martha's talent. She would be included among only six artists asked to appear near Greenwood at Florewood River Plantation on the Yazoo River, a state park in the Delta that is no longer open. "I hear your quilts are truly works of art," remarked the person from the commission who extended the invitation.[5] Martha was advised that she would be paid an honorarium of thirty-five dollars and any orders she took or items she sold during her appearance would be hers. But, as Martha said in a newspaper article in 1976, "I'm not a seller, but I enjoy getting other people started in quilting."[6] In fact, the only quilts Martha has ever sold have been to museums and manufacturers of quilt-related materials for their permanent collections, and there have been less than ten of those.

As early as 1972 and 1973, Martha had begun teaching for the Cooperative Extension Service, a U.S. Department of Agriculture program that was administered through Mississippi State University. In one session, she conducted a quilting demonstration for seventy-one leaders in Hinds County.[7] Eventually, she taught all over the state—at West Point, Natchez, Brookhaven, Raleigh, Louisville, Philadelphia, and at towns along the coast. Consequently, she has long had friends statewide.

Martha recalls being in Yazoo City because it was there that she taught Ollie Jean Lane, an Extension Service home economist. "Ollie Jean's dream was that some day when she retired, she'd be able to quilt. She said she would give it one year after retirement, and if she couldn't get really good at it in one year, she'd be through with it. As it turns out, she's one of the best quilters in the state. She's really

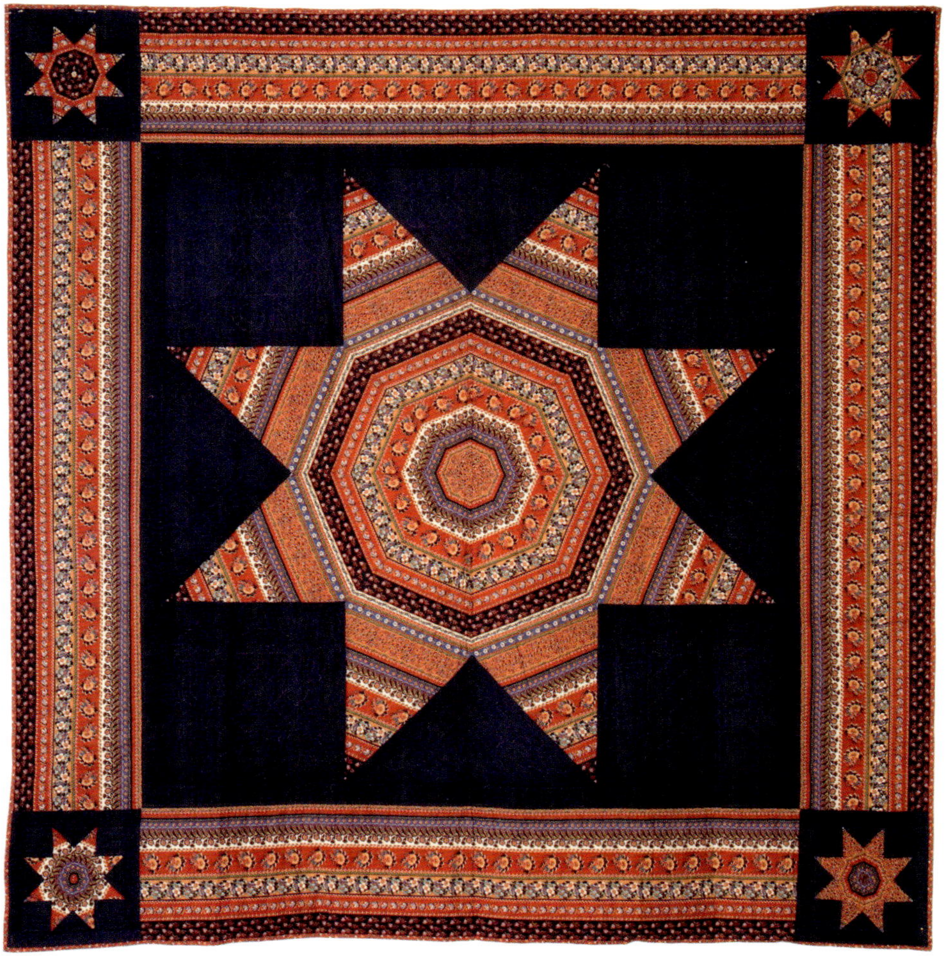

Quilt #68. "Star of Bethlehem" made in the mid-1970s; it is 82 inches wide by 82 inches long. It became popular in the mid-1970s to piece big eight-pointed stars such as this from striped or border-printed fabric. Each diamond had to be "fussy cut" so that the stripes would be exactly the same in each. Martha, always keen to stay abreast of the designs her quilting students were interested in, made up this "Striped Star" so that she could answer questions about it. The quilt was exhibited at the Museum of the City of Mobile. Collection of the maker.

good. I think it's meant a lot to her, and it's meant a lot to me to know her. That's really the value of the Extension teaching for me . . . that I got to know so many people in such a personal way, and to know that they were learning the skills to enjoy quilting as much as I do."[8]

The district leader of home economics programs for the Cooperative Extension Service wrote the following to Martha in 1981:

> Thanks so much for sharing your great talent for quilting with the ladies during the recent workshop. . . . You create the most beautiful quilts I have ever seen. With your love and enthusiasm for quilting, your workshops would have to be a success. In addition, you are an excellent teacher. . . . I sincerely appreciate the fine workshops you teach for our Extension Home Economists.[9]

Martha was very egalitarian in the sharing of her passion for quilting. She did not restrict her teaching to those professionals who would be teaching others: she also went into schools when she was invited and could schedule it, as this letter from a resource teacher in a middle school attests:

> It was such a treat to see you again and to see your beautiful quilts. You did a beautiful job of interesting the children in quilting as an activity. . . . Thank you for your interest in education and our students. You represent us beautifully wherever you go. And we are so proud of you. Thank you again for working with my students.[10]

Guilds across the Southeast invited Martha to hold workshops for them. She was a frequent visitor to Mobile because Ann Hope lived there, and she gave workshops for the Azalea City Quilt Guild from time to time. She also taught in Baton Rouge several times, judged quilt shows for the Patchwork Pelicans, and went to other guilds in Louisiana as well, including one in Alexandria. Other out-of-state teaching venues included Pensacola and Dallas, where she acquired additional fans in the guilds that hosted her.

After teaching a couple of workshops (one on hand piecing and another on piecing points and curves) at the American Quilter's Society show in Paducah in April of 1988, Martha decided that, although she enjoyed it, the show was too big and too crowded for her to enjoy personally if she was also teaching. "I had letters from people telling me how much they enjoyed the workshops and what it meant to them. They would write and ask me a question, and I'd write back. That was fun, but ultimately the teaching took away from the time I had at Paducah. I somehow just didn't really want to be one of those people who put all that pressure on themselves; I wanted to enjoy my quilting. I can enjoy it if I'm working with a group that doesn't put a lot of pressure. I wasn't interested in traveling all over the country or doing anything like that. I liked teaching all over the state. Most of the time I could leave early in the morning, could teach, and be back home for supper. I didn't feel like I was taking anything away from the children, when they were home, or from Alan. I didn't feel like I was cheating myself, and I sometimes think some of these [professional] teachers with children are cheating themselves. I don't see how they can handle all of that."[11]

Another project, for which Martha was originally responsible, that did a great deal to promote quilting in Mississippi was the State Fair Quilting Bee. She wrote in a July 1989 article for *Patchwork Quilts*,

> Attendance had been dropping at the Fair. In 1973 the State Commissioner of Agriculture and the Fair Commission decided to add some special events and family-oriented activities in an attempt to bolster attendance. Outdoors there would be a mule-powered mill grinding cane, the syrup would be cooked and served with hot biscuits on the spot, all free to onlookers. . . . [I]n the Exhibits Building would be an old-fashioned Quilting Bee. Area Extension Home Economists furnished lists of prospective quilters, and I was asked to coordinate the Bee. I was to provide the top, assembled and ready for quilting and then bind and finish at the Fair's conclusion. The same man made the set of [quilting] frames each year, and the quilters who volunteered to work on the quilt had a chance to win those frames as an incentive to work.
>
> Visitors were encouraged to ask questions of the "experts" at the quilting frames and to try their hand at stitching. Many of the older folks just liked to stand around and watch, reminiscing about life as it used to be, some telling how their mother or grandmother even hand-carded the cotton batts. They told of frames hanging from the ceiling. Talking to the visitors added a special dimension to the experience for all of us, and quilters returned year after year to take part.

> After the quilt was completed, it was returned to the Commissioner for final disposition. Governors and other state dignitaries have received quilts; one is in the collection of the State Historical Museum; and the Bicentennial Quilt belongs to the Agricultural and Forestry Museum in the state capital of Jackson.[12]

The Quilting Bee continues to be a feature at the Mississippi State Fair, and even after Martha was no longer in charge, the Fair maintained a practice she started at the very first one—the giving away of a quilt pattern to anyone who wanted it. It seems that quilters would send someone after the pattern if they couldn't get to the Fair themselves; many people are still collecting those free patterns, some thirty-five years later!

Eventually, a Fair quilt was presented to the commissioner of agriculture, whose idea it had been to institute the Quilting Bee. In a letter to Martha, he expressed his and his wife's pleasure at being the recipient of the quilt and made a point of saying that he had been told that a number of the quilters had suggested "this disposition" of that year's quilt. He added, "Since the Quilting Bee has been initiated, it has been one of my favorite Fair features, and I want to express my appreciation to you for making it the success it has been."[13]

When the Mississippi Arts Commission decided to form a state Craftsmen's Guild in the early 1970s, Martha was elected one of the original members. In order to be accepted into the Mississippi Craftsmen, one had to submit three pieces of work to be juried; exacting standards in each discipline had to be met. Members were obligated to present a public demonstration of their work once a year, in order to educate people about their craft, and they had to submit to being re-juried every three years. Martha was accepted on her first attempt, was renewed three years later, sat on the standards committee for the next three years, then was exempted from further jurying. "After I got so old," she laughs, "they told me that I didn't even have to pay my dues any more—I was paid up."[14]

When the Jackson Stitchery Guild mounted an exhibition at the Old Capitol Museum in June of 1974, Martha was already a contributing member. The group was made up of fine needleworkers, and they were interested in all of the needle arts. Originally, Martha had been invited by the Guild to teach some classes as quilting began to emerge as an area of interest across the country. In the beginning, she taught how to make things like small hand-pieced Christmas ornaments, and as time went by, she moved on to more challenging projects. Her association with the Guild lasted for about twenty years.[15]

The Appalachian Regional Commission, an organization of governors from nine states, in 1983 sponsored a conference entitled "Job Skills for the Future." The vice president of the United States, George H. W. Bush, was scheduled to attend the Jackson conference. Martha, as a member of the state's Craftsmen's Guild, was one of five people asked to demonstrate. (She was promised lunch, reimbursement for parking, and the opportunity to sell her work.) Martha remembers that she was introduced to each of the nine governors as they individually came to her quilt frame to watch her work. Afterwards, when she saw one of them on television, she enjoyed thinking, "I met him in Jackson."[16] She also found the men to be different from the audiences she was accustomed to, which were usually made up of women; they were, however, just as interested as any group for whom she had demonstrated. William Winter, the governor of Mississippi at the time, wrote and expressed his appreciation to Martha for her participation.[17]

Only three days after receiving the letter inviting her to participate in the Appalachian Regional Commission conference, Martha was given an opportunity to participate in another event not typically associated with quilting. An invitation to submit her work for inclusion in a show arrived from an art gallery in Sheboygan, Wisconsin. Sheboygan is the home of Kohler, the giant plumbing ware manufacturer, whose products depend on the expertise of ceramicists. As a means of acknowledging that the original success of the company had been dependent on the knowledge of skilled craftsmen, the John Michael Kohler Arts Center was established with the mission of publicizing the value of contemporary and traditional crafts. According to the *Milwaukee Journal*, the Center has been largely successful;

the paper cited exhibitions at the Whitney and the Guggenheim in New York City that featured crafts, as well as increased coverage in art journals.[18] The exhibition to which Martha was invited was held June 5 through August 14, 1983, and was entitled "Craft: An Expanding Definition." Her quilt, "Oak and Rose with Colonial Basket," (p. 60) was selected for display and was one of only two hundred objects in the show. Martha was thrilled because it was the first time her work would be shown in an *art* gallery, as opposed to a quilt show. She says, "After we began to have more of that sort of thing, people began to respect the fact that you were a quilter. They didn't think you were just a little old lady working down the street from them. You know a lot of the people still think that. I hear that all the time when I'm demonstrating—'My grandmother did that.'"[19]

Martha entered her first national quilting competition on July 25, 1979, when she submitted a block to Stearns & Foster, the parent company of Mountain Mist quilt batting, for their "Nursery Rhyme Quilt Contest." Several weeks later, a form letter arrived thanking all participants for their patience, explaining that they had received 712 entries, in contrast to the 300 to 350 that had been the norm in earlier contests. Finally, on January 9, 1980, a letter of congratulations arrived saying that, along with other winning squares, Martha's had been chosen to be stitched into a quilt that would then travel across the United States. The letter pointed out that the square became the property of Mountain Mist upon Martha's acceptance of the enclosed check for thirty-five dollars. In an effort to make sure her entry was different—not based on the overly familiar nursery rhymes—she went to the library and pored over books in the children's department. Her winning quilt block contained a robin in a cherry tree and was based on a little-known rhyme she located (and quickly forgot, once her block was made).

Martha began entering the different block contests sponsored by Mountain Mist and quickly had another design, a magnolia, accepted for the "State Flowers" quilt to be made of contestants' contributions. She was delighted when Mountain Mist allowed the finished "State Flowers" quilt to hang for several weeks at the Valley Department Store while her quilting classes were in session. It was great publicity for the store and the classes, as the *Vicksburg Evening Post* sent a photographer out to shoot the quilt for the paper.

When Mountain Mist decided to run a contest for full-size quilts in 1983, Martha and one of her dear quilting friends, Dr. Polly Sepulvado, decided they would each submit a quilt. Polly chose "Painted Poppies" and Martha picked out "Hollyhocks" from the catalog of Mountain Mist patterns. Despite the fact that the Mountain Mist contest had more entries than any quilt contest in the last fifty years,[20] both quilts were juried into the two hundred quilts that were accepted for the show at Houston that year. To Martha's great delight, one of Ann Hope's quilts, "Bunnies," was also accepted for exhibition. "Hollyhocks" took fifth place in the contest and was eventually bought by Mountain Mist for their permanent collection.

Martha's granddaughter, Jennifer Ann, was very disappointed when "Hollyhocks" went to Mountain Mist: "Grandma, you sold my quilt," she wailed to Martha. Martha had not known Jennifer was so enchanted with "Hollyhocks," and it made her feel "about two inches tall" that she had let it go. She and Jennifer did not speak of it again, but Martha quietly made a second "Hollyhocks," with fabrics left over from the first one—fortunately, there was enough. "I didn't do her out of it completely," Martha said, with a twinkle in her eye.[21]

The pattern Martha chose for her 1985 entry into the Mountain Mist contest was "Morning Glory." That year, she went with Ann Hope's Mobile quilt guild to Houston, where the winning quilts from that year's competition would be exhibited. As she and Ann entered the reception for the quilt show, they immediately noticed three quilts up on the stage. "There were two 'Morning Glory' quilts, and I don't remember what the other one was. I knew one of those was mine. You can't imagine how I felt, even though I didn't know who had taken what prize. It ended up that I had second prize, and the first prize was the other 'Morning Glory' quilt. The judges said they were so close they had a hard time telling which one to give what prize to. It didn't matter to me. If I had gotten that close [to first], I was so proud."[22] This win came with a cash prize of $750, plus a Caribbean cruise for two. (Martha gave the cruise to Gordon and his wife.)

Martha's outstanding talents, not surprisingly, caught the attention of Pamela

Reising, national sales manager for Mountain Mist. Several times over the next few years, she engaged Martha to make quilt tops for her, although Martha declined to quilt them, citing lack of time to get her own quilting done.[23]

Martha's association with the American Quilter's Society (AQS) in Paducah began with her "New York Beauty" quilt. The design had first attracted her attention at a quilt documentation day in Mobile in early 1984. She was serving as an evaluator and began to notice that there were a quite a few examples of "New York Beauty," plus variations, among the quilts brought in that day. Subsequently, she began paying closer attention when she saw the design in other places, and finally decided that she was going to make it. "I got my fabrics together, looking for whatever I had that would be enough for the quilt. I had pieces of a red print that I had bought at the Valley probably two or three years before; it was not on a bolt, but was several flat-folded pieces. I'd get it out to use it and then I'd say, 'There's not quite enough, or it's a little too much, so I'd put it back. I decided this was the time to use it—that it was right for this quilt. I really liked the fabric. I can pretty well judge how much fabric it's going to take and how I'm going to cut my pieces. I'm pretty thrifty, because I grew up in the Depression and learned to be careful with what I had. I don't mind if I get to the end and have to piece something a little bit. After all, if my grandmother had been working on it, she would have pieced if she needed to, to finish out a little bit of sashing or any other part of the quilt, so I do the same thing. After I chose my fabrics, I decided on how I wanted to set the blocks together. The pattern gave a choice of straight or diagonal set. I picked the diagonal set, and extended the lines so that the stars were complete at the ends of the sashing rather than being just partial stars. I pieced it by hand, and I enjoyed working on it because the pieces were little. I like to work on something that's not just simple piecing, but makes me pay attention to what I'm doing. I used lots of quilting in the solid areas of the pattern to bring out the design."[24]

The year following "New York Beauty," Martha made her "Chips and Whetstones" for the AQS contest. It took second place in its category in 1988. Martha explains that it was based, like so many of her quilts, on an old quilt that she altered slightly to please her eye. Because the pattern is old enough to be considered in the

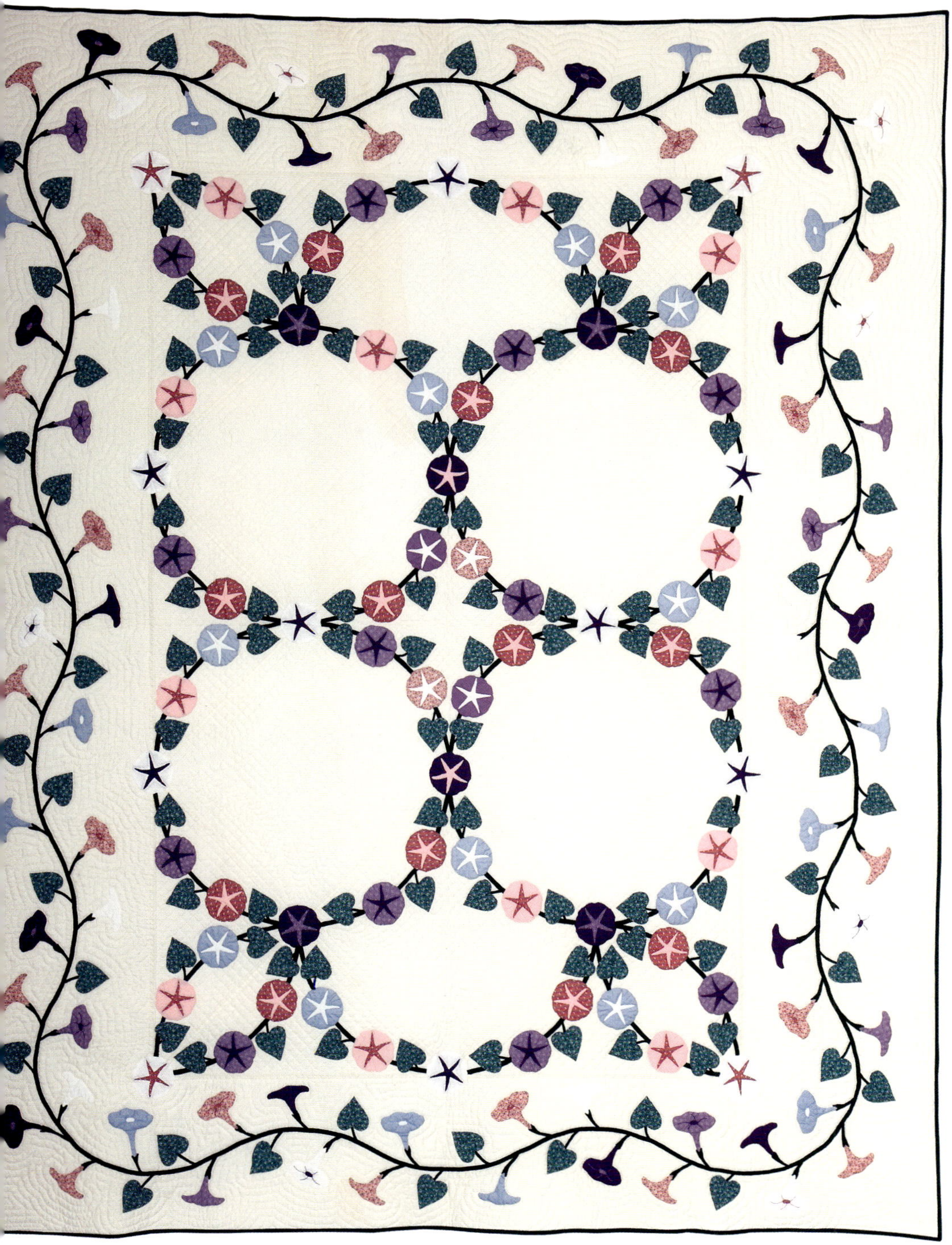

Quilt #151. "Morning Glory" made in 1985; it is 76 inches wide by 96 inches long. This quilt, made from a pattern copyrighted by Mountain Mist in 1933, won second place in the 1985 Mountain Mist contest. It was exhibited in Kentucky Oaks Mall in Paducah and published in the December/January 1997 issue (No. 115) of *Patchwork Quilts*. It was later purchased by Mountain Mist for their permanent collection. Photograph by Brian Loden. Quilt provided courtesy of Mountain Mist.

public domain, Martha points out, she could use the design without infringing on anyone's copyright. The blocks are pieced, following the design from one antique quilt, and the appliquéd border is from a different antique quilt she had seen in *Lady's Circle Patchwork Quilts*. It is a scrap quilt, as nearly all of hers are.

"I've submitted an entry almost every year to the AQS contest in Paducah," Martha says. "Any that I have entered have been accepted; I have never been turned down on a quilt, and I'm really proud of that."[25] The founders of the American Quilter's Society, Bill and Meredith Schroeder, were as quick as Pam Reising of Mountain Mist had been to recognize a truly outstanding talent, and quilts they purchased from Martha became regular features in their publications and promotional materials, just as her quilts for Mountain Mist had been shown on the wrappers for quilt batting and pattern catalogs. And although Martha had declined (ever so graciously) to do any more workshops for AQS, she continued to enjoy going to the show each year and taking classes from other teachers.

By the end of the 1980s, Martha was firmly established as the "go-to" person in the state of Mississippi if you wanted to know anything about quilting; organize a project, meeting, or event that had to do with the craft; or get encouragement for your own work. She had made it a point to join as many organizations as possible that would support her love of quilting and that would encourage her to share that love. It is doubtful that she missed any chance to enter a contest, give a demonstration, or speak to a guild. Surely one of the reasons for her success and acceptance has been her willingness to involve herself in any and all opportunities having to do with quilting. Although quilts may have a component of "solitary work" while under actual construction, they can also be tickets to a very wide world, as Martha proved early in her life, even at a time when quilting was considered "an unusual craft." It is safe to say that Martha's reputation as "The Quilt Lady" of Mississippi had been firmly established by the end of the 1980s.[26] She was entering her sixth decade with a wonderful reputation and a rosy outlook toward the future.

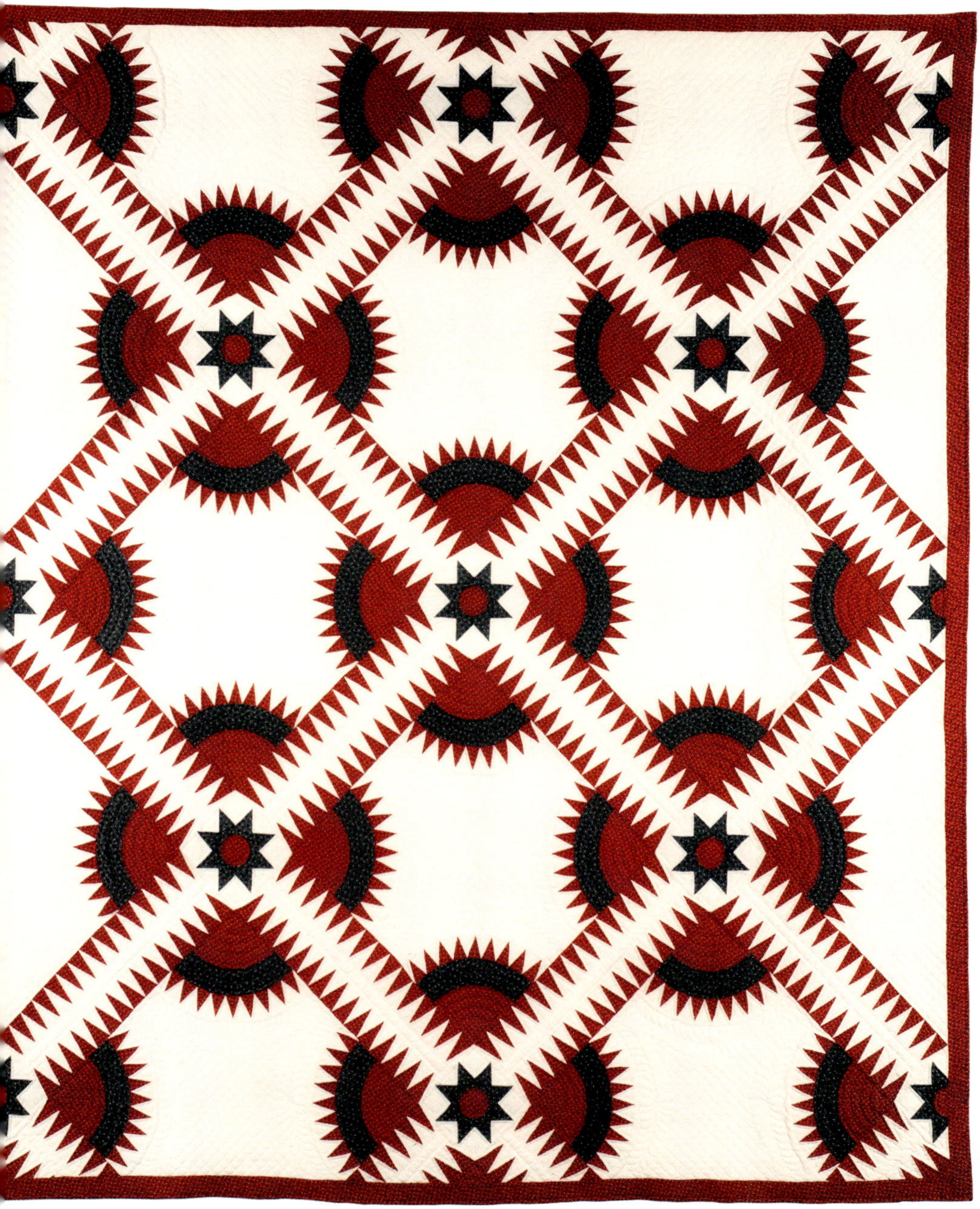

Quilt #152. "New York Beauty" made in 1986 and 1987; it is 77 inches wide by 90 inches long. Perhaps the most honored of all Martha Skelton's quilts, this exquisite piece won first place in the "Traditional Pieced, Professional" category in the 1987 American Quilter's Society Show and Contest in Paducah, Kentucky. It was exhibited at the Cotton Patchers' Quilt Show on May 10, 1987; featured in *The American Quilter*, fall 1987 (vol. 11, no. 3); and published in both editions (1991 and 2001) of MAQS [Museum of the American Quilter's Society]: *The Permanent Collection, QUILTS*; in *Award-Winning Quilts and Their Makers*, vol. 1, by Victoria Faoro (1991); in *Quilts: A Living Tradition*, by Robert Shaw (1995); in *Country Living* magazine (September 1991, "Quilter's Notebook"); and in *American Quilt Making, 1970–2000*, by Eleanor Levie (2004). It appears on the cover of the American Quilter's Society brochure and was chosen as one of the first quilts used in a series of jigsaw puzzles produced by AQS in October 1992. It is now in the Founders Collection of the Museum of the American Quilter's Society in Paducah, Kentucky (accession no. 1997.06.44). Photograph courtesy of MAQS.

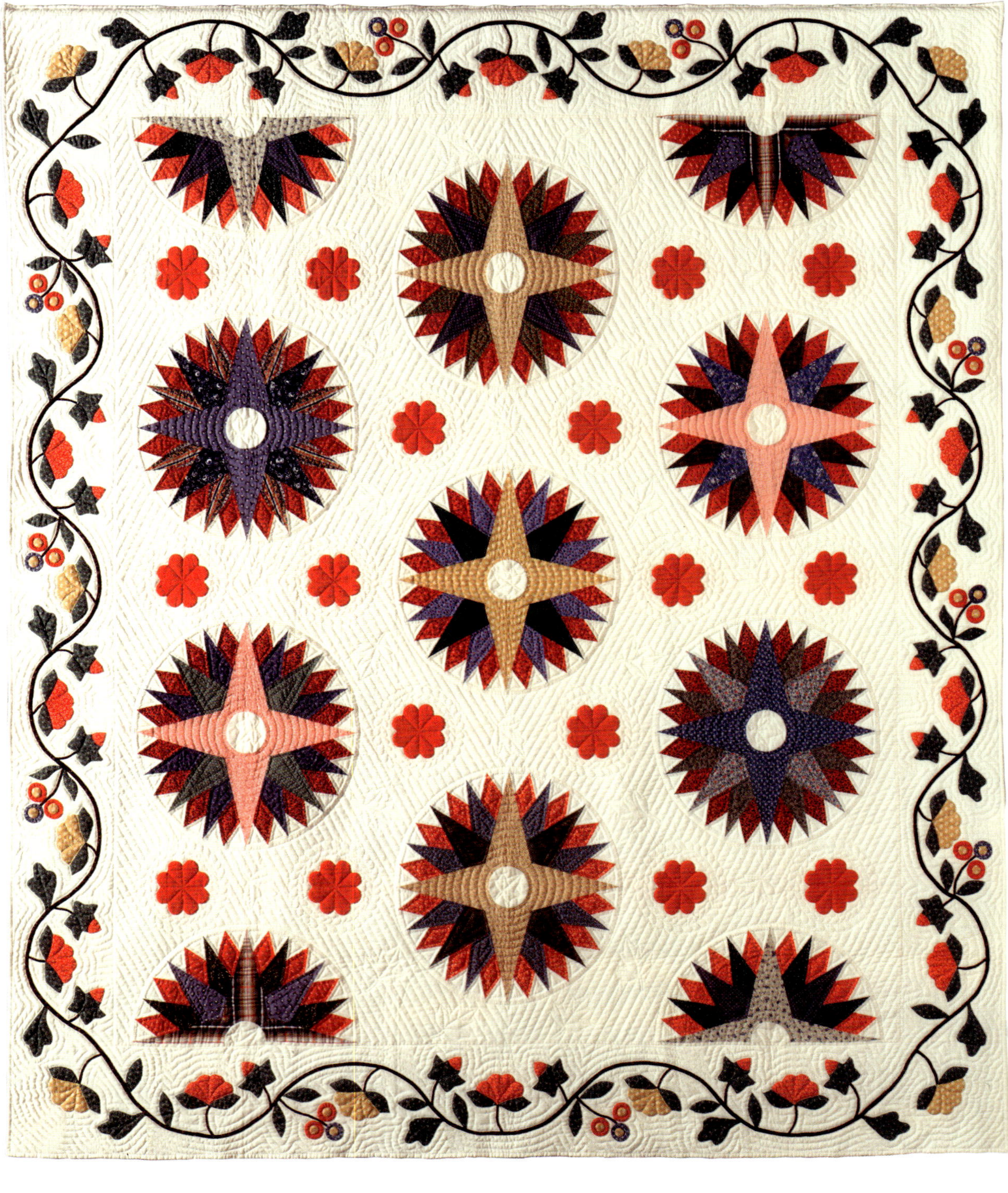

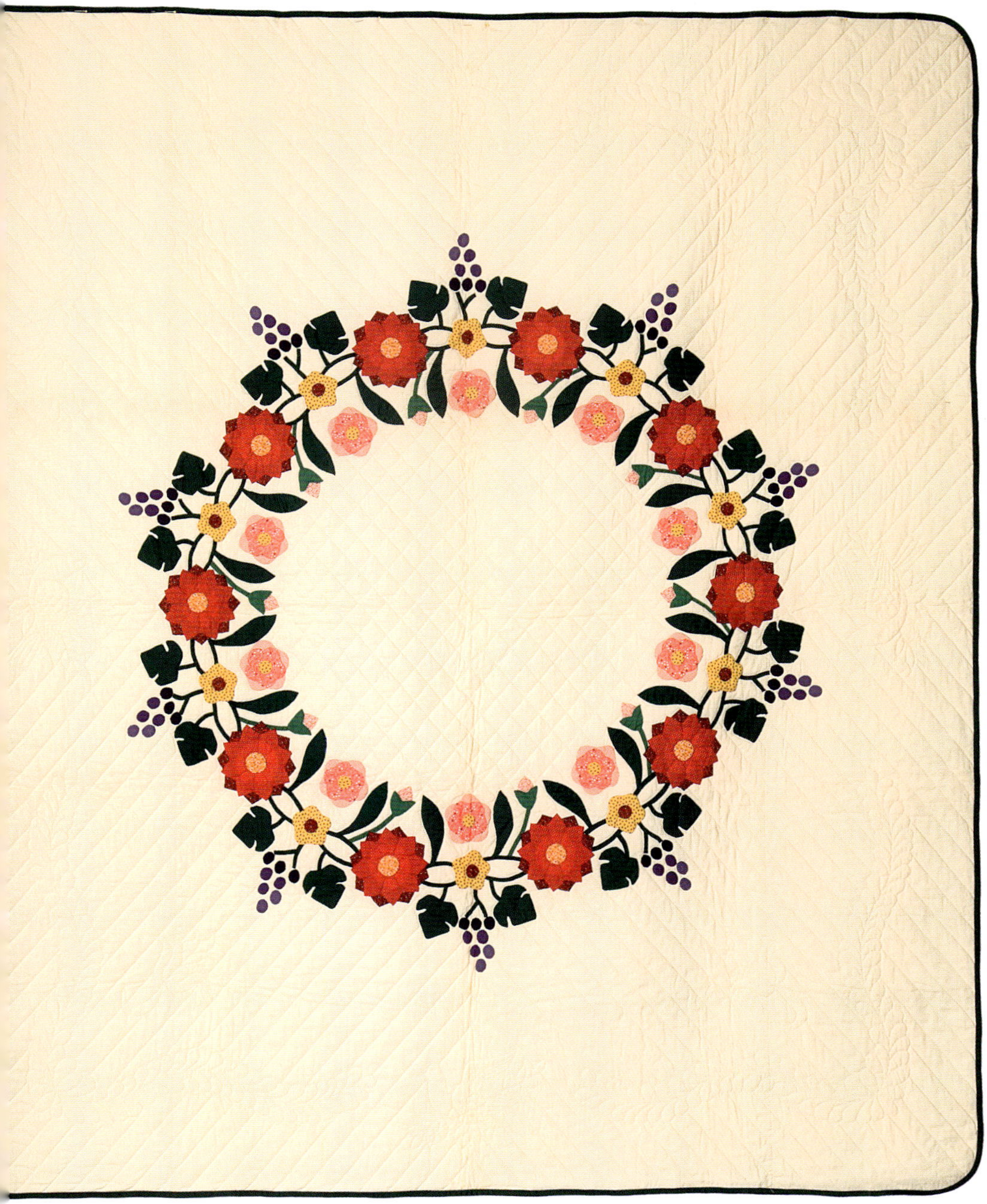

Quilt #153 (preceding page). "Chips and Whetstones" made in 1987; it is 80 inches wide by 89.5 inches long. This is probably the most widely recognized of the quilts Martha has made. "Chips and Whetstones" won second place in the "Traditional Pieced, Professional" category at the 1988 American Quilter's Society show in Paducah, Kentucky; it was on the cover of the winter 1989–1990 issue of *Quilt Digest*. It was published in *American Quilter* in fall 1988, and again in winter 1995 as the cover; in a Museum of the American Quilter's Society's publication, *Award-Winning Quilts and Their Makers*, in 1992, 1995, and 2001; and in Phyllis D. Miller's *Encyclopedia of Design for Quilting* in 1997. It is now in the Founders Collection of the Museum of the American Quilter's Society in Paducah, Kentucky (accession no. 1992.02.01). Photograph courtesy of MAQS.

Quilt #23. "Indiana Wreath" made in 1982; it is 73.5 inches wide by 84 inches long. Martha copied the pieces for this appliquéd quilt out of a book. "Indiana Wreath" was featured on page 25 in the July 1985 *Lady's Circle Patchwork Magazine*. Collection of the maker.

Quilt #35. "Oak and Rose with Colonial Basket" made in 1983; it is 75 inches wide by 88 inches long. This quilt was exhibited in "Craft: An Expanding Definition," at the John Michael Kohler Arts Center, governed by the Sheboygan Arts Foundation, Wisconsin. Collection of the maker.

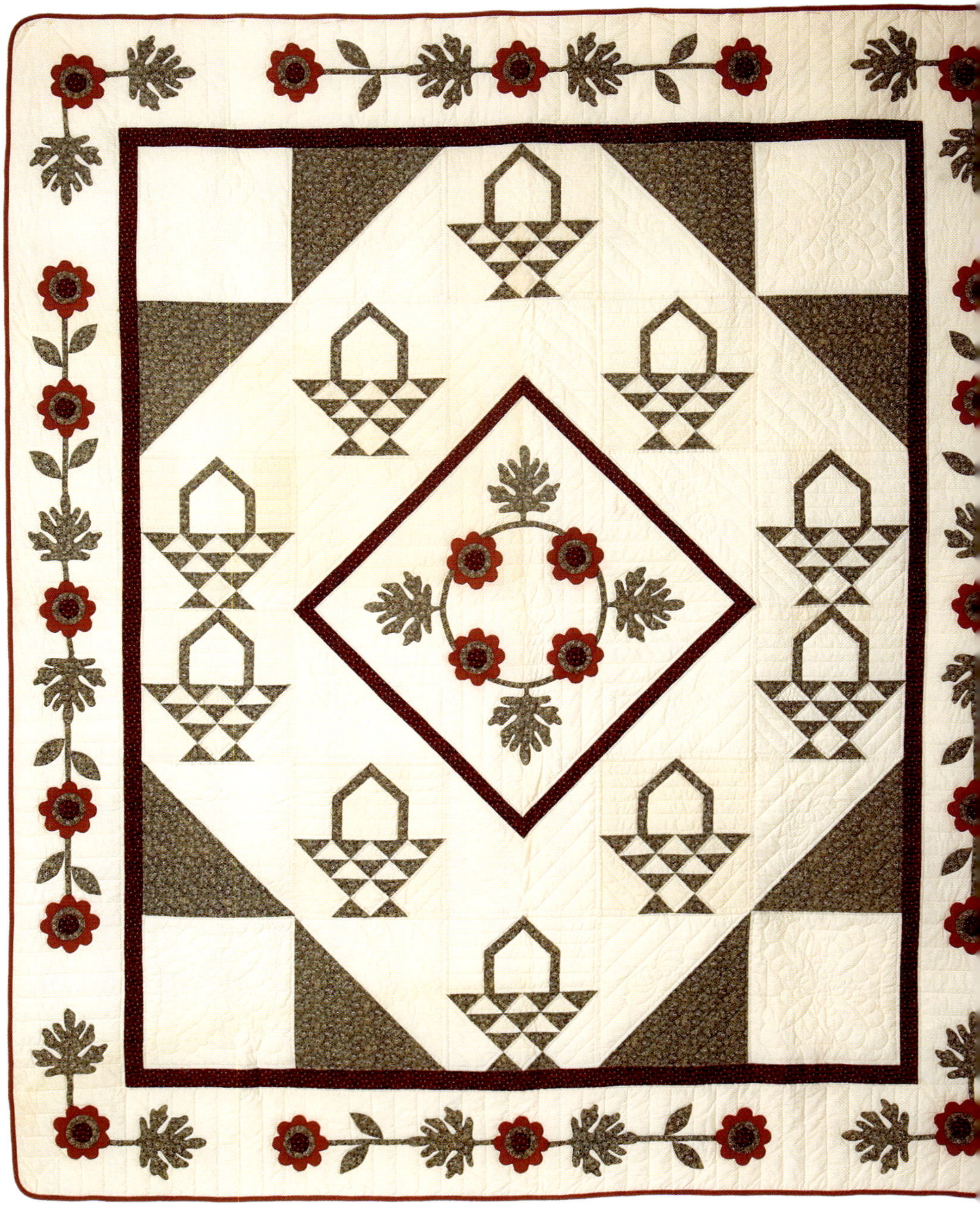

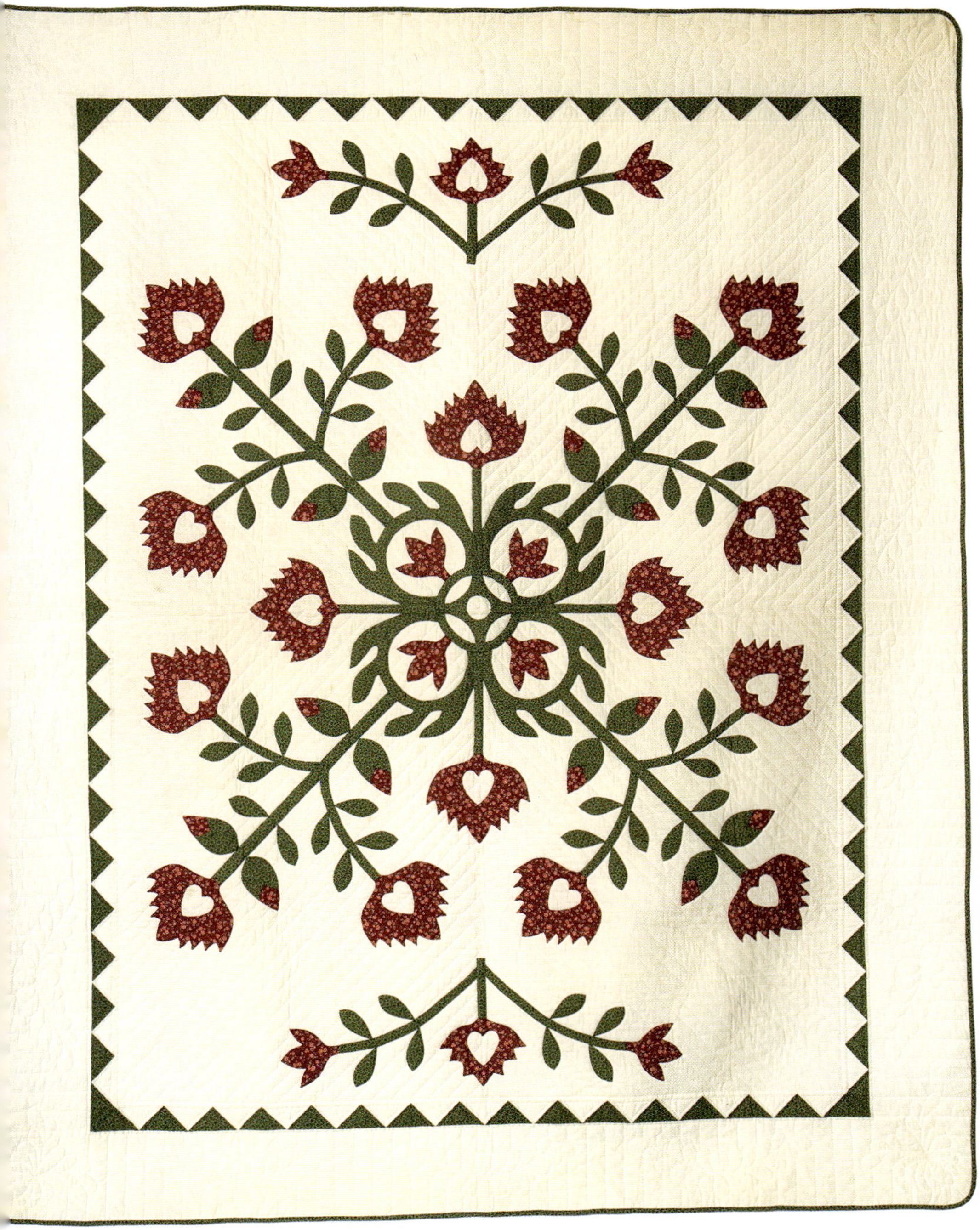

Quilt #154. "Cut-Paper Coxcomb, Folk Art Style" made in the 1980s; it is 80 inches wide by 95 inches long. Martha was taken by the beauty of a quilt she saw in a book by her friend Carter Houck, *American Quilts and How to Make Them*, and she pretty much replicated it in this quilt, except for the appliquéd border, which are her original touch. It was exhibited at the Museum of the City of Mobile in either 1984 or 1986. Collection of Gordon Skelton, Madison, Mississippi.

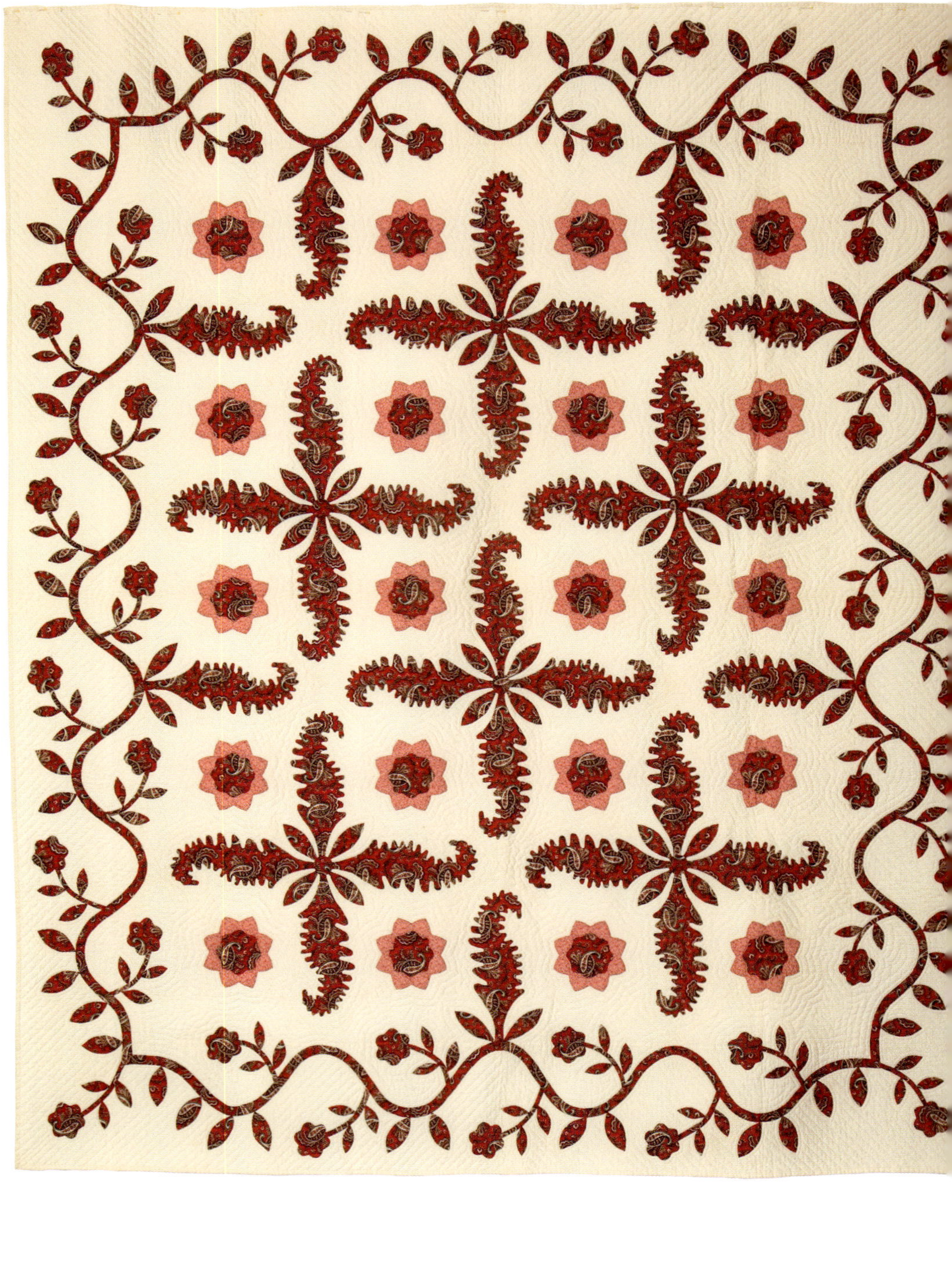

Quilt #81. "Feathers and Rose" made in the 1980s; it is 76 inches wide by 88 inches long. This quilt is based on an antique quilt Martha saw in a book; she then drafted a pattern. It has been exhibited in Paducah and in "Martha Skelton: A Retrospective," at the River Oaks Square Arts and Crafts Center in Alexandria, Louisiana, September 9–29, 1989, sponsored by Rapides Regional Medical Center. Collection of the maker.

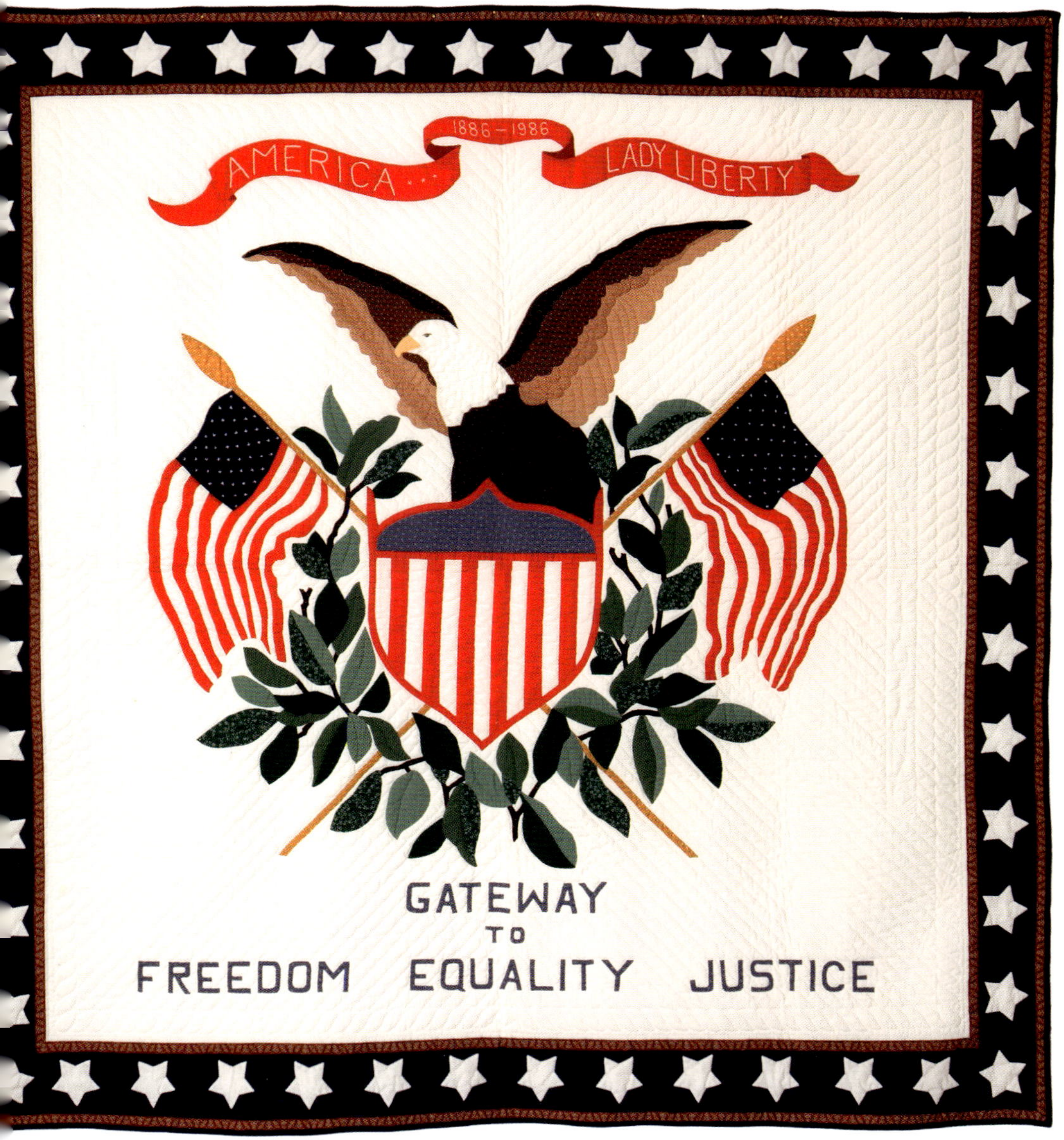

Quilt #160. "America and Lady Liberty" made in 1985 and 1986; it is 70 inches wide by 71 inches long. The Museum of American Folk Art in New York City sponsored a "Statue of Liberty" quilt contest in 1986: this is Martha's entry, her original design. Collection of Gordon Skelton, Madison, Mississippi.

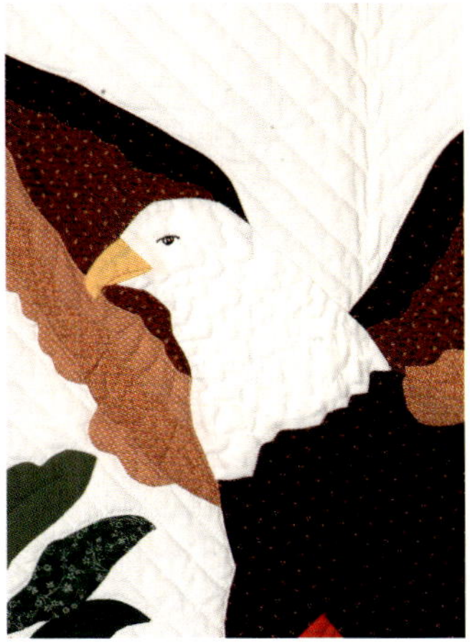

Detail of quilt #160. The eagle's right wing utilizes four different fabrics to achieve a realistic impression of feathers.

Quilt #73. "Baltimore Album Quilt" made in 1986; it is 77 inches wide by 94.75 inches long. When *Woman's Day* magazine offered a packet of patterns at 50 cents for a beautiful appliquéd design known as "Baltimore Album" (for the city that made it famous), Martha embarked on her first quilt of this type. She remarked that the patterns had to be enlarged "the old-fashioned way—by hand." The quilt has been exhibited at the Mobile Museum of Fine Art and the Gulf States Quilting Association Show. Collection of the maker.

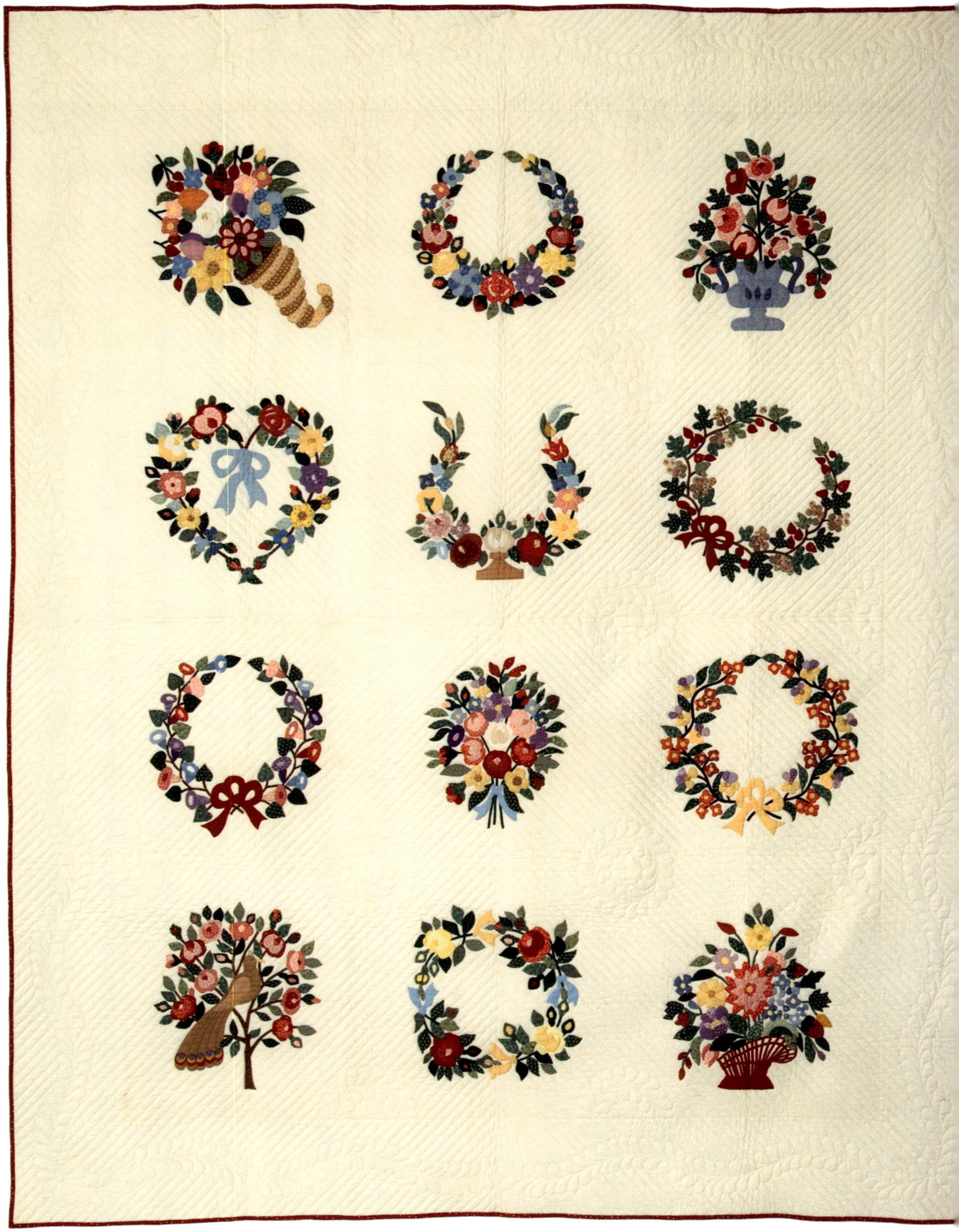

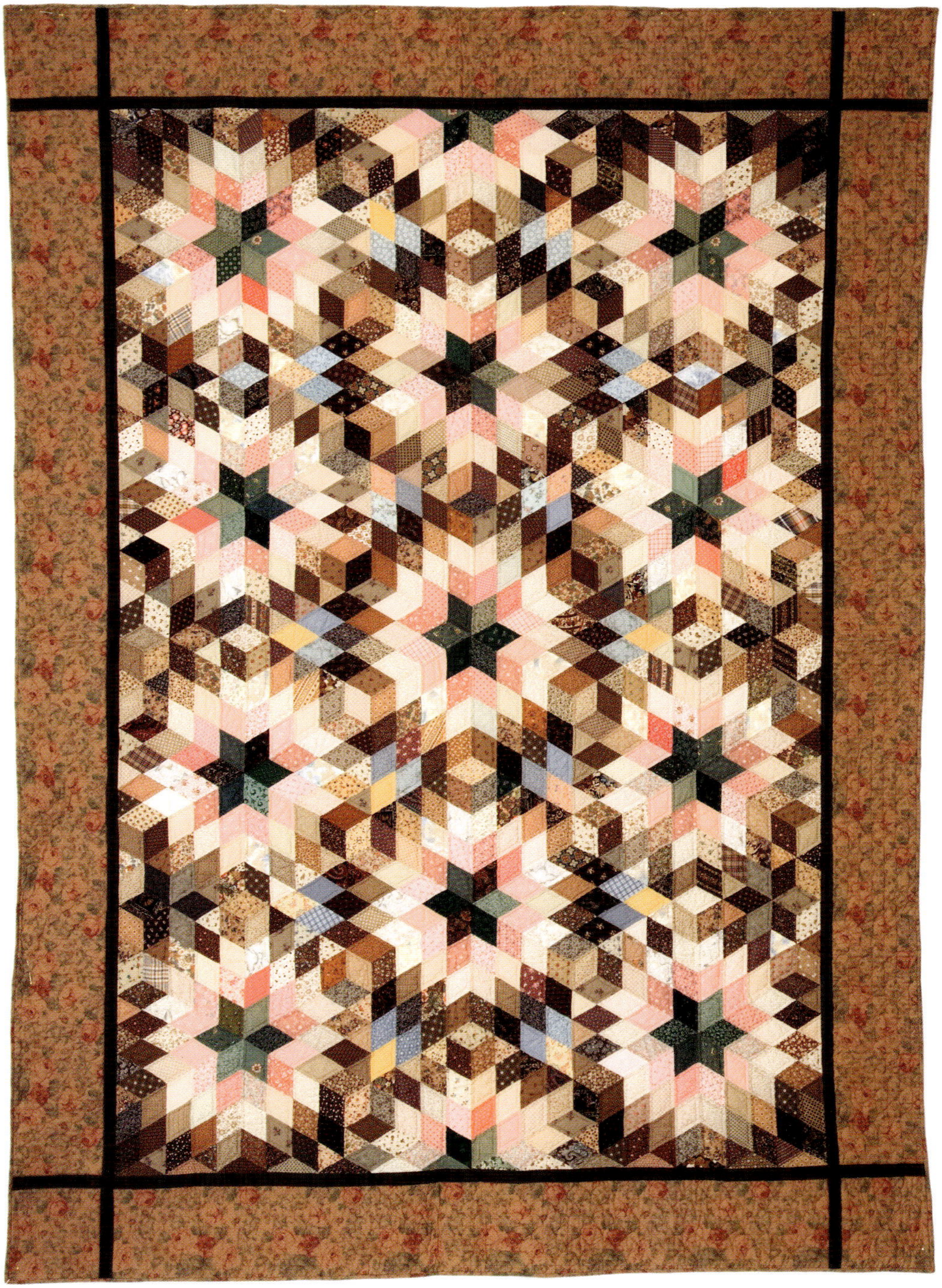

Quilt #36. "Canadian Star" made in the 1980s; it is 70 inches wide by 95 inches long. As she perused a Canadian quilt magazine one day, Martha's attention was attracted to this design, so she immediately wrote for more information and a photo of the quilt. Sharp eyes will recognize the border fabric as being the same as that on "Hexagon Star" (page 38), which Martha remembers purchasing from a Vicksburg quilt shop.

Quilt #112. "Star of Chamblie" made in the 1980s; it is 79 inches wide by 91 inches long. Martha kept up a lively correspondence with a Kansas quilter, Helen Ericson, who had bought Mrs. Scioto Imhoff Danner's (1892–1974) pattern business, Mrs. Danner's Quilts. When Mrs. Ericson re-drafted this pattern from Mrs. Danner's original, she thought Martha would enjoy it. Martha made it up as a tribute to the impressive contribution that Kansas quilters have made to American quilting. Collection of the maker.

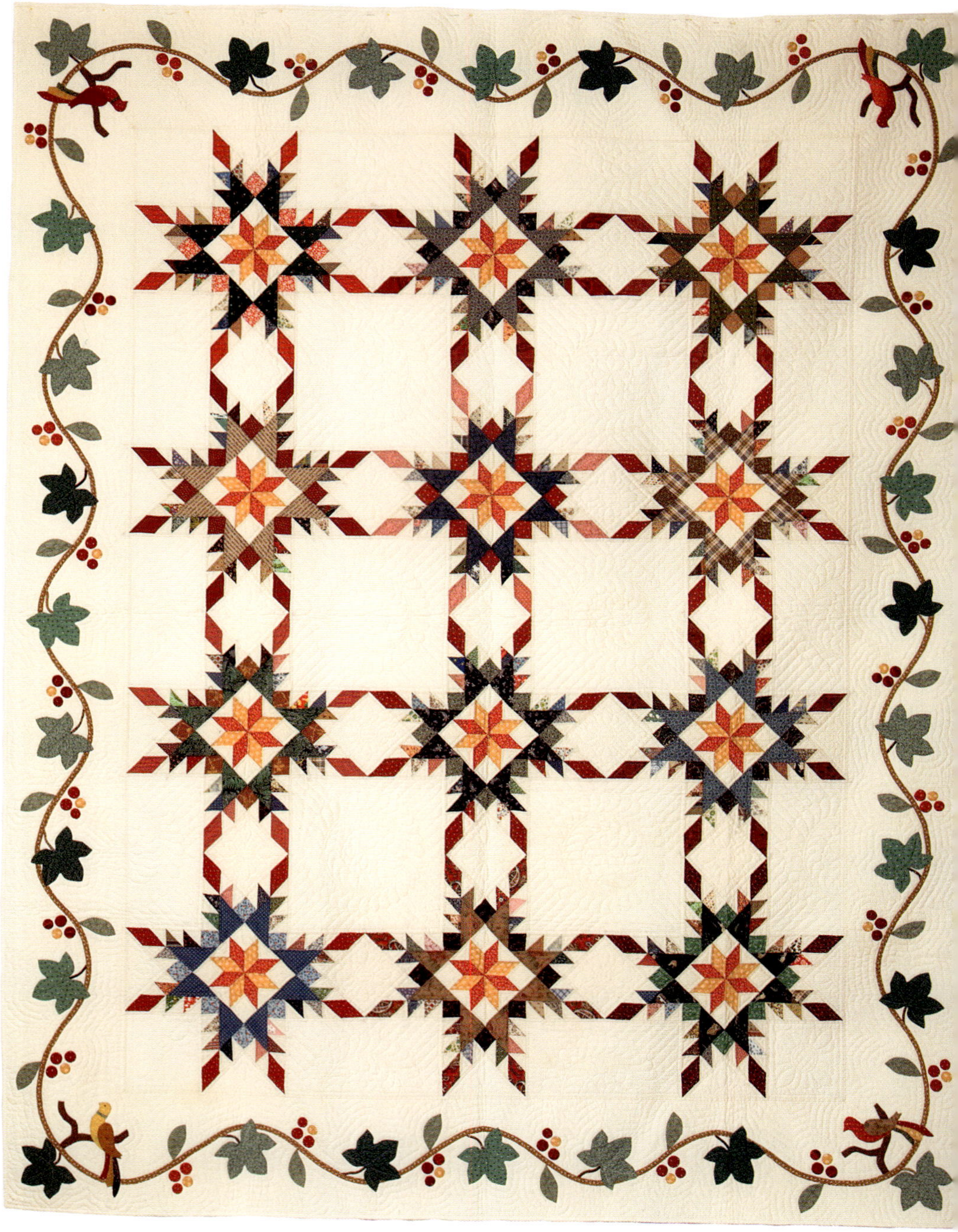

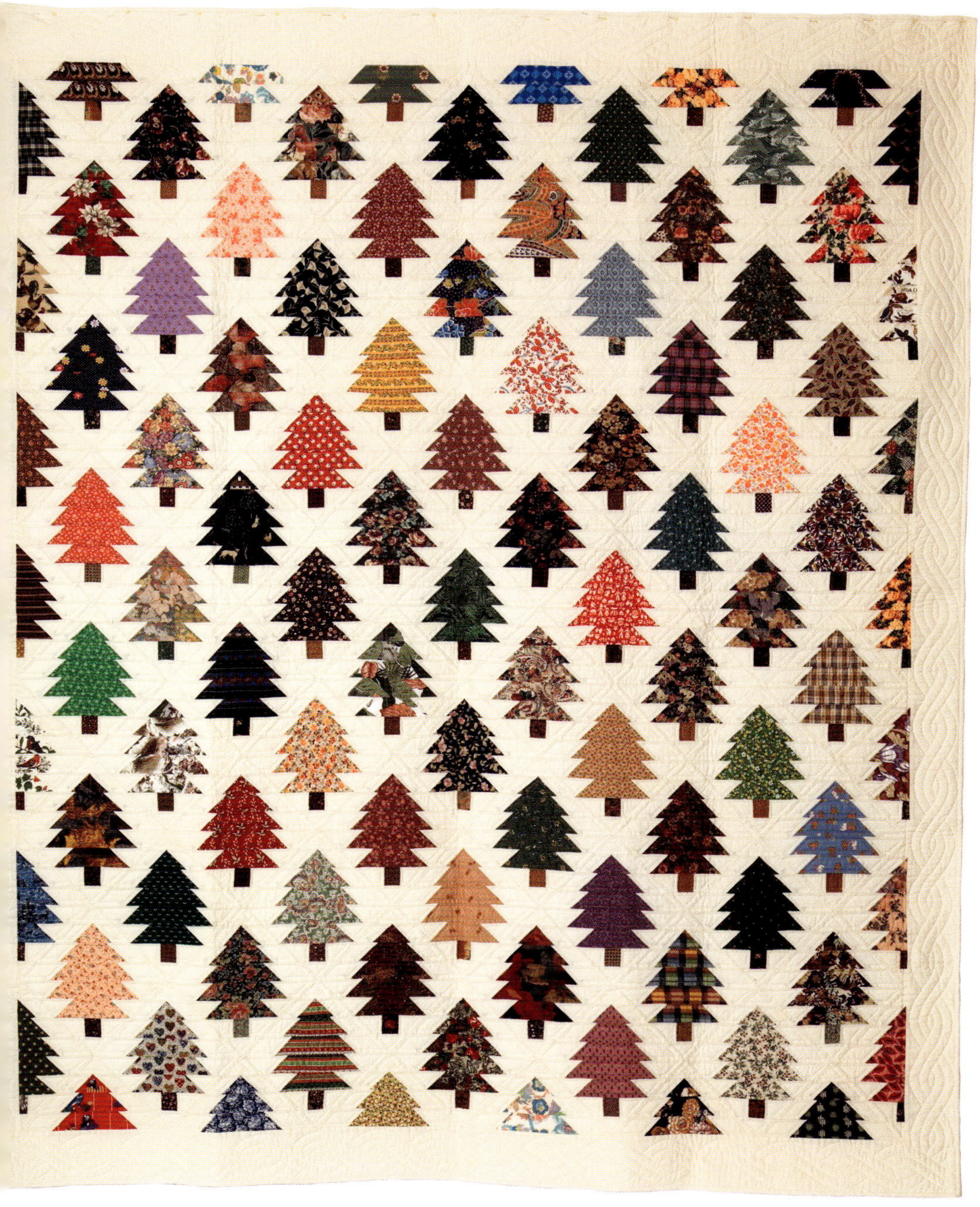

Quilt #100. "Little Trees" made in the 1980s; it is 75.5 inches wide by 88 inches long. When she saw a picture of an old quilt in a book, Martha knew this was a quilt she wanted to make to express her particular love of trees. She drafted the pattern herself and picked carefully through the fabrics in her scrap bag to get exactly the right ones to give the impression of different types of trees. The quilt has been exhibited at the Jackson Quilter's Show and the Craftsmen's Guild Winter Show. Collection of the maker.

Quilt #10. "Flower Reel" made in 1987 and 1988; it is 70.5 inches wide by 87 inches long. It is another of Martha's quilts honored by wide publication—in the *Quilt Art Calendar* for 1989 as the May quilt; in *Great American Quilts 1995* (Carol L. Newbill, 1994); in *Encyclopedia of Classic Quilt Patterns* (ed. Patricia Wilens, 2001). Following her own tradition, Martha used fabrics from her scrap bag for the colorful designs; the only fabric she purchased was muslin for the background. Collection of Jennifer Ann Fentress, Baton Rouge, Louisiana. Photograph by Brian Loden.

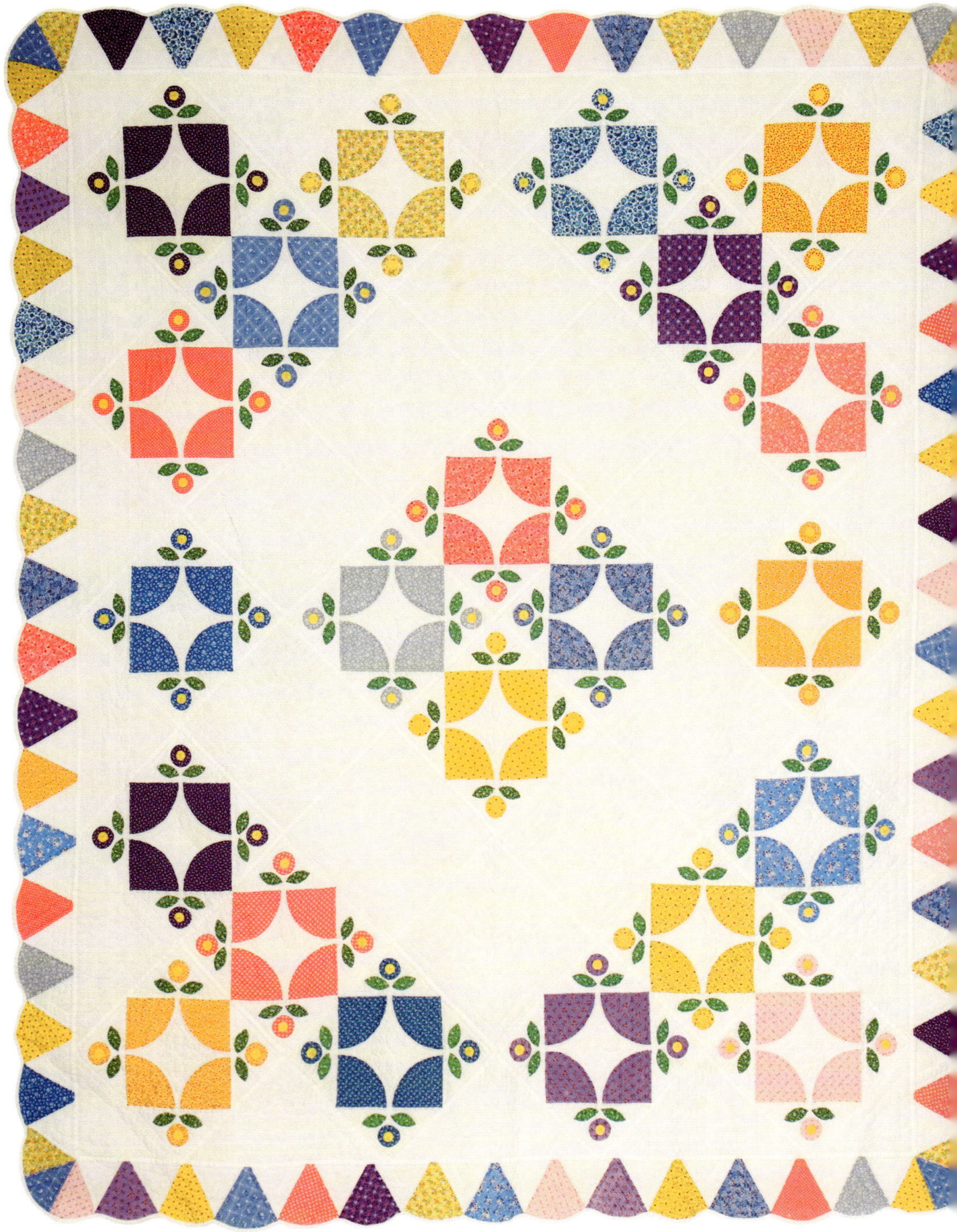

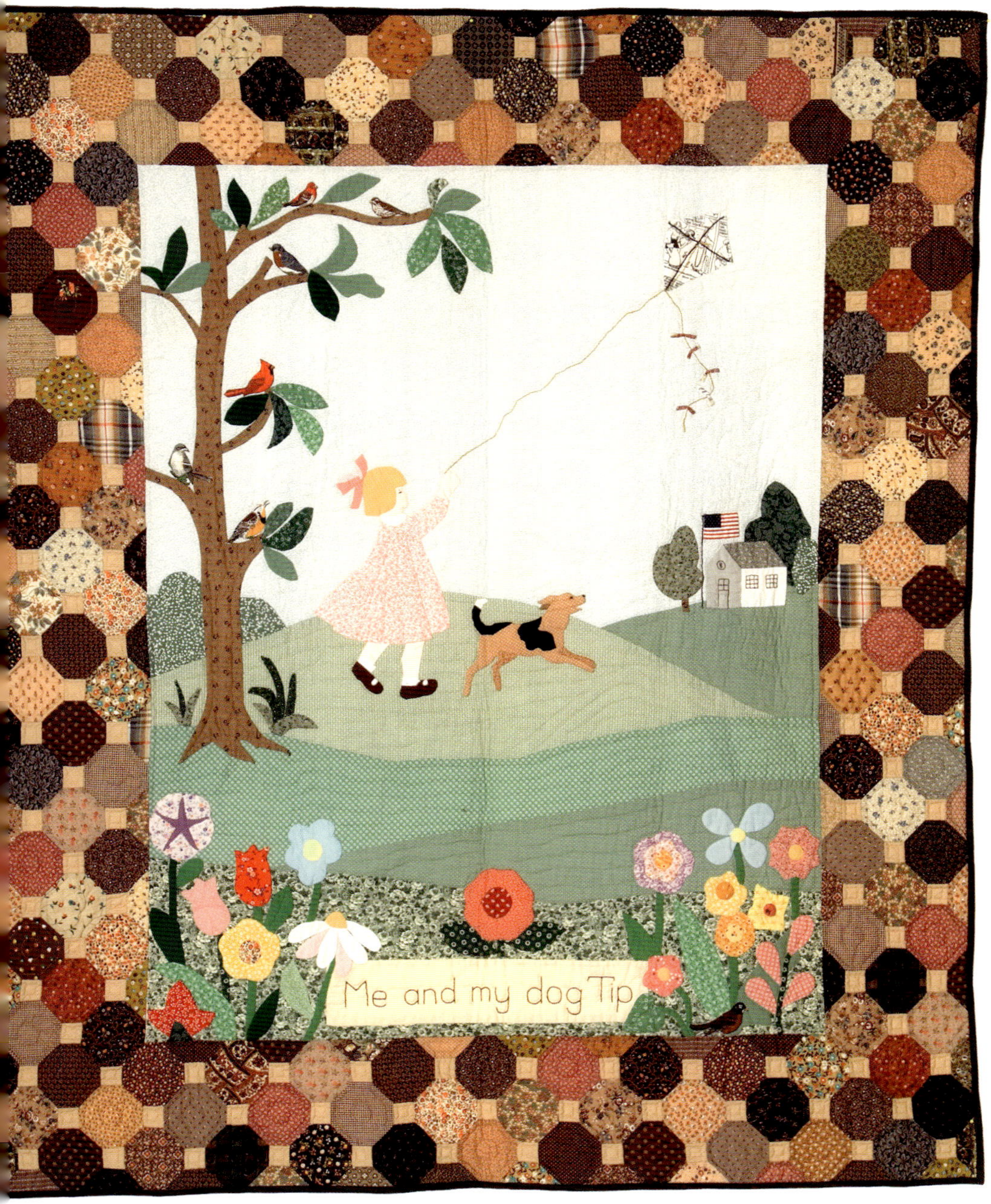

Quilt #59. "Me and My Dog Tip" made in 1988; it is 46.5 inches wide by 54.5 inches long. Jennifer, Martha's granddaughter, loved hearing stories about the dog her grandmother had owned as a child. "Tip" was very protective of all children and would accompany Martha on her one-mile walk to grammar school in Carthage, Missouri. Then he would be waiting for the children at the end of the school day to walk them back home. (There was even a story about Tip protecting the family from wolves!) To Jennifer, Tip seemed a natural subject for a quilt entry into a contest, "Memories of Childhood," announced by the Museum of American Folk Art. A six-year-old Martha, the one-room schoolhouse she attended, and a kite made out of the "funny papers" go with Tip's romp across the flower- and bird-filled fields. The patchwork border, in a pattern called "Cobblestones," represents the fences of the area. The quilt was selected by the Museum of American Folk Art to be in its traveling exhibit of crib quilts that toured the country in 1989. It was also published in *Family Circle* magazine. Collection of the maker.

Quilt #80. "Pink Poppies" made in 1988; it is 80 inches wide by 89 inches long. In early 1988, *Lady's Circle Patchwork Quilts* published this Marie Webster pattern from the 1920s. Mrs. Webster was one of the first designers of commercial quilt patterns, and Martha admired Webster's realistic appliquéd flowers. Although she worked up her poppies much as the pattern showed them, she introduced some ideas of her own in the quilting. It was published in *American Quilter* magazine, summer 1990 (vol. 4, no. 2), in an article named "How Does Your Garden Grow?" and in the book *Award-Winning Quilts and Their Makers*, 1991. Collection of the maker.

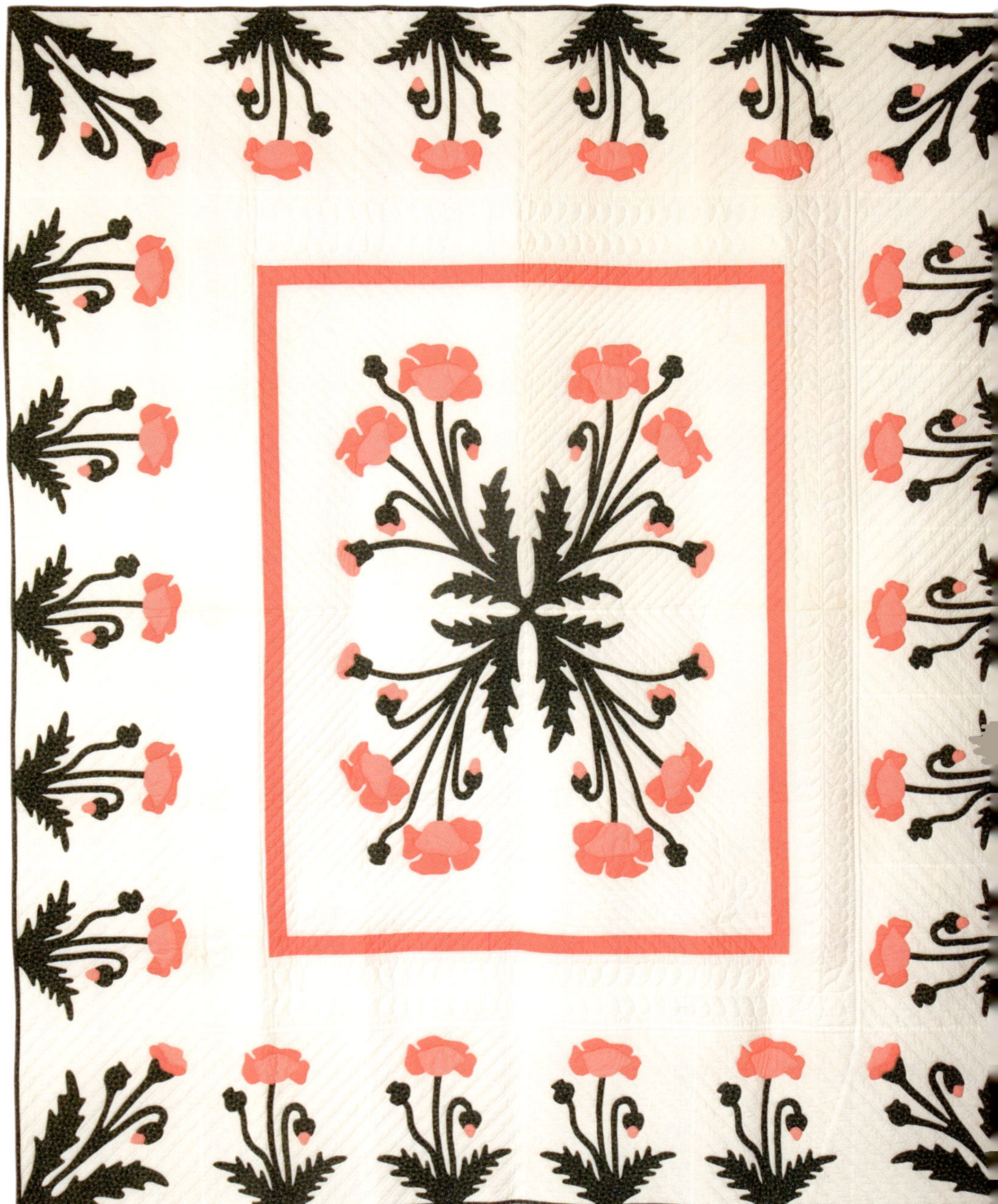

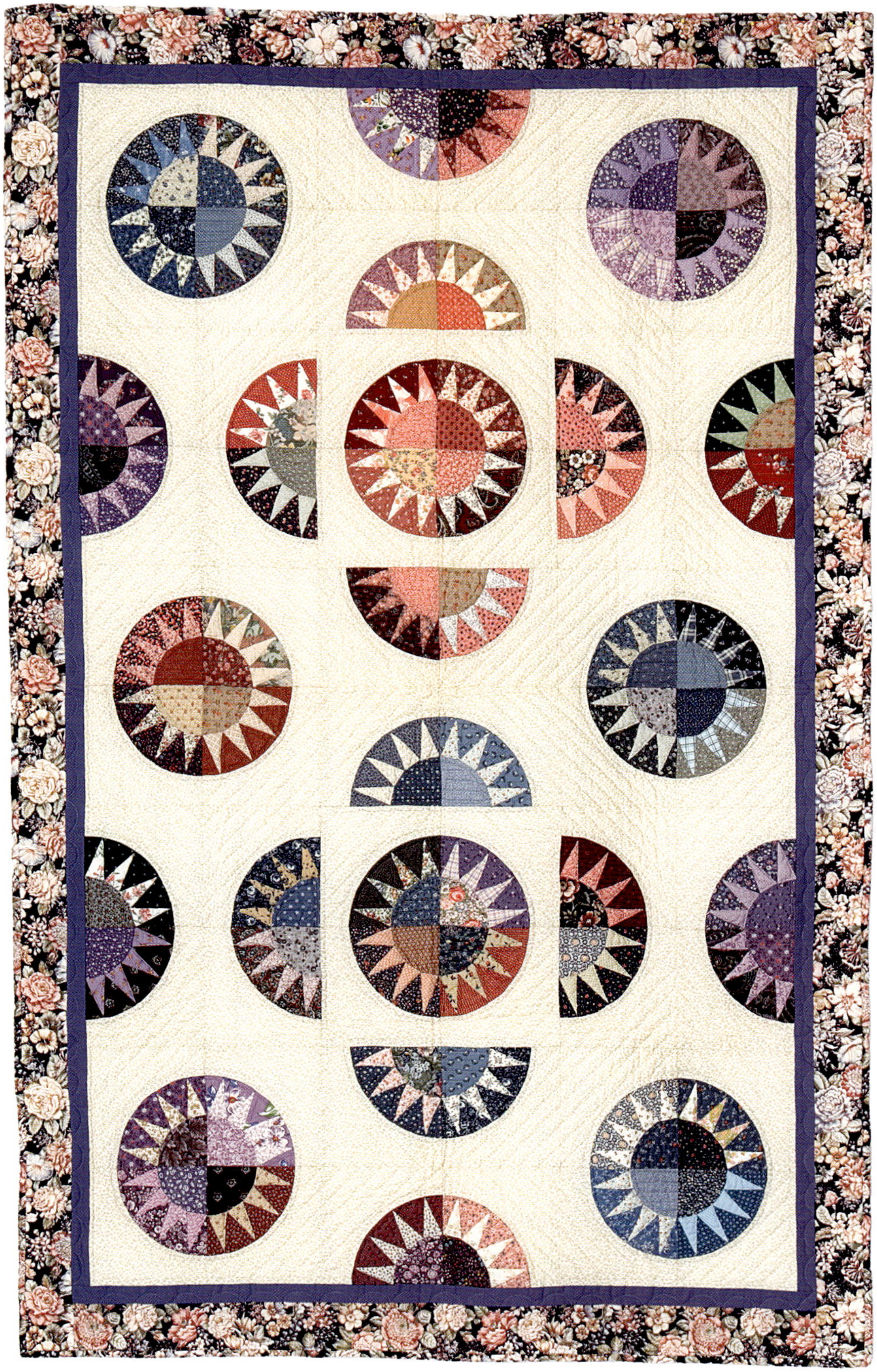

Quilt #58. "Scrappy Baby" made in 1988; it is 42 inches wide by 65.5 inches long. Upon being invited to teach a class about the challenges of curves and points at the American Quilter's Society annual show in Paducah, Martha pieced this as a teaching sample. It was juried into the quilt show that ran simultaneously with the annual meeting. Collection of the maker.

Quilt #17. "Rose of Sharon" made in 1989; it is 79 inches wide by 94.5 inches long. The open background in this Mountain Mist version of a familiar pattern is what attracted Martha; she wanted to do some elaborate quilting to demonstrate how an appliqué design can be enhanced with the textural quality of wonderful stitching. The quilt was juried into the Sixth Annual American Quilter's Society Show and Contest in 1990, as was her pieced "Fall Blooming Asters." Collection of the maker.

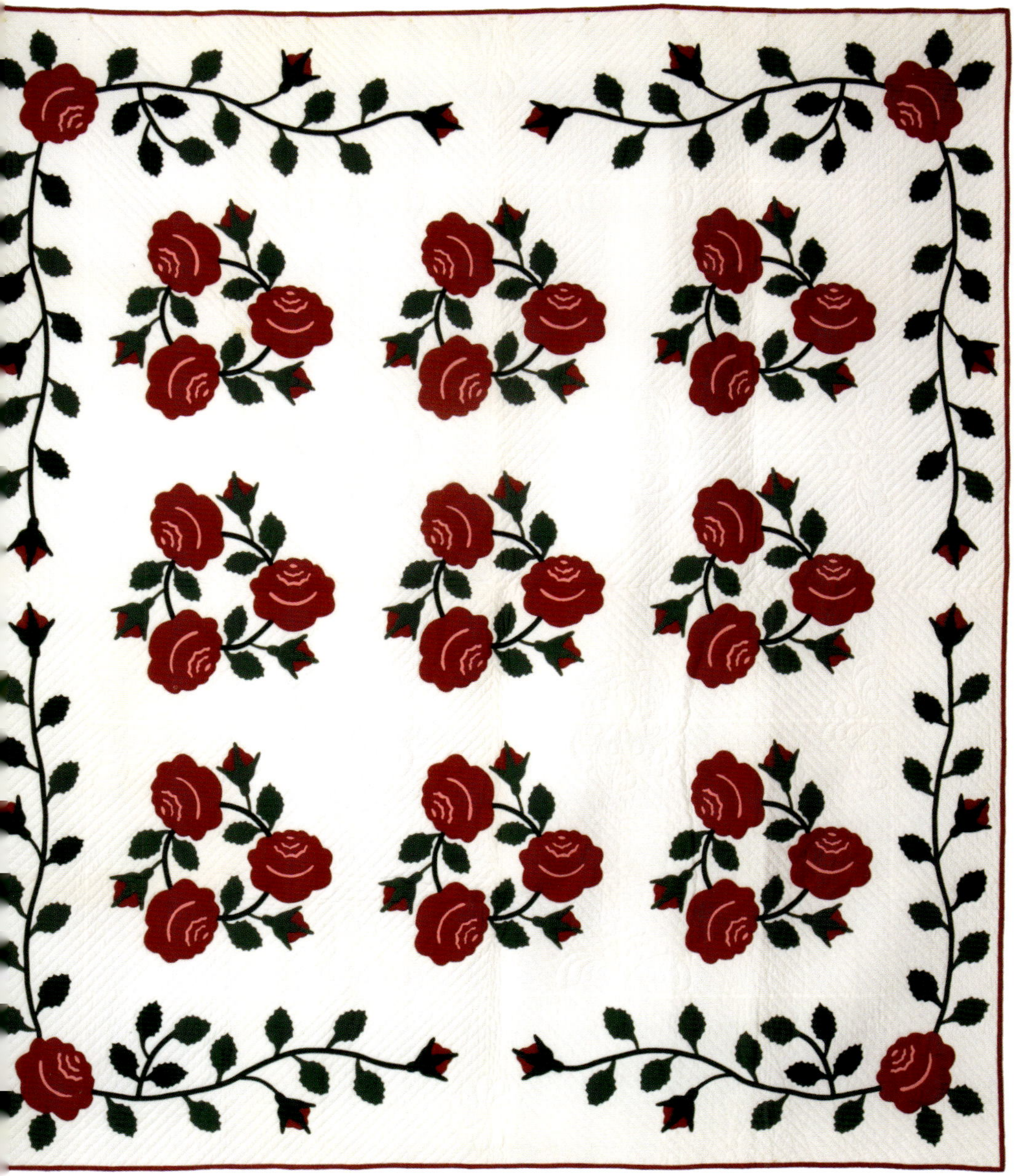

Quilt #110. "Victorian Rose" made in the 1980s; it is 78 inches wide by 86.5 inches long. The pattern for this quilt appeared in *Lady's Circle Patchwork Quilts*, and when the magazine organized an exhibition for the 1991 International Quilt Market and Festival in Houston, the staff chose Martha's example for inclusion. This quilt then traveled to the Quilts Europe show in 1992 at The Hague in the Netherlands. The roses demonstrate Martha's ability with reverse appliqué, a skill not often brought into the quilt maker's repertoire. Collection of the maker.

Quilt #97. "Glittering Stars" (detail) made in the late 1980s; it is 72 inches wide by 83 inches long. Martha really enjoyed reading *Nancilu Burdick's Legacy: The Story of Talula Gilbert Bottoms and Her Quilts* (see bibliography). Talula was born 1862 in Fayette County, Georgia, died in 1946 in Athens, Alabama, and made between two and three hundred quilts in her lifetime. (Perhaps Martha recognized a kindred spirit in this woman whose creative passion from early childhood was quilts.) When Martha saw a quilt of Talula's in *Legacy* that she wanted to make, she drafted her own pattern from the photograph—no patterns were included in the book. Collection of the maker.

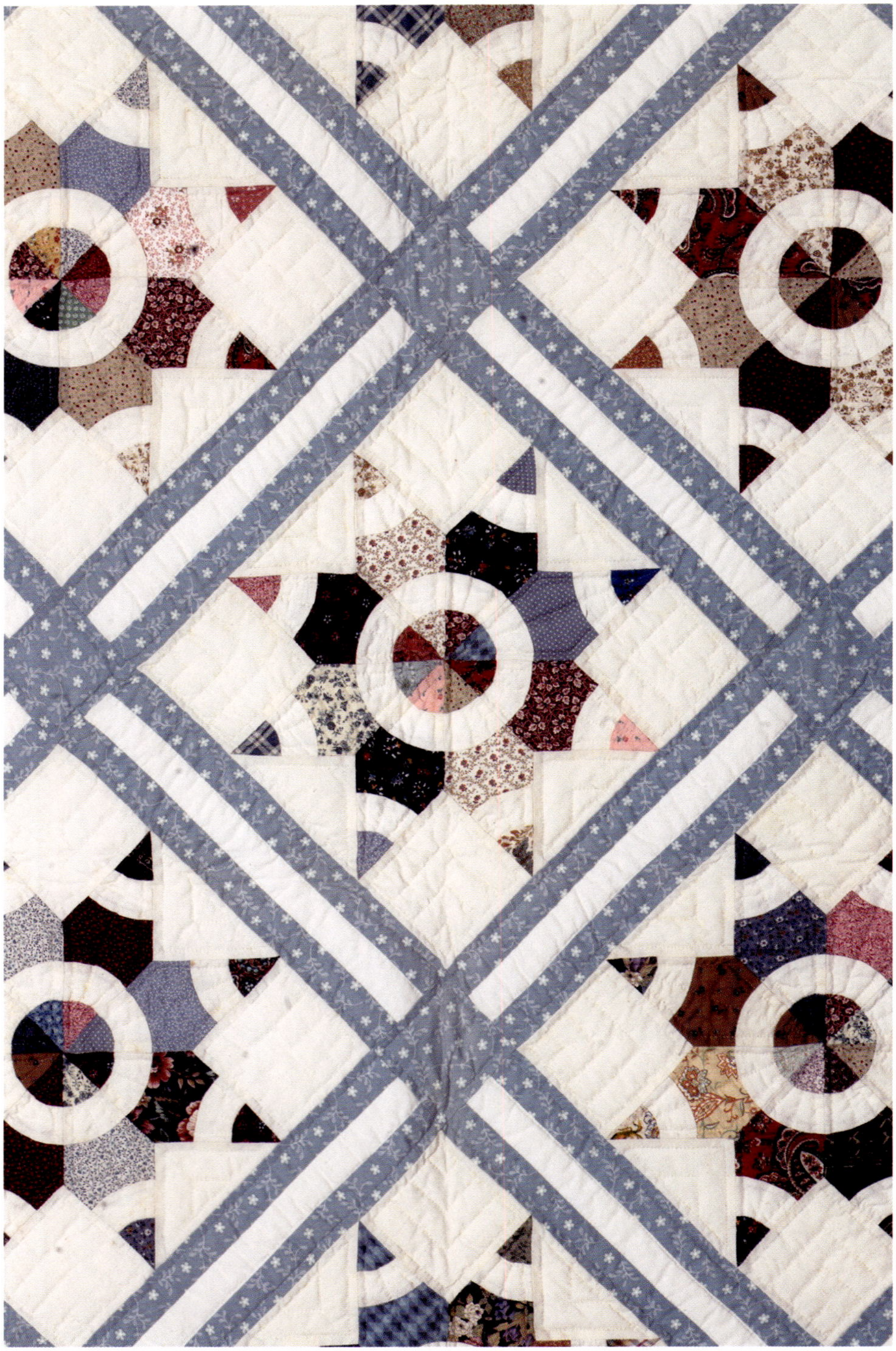

Additional Quilts Made between 1980 and 1989

"Pine Tree" table runner, 1980[27]
"Johnny Jump-Up," 1980[28]
"Friendship Quilt," 1980[29]
"Peony," pieced in 1979, quilted in 1984[30]
"Rose of Sharon" pillow, 1982[31]
"Christmas Sampler," 1984[32]
"Hole in the Barn Door with Cotton Boll Appliqué," early 1980s[33]
"Fantasy Garden," early 1980s[34]
"Pink and White Sampler," early 1980s[35]
"Inner City," early 1980s[36]
"Pinwheel/Barbara Fritchie's Star," early 1980s[37]
"Tumbling Blocks," early 1980s[38]
"Sunflower" center with "Bright Hopes" border, early 1980s[39]
"Cotton Patchers' Challenge," wall quilt, early 1980s[40]
"Magic Vine," early 1980s[41]
"Pickle Dish," 1980s[42]
"Wheel of Fortune," with appliquéd bird and vine border, 1980s[43]
"Log Cabin," 1980s[44]
"Double Hearts" wall hanging, 1980s[45]
"Little Hearts" mini quilt, 1980s[46]
"Bird and Urn," 1980s[47]
"Mariner's Compass" wall hanging, 1980s[48]
"Bleeding Heart," 1980s[49]
"Friendly Pleasures," 1984[50]
"Swallows and Smilax," late 1980s[51]
"Glittering Stars," late 1980s[52]
"Square in a Square," 1988[53]

A Statewide Organization: More Quilts than Ever in the 1990s

Quilters across Mississippi will surely agree that the Mississippi Quilt Association has been a great way of bringing them together to get to know one another, to learn and share, and to accomplish things much greater than any one guild could do on its own. In addition to numerous symposiums (called "Gatherings"), the association has published a significant book on the history of quilts in the state, *Mississippi Quilts.* Martha recalls the germination of the organization in early 1991: "I had been to various quilt symposiums and had heard about other state organizations, and I was beginning to think that Mississippi needed one really badly. We didn't have any way of knowing who other quilters were. I knew there were lots of quilters I'd like to know if I had a chance to meet them in a big group. I was teaching around and I talked to lots of different people. I knew there was not a formal organization in the state, or I would be in it.

"Chris Dahlman was a girl who had moved to Mississippi from Nebraska. She was a home economics major in college and interested in all kinds of fiber work. She had been looking around for quilters and called me one day and said that every place she talked to people about quilting, they would ask her if she knew me, so she wanted to get acquainted. We talked and found out that we were both interested in developing a state organization for quilters. Chris had talked with a friend of mine, Ann Root, and had visited her quilt shop in Clinton. At the same time, the Pine Belt

Quilters had become a pretty active group in Hattiesburg. As it turned out, Chris and Martha Ginn of Hattiesburg, Ollie Jean Lane of Yazoo City, and I decided that we would pull together the people we knew who were interested in forming a state organization, and Ann volunteered her shop for that meeting. We had probably twelve or fifteen people there, because I remember that all of us fit around one of the big tables in the workroom. We all agreed to go out and talk to other people and meet up again in a month or so. The next time or two we met, we got to the place where we were ready to go ahead and begin making a formal organization. It all grew out of those first two or three meetings we had; it didn't take it long for the organization to grow. . . . Martha Ginn was our first president, because she is a good organizer, and she's a good one to put in if you're trying to get something off the ground."[1]

The *Hattiesburg American* carried the following item on Sunday, March 31, 1991, complete with a photograph of Martha Ginn speaking from a podium and Martha Skelton standing nearby, smiling.

> Quilters from throughout Mississippi have formed the Mississippi Quilt Association to identify quilters, to help them improve their techniques, and to preserve and promote the art of quiltmaking.
>
> Organizational meetings were held in October, and the first response to the formation of the MQA was a Quilter's Gathering held February 9 at Paul B. Johnson State Park near Hattiesburg. Pine Belt Quilters of Hattiesburg hosted the event and approximately 180 people attended the demonstrations and educational displays arranged by Martha Skelton of Vicksburg.
>
> Officers selected for the organization include Martha Ginn of Hattiesburg, president; Suzanne Schutt of Clinton, secretary; Miriam Rice of Brandon, treasurer; and Ellen Hall of Hattiesburg, membership coordinator. Dues are $10 per year ($7 for people 65 and older).
>
> Future plans include a newsletter, regional gatherings, and an annual statewide meeting, beginning in the spring of '92. Future Quilter's Gatherings are planned for June 15 at Mississippi Delta Community College at Moorhead and for November in Picayune.

Barely four years later, on January 5, 1995, the executive board of the Mississippi Quilt Association approved a proposal to establish a quilt documentation project, which had been a priority with the members from the beginning and stated in the objective of "preserving and promoting the art of quiltmaking." Carol Vickers, chairman of MQA's Heritage Quilt Search Project, writes in the introduction to the book that resulted from the search, *Mississippi Quilts*,

> In retrospect, what has been accomplished seems nothing short of phenomenal. At the time, the prospect of traveling the state to look at hundreds of quilts seemed exciting. Little thought was given to the toll that the work ahead would take.
>
> At the first search day (in 1995), a photograph of the search's core team was taken. At the end of the search, a final photograph was made (October 17, 1997). As one member commented, "When we began, we all looked thinner, younger, and more naïve." Had the individuals involved thought of the hundreds of hours required, the time spent away from families, the frustrations and sometimes back-breaking work, the project might never have been undertaken.

Martha, one of the search's core team, agrees that it was hard work. "By the time the day was over, you had spent a lot of time standing up, plus bending over quilts. It was a hard job; you worked real hard. There is so much to go into when you're having a documentation day. I was an analyst. I looked at the quilts and got to measure them. We counted the stitches . . . only the ones on the top . . . to get an idea of the quality of the quilting. We determined the fiber content of the quilt top—that varied from quilt to quilt. We had to determine the batting of the quilt, and we told about the backing, or the lining, of the quilt. We told about how it was bound. We determined the name of the pattern if we could, using as a reference Barbara Brackman's *Encyclopedia of Pieced Quilt Patterns.* It has lots and lots of quilt patterns, although not all of them. We also tried to decide if the quilter had worked with scraps or had purchased fabric especially for the quilt. I came to feel really close to the girl who scribed for me so much—Nancy Braswell. We traveled together and had the best time. The members of MQA who worked on the documentation really formed close friendships. I think it strengthened the organization and made it better. I learned a whole lot while I was documenting, and I think many of the younger women did as well. The whole thing was really a wonderful learning experience for all of us."[2]

Other personal memories Martha shared about her attitude toward and participation in the MQA Heritage Quilt Search Project have to do with her first experience with a documentation project and the way it made her feel about the owners of the quilts. "I had had a chance a number of years earlier (in 1984) to go down to Mobile for a documentation project sponsored by the Azalea City Quilt Guild and the Mobile County Cooperative Extension Service. That was when Mary Elizabeth Johnson and [quilt collector] Robert Cargo and I were the three who looked at all the quilts and determined the age when we could, as well as the pattern and that sort of thing.[3] I saw what kind of opportunity it was and how interested the quilt owners were to be able to have their quilts examined and their questions answered. They were willing to wait all day, if they had to, for the opportunity to have their quilt come up for viewing and analysis. When the MQA was conducting its documentation days, often one of the women interviewing the quilt owners would come and ask if I would talk to so-and-so and tell them something—they needed an answer about their quilt. I always said yes, and in that way I got to talk to lots of people who owned quilts around the state."[4]

The Mississippi Quilt Association's Heritage Quilt Search Project documented 1,769 quilts and in 2001 published *Mississippi Quilts.* In the final chapter of the book, entitled "The Tradition Continues: 1945–2000," Martha Skelton's biography is the first of those of thirteen outstanding contemporary Mississippi quilters, and she is the only person to have a "new" (1995) quilt prominently displayed in the book.

Simultaneous to the formation of the Mississippi Quilt Association and its quilt documentation project, things for Martha were proceeding in a fashion that, over the preceding decade, had become more or less commonplace. The established patterns of interaction with the American Quilter's Society, the Craftsmen's Guild, the Mississippi State Fair, the Cotton Patchers, the Stitchery Guild, and the teaching and demonstrating in a host of venues would continue throughout the last ten years of the century. The events of 1990 and 1991 were typical of the years that followed, although every once in a while a completely new and different opportunity would arise.

In late February 1990, a letter arrived from AQS informing Martha that one of her quilts would be in the summer 1990 issue of *American Quilter;* four or five days later, two more letters from AQS told her that two of her quilts had been juried into the 1990 show, to be held April 26–29. The Craftsmen's Guild of Mississippi wrote on April 16 to confirm Martha's appearance at the Chimneyville Crafts Center in the Mississippi Agriculture and Forestry Museum in Jackson on May 12. Later that year, there was an invitation from the Old Kentucky Home Quilters of Bardstown, Kentucky, to exhibit a quilt "made after 1982." (Although Martha participated in the festival that time, she declined thereafter, citing the bother of insuring, packing, and shipping the quilts.)

The year 1991 continued with more of the same, with added excitement brought about by the opening in Paducah of the new Museum of the American Quilter's Society on April 27, in which Martha's "New York Beauty" was prominently displayed. Concurrently, AQS published *Award-Winning Quilts and Their Makers:* Volume 1, *The Best of AQS Shows, 1985–87*, which showcased Martha and "New York Beauty" on its pages. (Martha was also included in volume 2, with "Chips and Whetstones," and in volume 8, with both of the quilts.) Two more of Martha's quilts were juried into the AQS annual show. In October, Martha's "Coxcomb" was a local winner in the "Labor of Love" quilt contest and was exhibited at the Seventeenth International Quilt Market and Festival in Houston. The Mississippi State Fair that year included a new feature: *Better Homes and Gardens* magazine sponsored a quilt contest alongside the one the Fair always held, and the same team of judges served both competitions. Martha took a blue ribbon for appliqué, which was accompanied

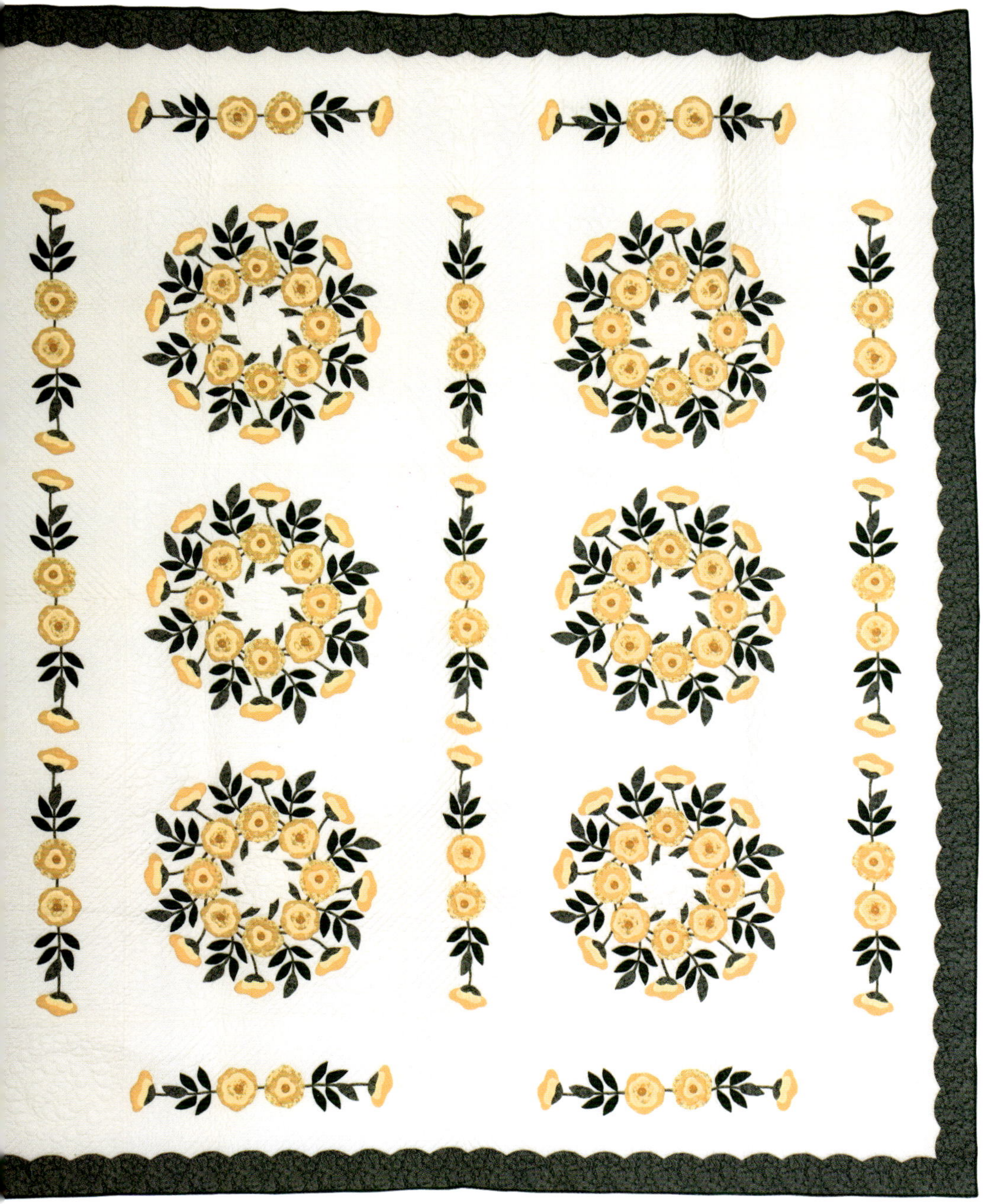

Quilt #19. "Yellow Rose for Peace" made in 1990; it is 75.5 inches wide by 86 inches long. Martha made this quilt during the Desert Storm war, when yellow ribbons were tied "everywhere." Photographs of quilts from Marie Webster provided the original idea for the quilt, but Martha worked out her own design for the setting of the six rose wreaths. It was exhibited in the 1991 American Quilter's Society show in Paducah. Collection of the maker. Photograph by Brian Loden.

Quilt #108. "Touching Stars" (aka "Patchwork Stars") made in 1990; it is 73 inches wide by 90 inches long. The appliquéd border of this traditional pieced star was based on an antique quilt. This was the first quilt Martha submitted to *American Patchwork and Quilting Magazine*, and in addition to publishing it in their March 1993 issue, they used it on a brochure to attract subscribers. It was the cover of *Traditional Quilts* in 1996. Collection of the maker.

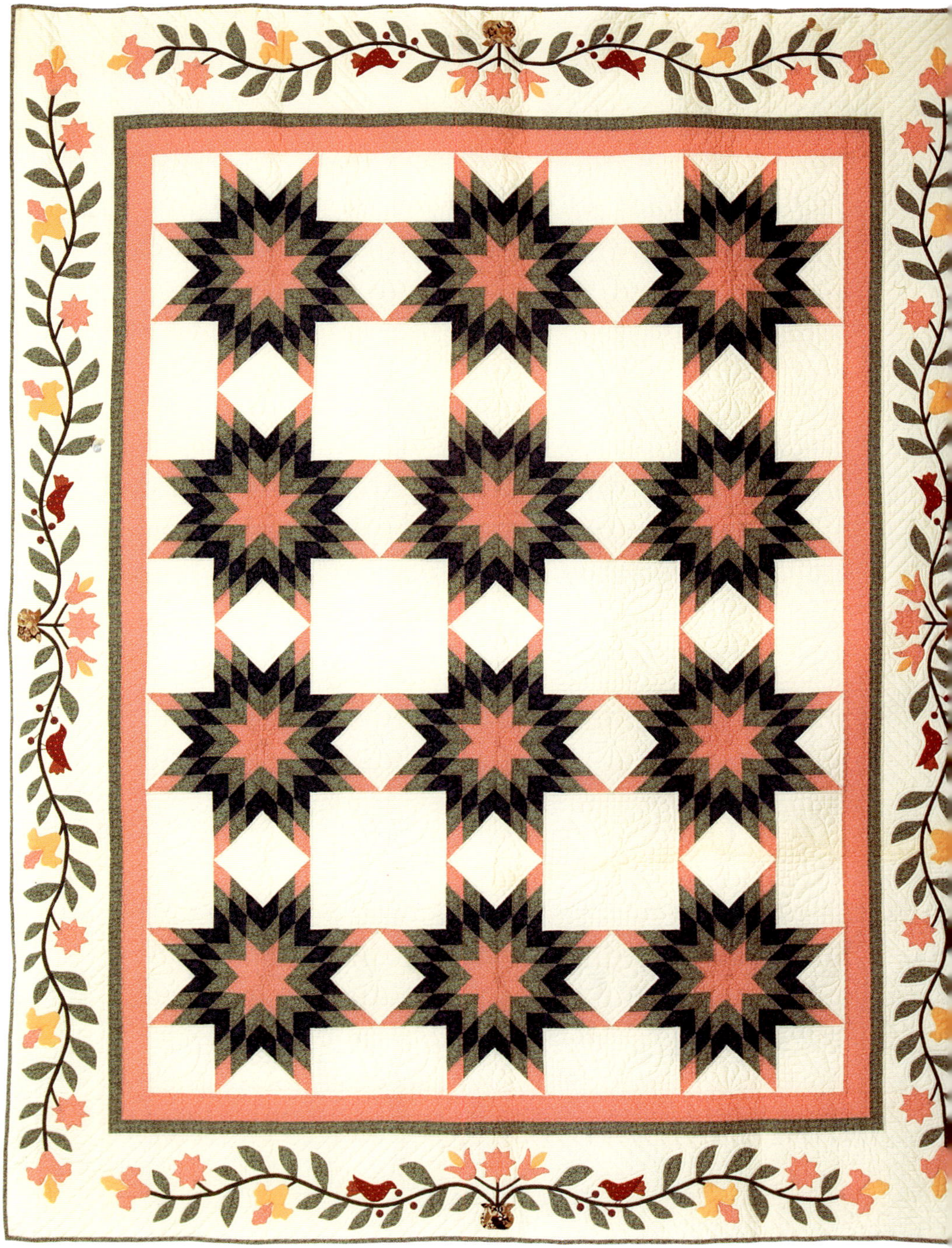

by a one-hundred-dollar check; her quilt was automatically entered into the 1992 national competition. As a result, a relationship with another publisher began: by October 1992, Martha was contributing her "Patchwork Stars" to *American Patchwork and Quilting*, the new magazine being started by *Better Homes and Gardens*. Five years later, in 1997, an editorial assistant wrote to Martha:

> I received a letter from a lady that would really like to see more of your work in *American Patchwork and Quilting®* magazine. She tells us that you have done some beautiful quilts and started *American Patchwork and Quilting®* magazine with the October 1995 issue where your "Garden Mosaic" was on the cover. [Martha's admirer didn't quite have her facts straight.]
>
> Enclosed are our writer's guidelines for your convenience. We would enjoy seeing your work also. Please let us hear from you with any new projects you wish us to consider for publication.

In 1992, Martha was asked to judge a quilt show at the Cultural Crossroads in Port Gibson, Mississippi. The show, remarkably, included both African American and European American quilts, new and experienced quilters, heirloom and contemporary quilts: all were welcome (and continue to be, to this day). The other two judges were Roland Freeman, a freelance photographer from Washington, D.C. (who, in 1996, published a ground-breaking book on African American quilt-making named *A Communion of the Spirits: African-American Quilters, Preservers, and Their Stories)*, and Mary Lohrenz, an established quilt scholar and curator of collections at the Mississippi State Historical Museum, based in Jackson. On the day that the awards were handed out, the three judges participated in a forum in which the public could ask questions about the quilts. It provided a good give-and-take with the audience, and was just the sort of thing Martha has always enjoyed.

"The goal of Patty Crosby, the director of Cultural Crossroads, was [and still is] to provide a way for the women to earn some income from the quilts they make. There is, as we know, sometimes a difference in the European American and African American styles of quilting. That difference centers on the way the women approach their material. I used to work with the African American quilters to help them become a bit more careful in their construction and make their quilts a little more durable. I told them I didn't want to change the way they handle color, because they were very good with it, but their sewing techniques did need a bit of improvement, mainly to make their quilts last longer. The better you make a quilt, the better it lasts. Quilts are made to be used, but they do need to be well-constructed. [Helping with their sewing skills] was the personal goal I had as I worked with them. I went down there for ten to twelve years, until I got to the place where I simply couldn't any longer manage the time to do it. I really enjoyed getting to know everyone. Some of the quilters, especially Hystercine Rankin, did quite wonderful story quilts, and they had a good program for the children."[5]

Although it never became routine to Martha that her submissions to the AQS show were *always* accepted and that she *always* took one of the top prizes in the many contests she entered *and* that her work was regularly published, she was nonetheless flattered and pleased to be singled out for other special acknowledgment in the 1990s. To begin with, in 1992 the Mississippi Department of Archives and History mounted an exhibition entitled "Pieced Together: Mississippi Quilts," curated by Mary Lohrenz and held at the "Old Capitol," the State Historical Museum in Jackson. Martha's quilt "Mississippi: The Magnolia State," one of three of hers owned by the Museum, was on display for the entire run of the show, September 20, 1992, through January 17, 1993. (The other two quilts by Martha in the Museum's collection are "Mississippi Spring" and "Hope of Hartford.")

Next, Martha was a subject of the documentation effort mounted throughout 1996 by the Craftsmen's Guild of Mississippi as folklorists photographed and interviewed traditional craftspeople whose training had been passed down to them from earlier generations. The documentation culminated in an exhibition and symposium on March 22, 1997. Martha's photographic portrait, along with quotes from her interview, were included in the exhibit, which traveled to schools, libraries, and museums in Mississippi. The full transcription of the interview was archived by the Oral History Program of the University of Southern Mississippi.[6] Four months later, on July 17–18, 1999, the Craftsmen's Guild presented Martha, demonstrating her quilting techniques, to the visitors who stopped by the Mississippi Crafts Center on the Natchez Trace Parkway.

Most exciting, perhaps, was the second invitation from the Smithsonian Institution to come to Washington for the Festival of American Folklife in June of 1997. The Mississippi River Delta, from Vicksburg to Memphis, was the geographic area of concentration, so the states of Mississippi and Louisiana both contributed craftsmen, cooks, and musicians. For two weeks, in a nice little tent with lattice walls on which their quilts were hung, Martha demonstrated European American quilting and Henrietta Taylor from Greenville showed the African American style. A Smithsonian folklorist interviewed them, individually and together, on a little stage built to look like the front porch of a farm cabin, with a rapt audience seated on rustic-looking seats facing them.

One lady came several times to ask questions: she was just learning how to quilt, and she had found no one in the Washington, D.C., area to guide her. When she came her final time, Martha had stepped away from the booth to eat lunch, so the visitor left a gift of a couple dozen glass-headed pins stuck through a piece of paper, a souvenir thimble, and "a spool of inexpensive thread. It was what she worked with, and she wanted to share it with me. I felt bad that she had given away what she had, because you hate for people to do this. She left a note saying that I taught her so much in such a little while, and she wanted me to know that. It was a treat to talk to so many people and to know that they enjoyed it and what the festival meant to them."[7]

Publicity attending the Smithsonian Festival and Mississippi's place in it motivated the town of Greenville (with help from the Smithsonian) to hold its own Folklife Festival on May 1–4, 1998. Proving the adage that "imitation is the sincerest form of flattery," the organizers set up the Greenville festival to be almost exactly like the one at the Smithsonian the previous year; many of the same participants were there, including "Martha B. Skelton, Quilter." It took place on a ten-acre site along the levee immediately south of downtown, with two large music tents, a dem-

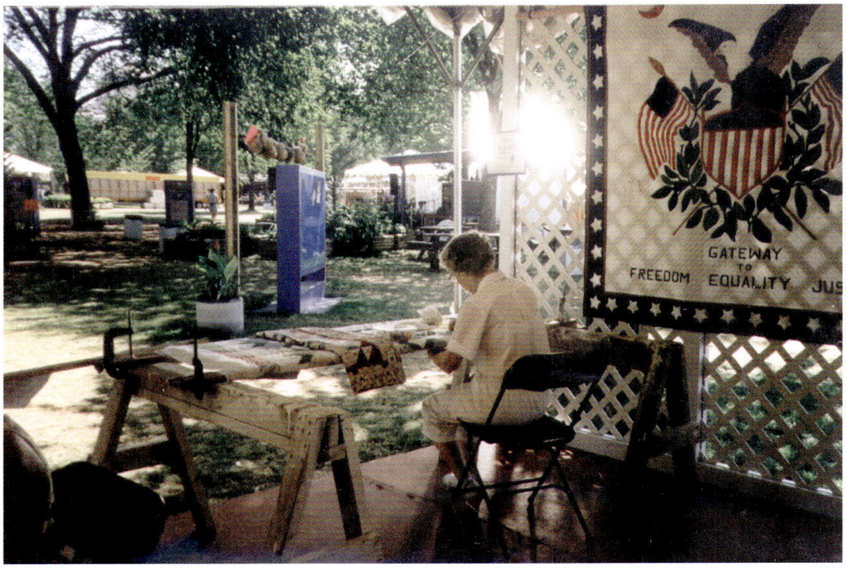

Thousands of people over the years have learned from Martha's public demonstrations of quilting, like this one at the Festival of American Folklife in June of 1997. Although she works steadily on her quilt, she loves talking to people about her lifelong passion and showing how it is done.

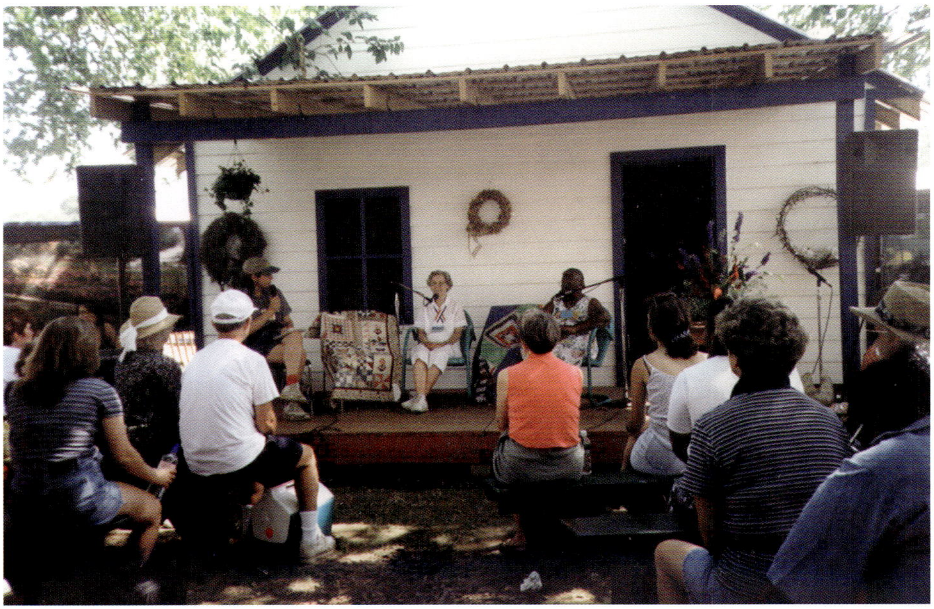

In Washington, D.C., for the Smithsonian Institution's Festiva of American Folklife in June of 1997, Martha Skelton (center) of Vicksburg and Henrietta Taylor from Greenville, Mississippi, are interviewed. A sizeable audience listens raptly to the women discuss their approaches to quilting Each has an example of her wor beside her.

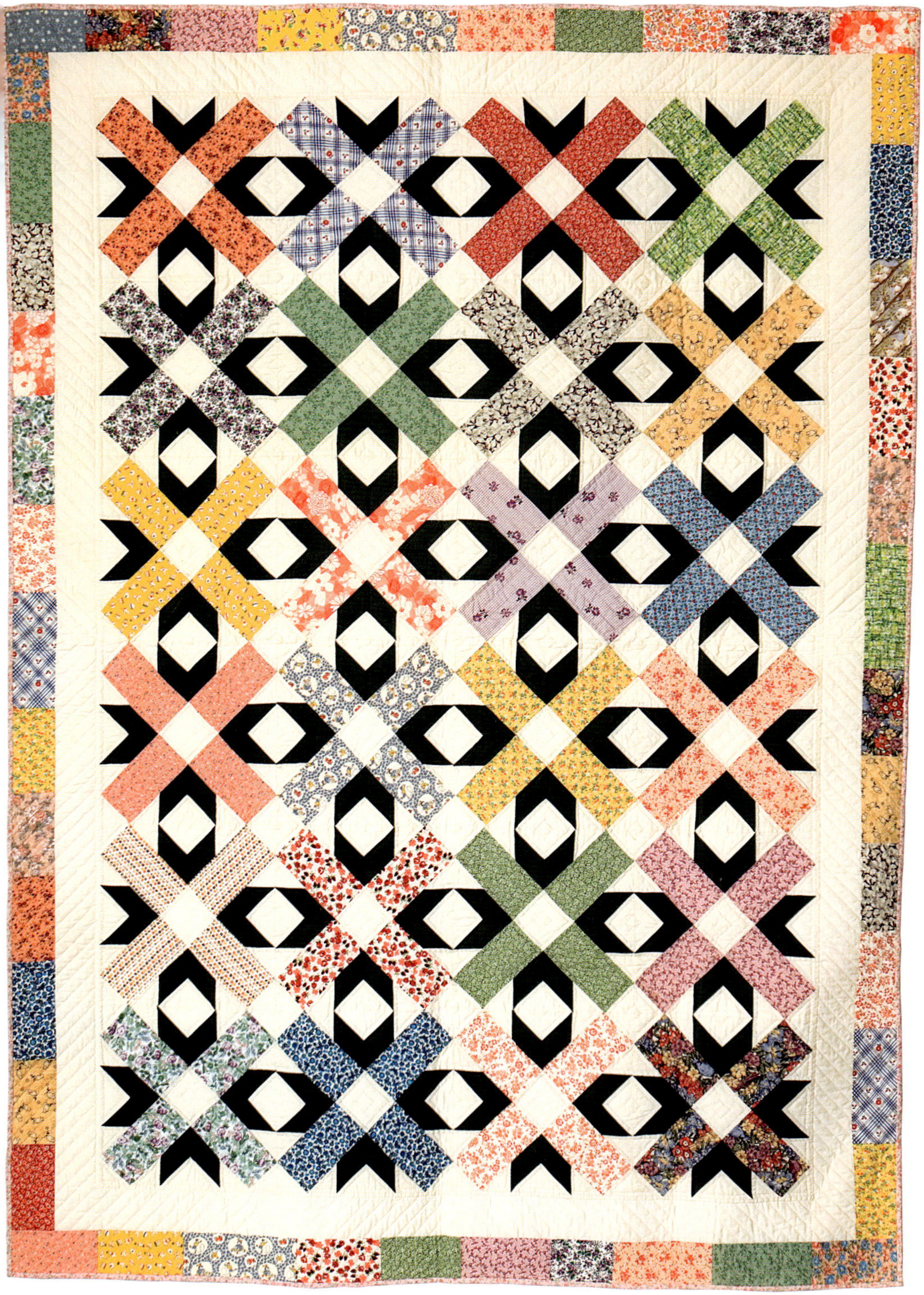

Quilt #119. "Swing in the Center" made in 1995; it is 60 inches wide by 83 inches long. This is the quilt that was in Martha's frame at the Festival of American Folklife in June of 1997. Because she was so busy answering questions, she did not get much done on the quilt during the two weeks on the mall. She had pieced the top completely before heading for Washington, having seen a similar quilt on page 19 of the book *Soft Covers for Hard Times*, by Merikay Waldvogel. Collection of the maker.

Quilt #18. "Folk Art Album" made in 1993; it is 73 inches wide by 93 inches long. Intriguing by virtue of the many wonderful appliqués depicting flowers, leaves, birds, a bunny, and a squirrel, the visual depth of this quilt is increased by the background squares pieced in a "Nine Patch" pattern of tan and white fabric. This quilt was displayed in Martha's tent on the mall at the 1997 Festival of American Folklife. Collection of the maker.

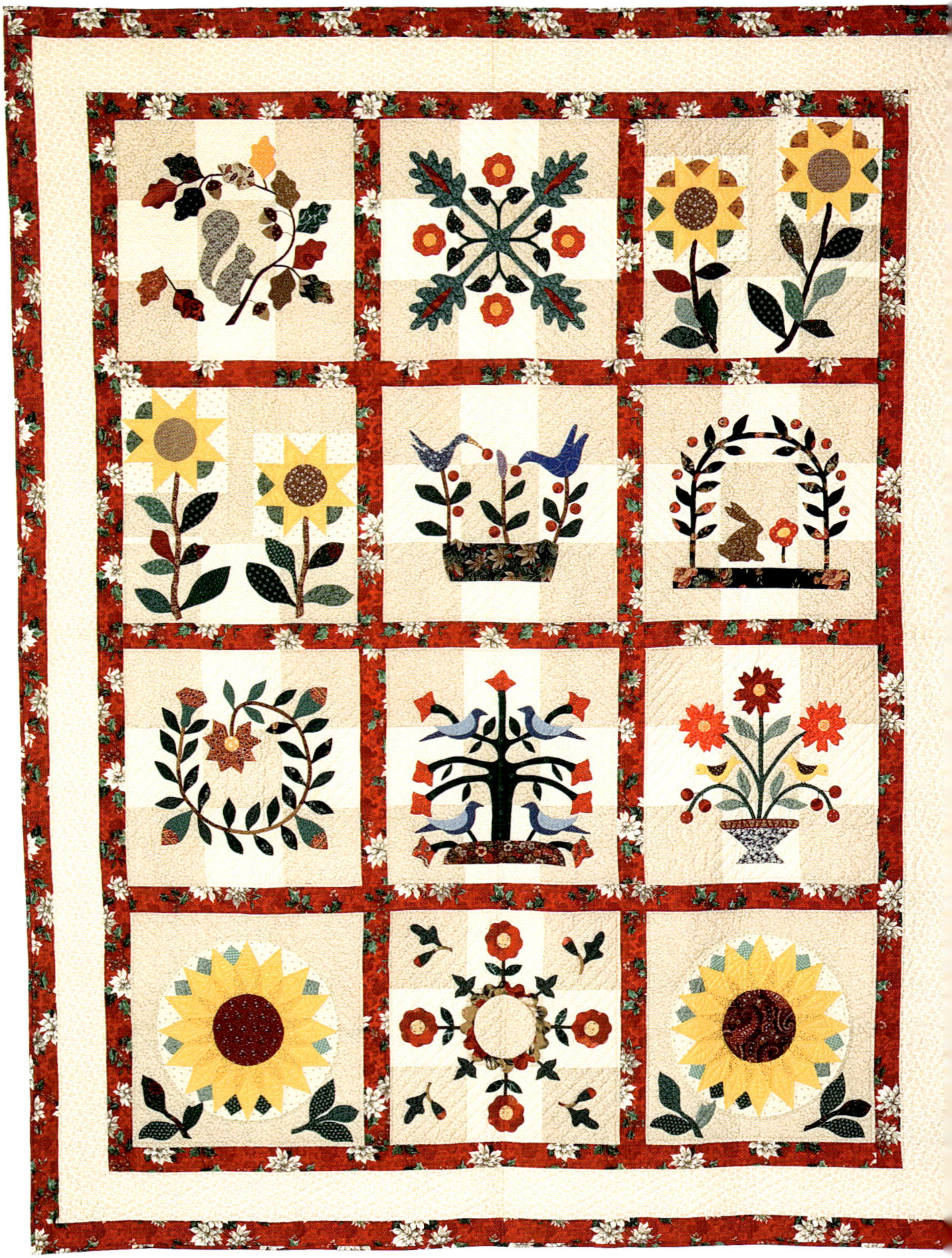

onstration kitchen, and two buildings; the front porch of a small house, typical of the Delta, was the narrative stage for home crafts and traditions, while a re-creation of a hunting camp cabin was the stage for discussions about farming, hunting, crop-dusting, and fishing. There were tented areas where craftsmen demonstrated their work and talked with visitors about their crafts.[8]

In a letter to the editor of the *Vicksburg Post* on March 22, 1998, a festival fan from Hollandale wrote to say:

> I just have to tell someone "in authority" that I think the Mississippi Folklife Festival was wonderful! My favorite parts were the extraordinarily beautiful quilts, the French hand-sewing, and the awe-inspiring gospel music (especially the talent displayed by the Mississippi Delta Mass Choir). Every part of the festival was wonderful; others in my group had entirely different favorites.

Years later, Martha admitted she was embarrassed at sweeping the awards at the 1993 quilt show sponsored by the Gulf States Quilting Association, called "The Heart of Quilting," which had been held in New Orleans. Her "Sunburst" took first place and Best of Show. Her "Autumn Leaves" took second place and the Lois King Award for most outstanding needlework skills. "Hexagon Mosaic" won first place in the "Traditional Quilts" category. Earlier in 1993, at the Pine Belt Quilters' show in Hattiesburg, "Sunburst" had taken Best of Show and tied for first place in the "Mixed Techniques" category, and "Autumn Leaves" had taken Judge's Choice and second place in the "Appliqué" category. "Autumn Leaves" was chosen for exhibition at Quiltfest USA in Louisville, Kentucky. With characteristic modesty, she says, "I think a quilt that won't get any recognition in one show can go some place else and, my goodness, it takes all kind of credit and everything."[9]

By our count, Martha made a minimum of forty-eight quilts during this ten-year span. That averages out to nearly five quilts per year, and this decade was vibrant with other activity: working with the Mississippi Quilt Association in its Heritage Quilt Documentation Project, attending the Smithsonian Festival of American Folklife for the second time, participating in the Folklife Festival on the levee in Greenville, quilting with the Cotton Patchers, traveling across the state to teach and demonstrate as often as time would allow, and developing a relationship with the Cultural Crossroads in Port Gibson. We must remember also that Martha had a lively correspondence and made it a point to respond to all the letters she received from students, fans, editors, and fellow quilt scholars and enthusiasts all over the world. She continued to make her own clothes, to garden, and, while sharing the tent at the Smithsonian Festival of American Folklife with a woman who excelled in a beautiful old needle art, had renewed her interest in tatting!

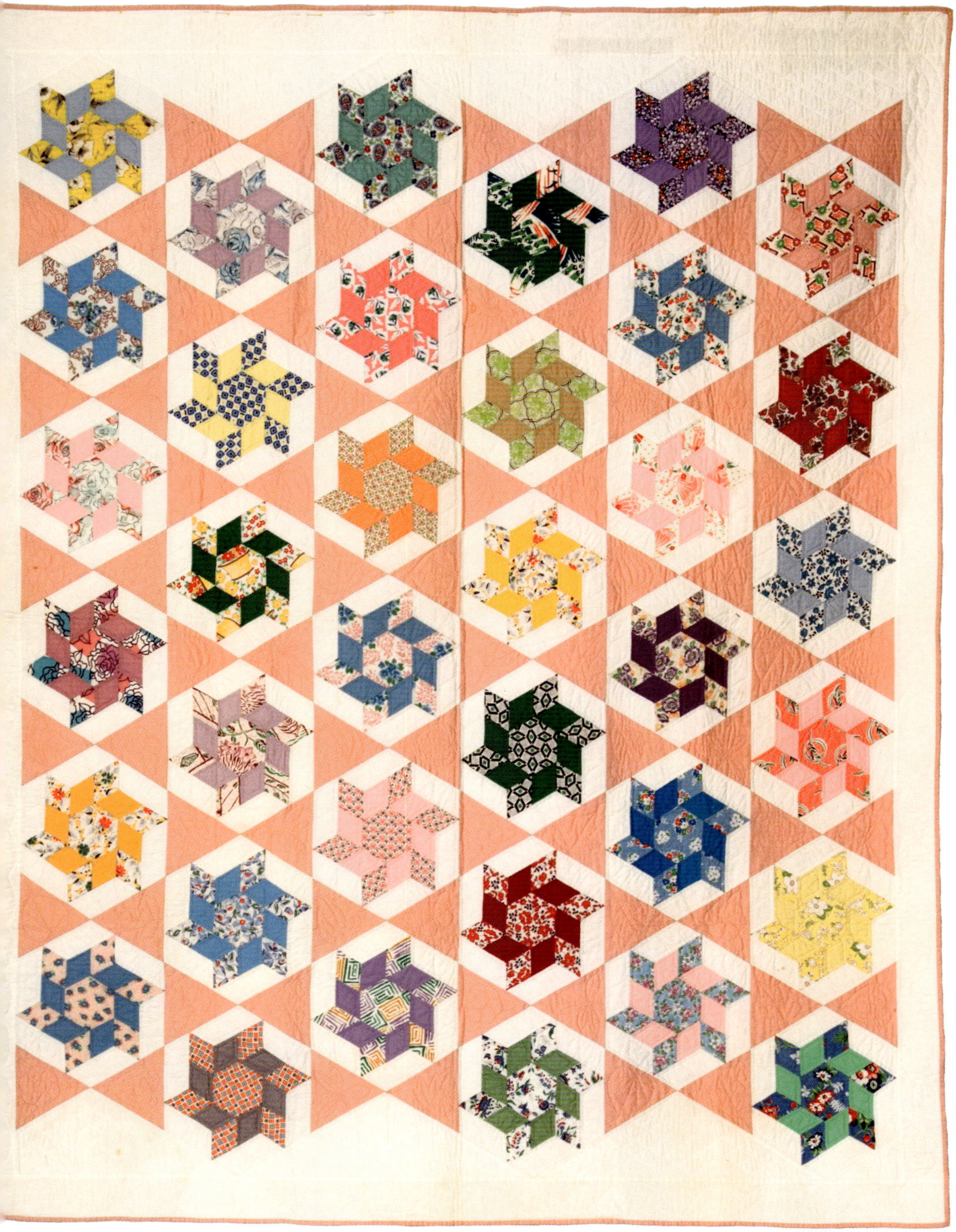

Quilt #52. "Pinwheel" made in 1989 and 1990; it is 67 inches wide by 83 inches long. The fact that this was an original Kansas City Star quilt pattern, and that she saw it while attending a quilt symposium in Kansas City, convinced Martha to buy the pattern. She used feed sacks for the printed pieces in the quilt. Collection of the maker.

Quilt #95. "Six-Pointed Star" variation made in 1990; it is 78 inches wide by 88 inches long. Ollie Jean Lane and Martha had both noticed this quilt in a magazine; each of them made one. Martha put a white diamond between each star; in the quilt she copied, that diamond was printed fabric and the stars didn't stand out so well. Collection of the maker. Photograph by Brian Loden.

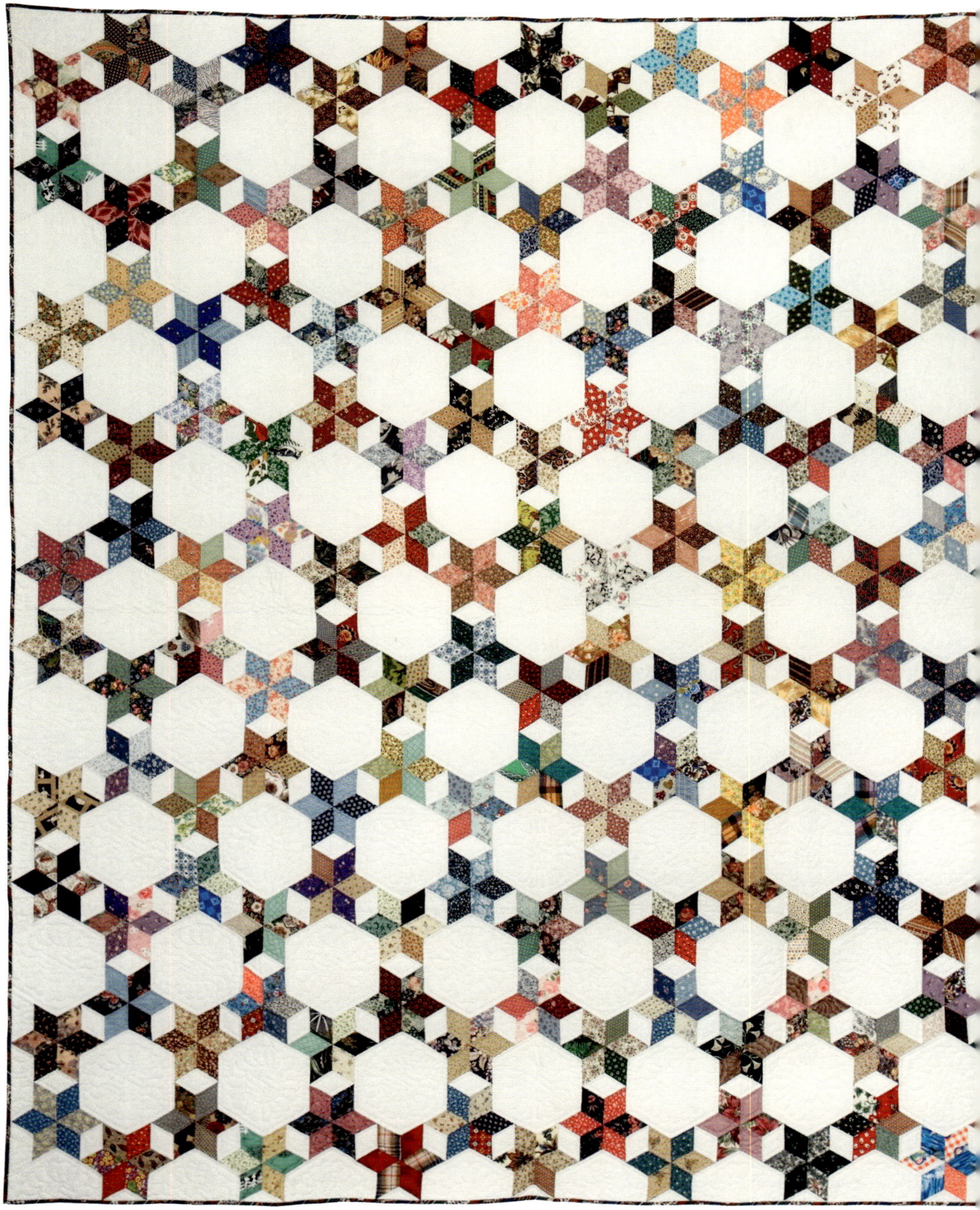

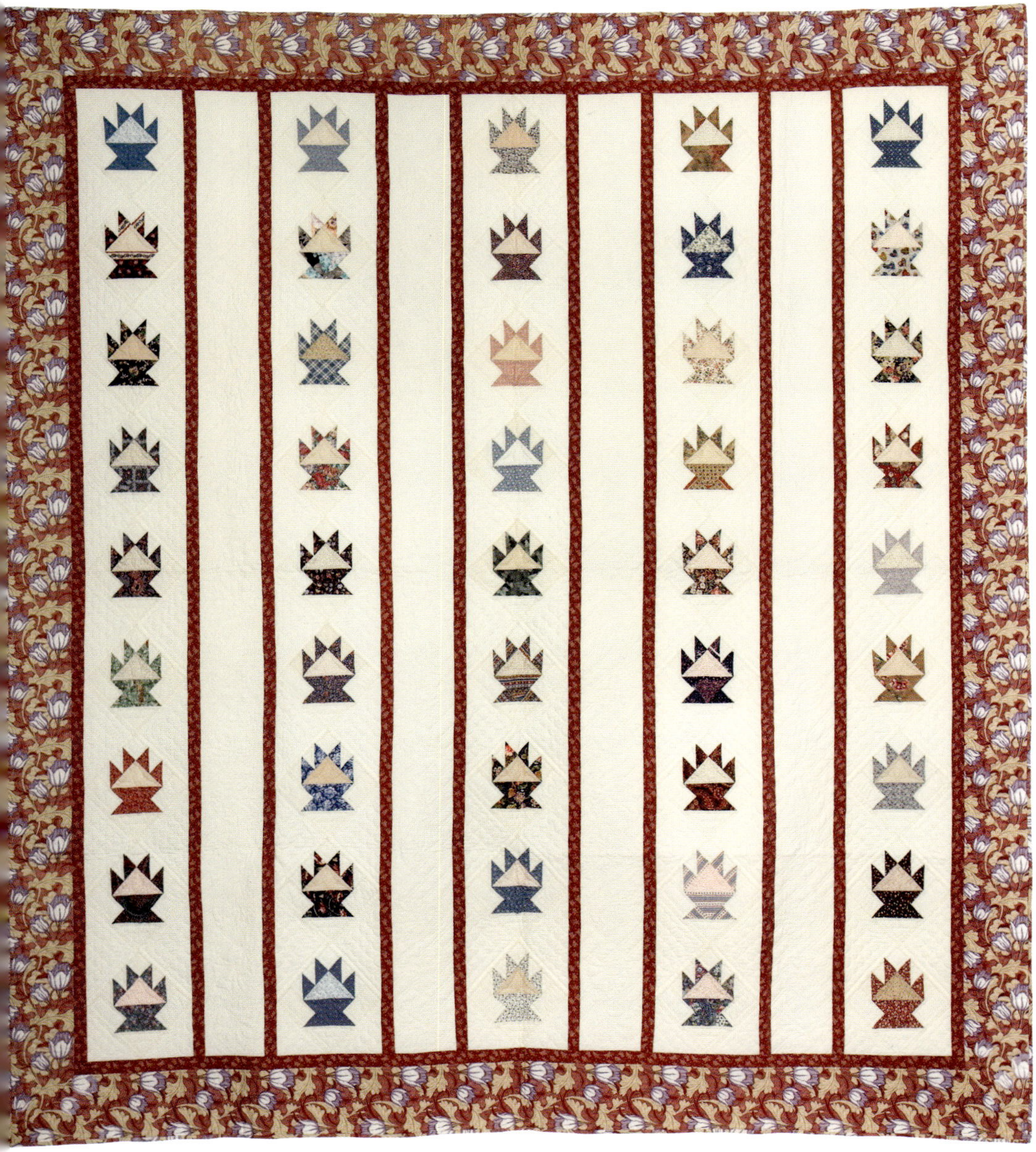

Quilt #79. "Little Baskets" made in 1991; it is 80.5 inches wide by 87 inches long. The small baskets, in six-inch square blocks, of an antique quilt provided the motivation for this quilt, which Martha decided to set in strips so that she could quilt a vine in the open white areas. It was exhibited at the 1992 American Quilter's Society show in Paducah and published in *American Quilter*, winter 1995. Collection of the maker. Photograph by Brian Loden.

Quilt #25. "Currants and Coxcomb" made in 1991; it is 80.5 inches wide by 85 inches long. Through quilt shops, the International Quilt Festival in Houston sponsored an annual "Labor of Love" contest for three years or more, and one of the rules was that at least half the fabric in the quilt should be bought from the shop through which the quilt would be submitted. Martha bought her fabrics at her friend Ann Root's quilt shop in Clinton, choosing a palette of blue and red rather than the more familiar green and red for the design she had seen in Cyrus Nelson's *Quilt Engagement Calendar*. When it took first place, Ann Root shipped the quilt to Houston, where it was exhibited in 1991, and then it went to the International Quilt Exposition in Karlriche, Germany. It was published in *American Quilter*, winter 1995, and in the letters column of the December 1991 *Quilter's Newsletter Magazine*. Collection of the maker.

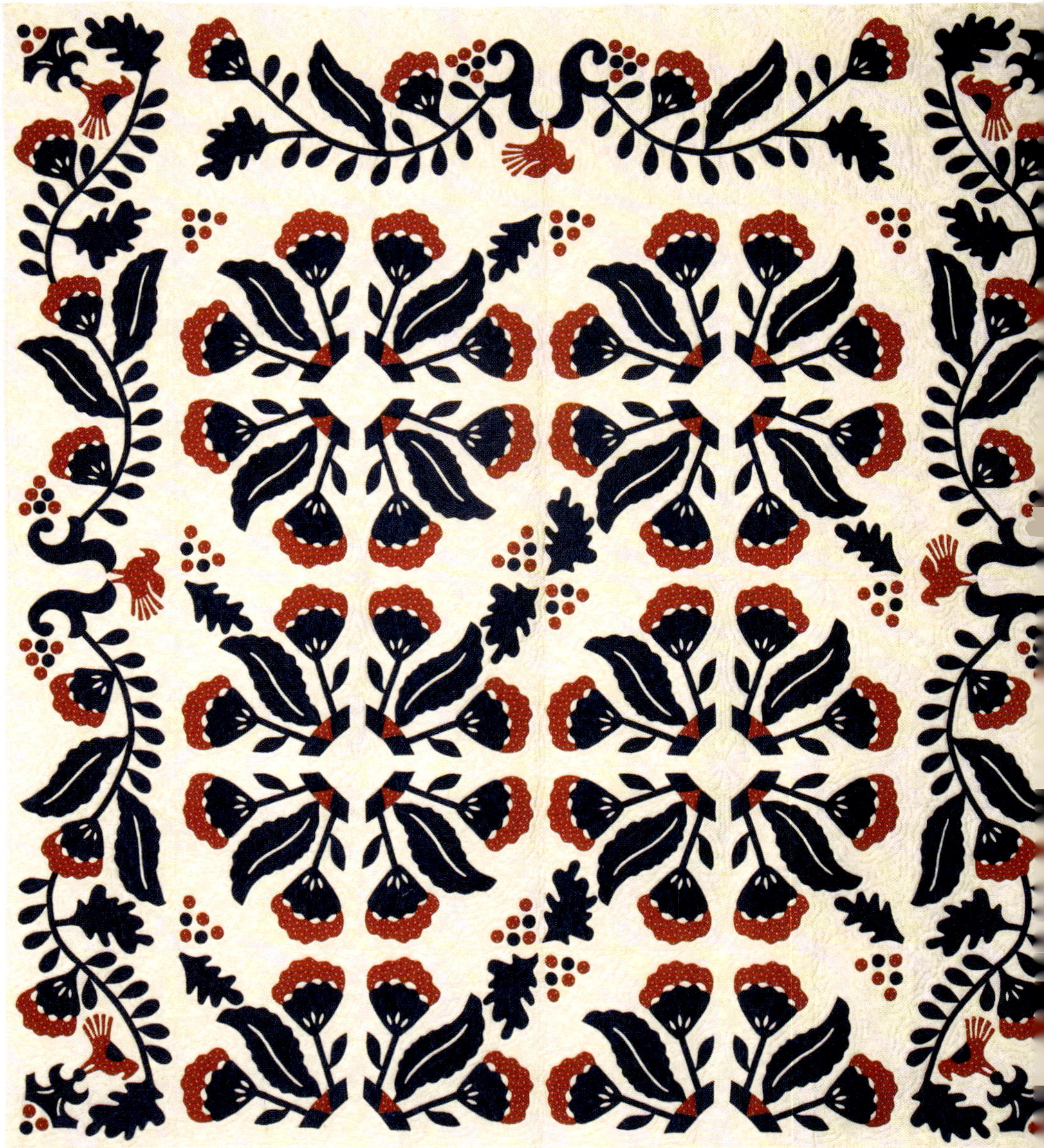

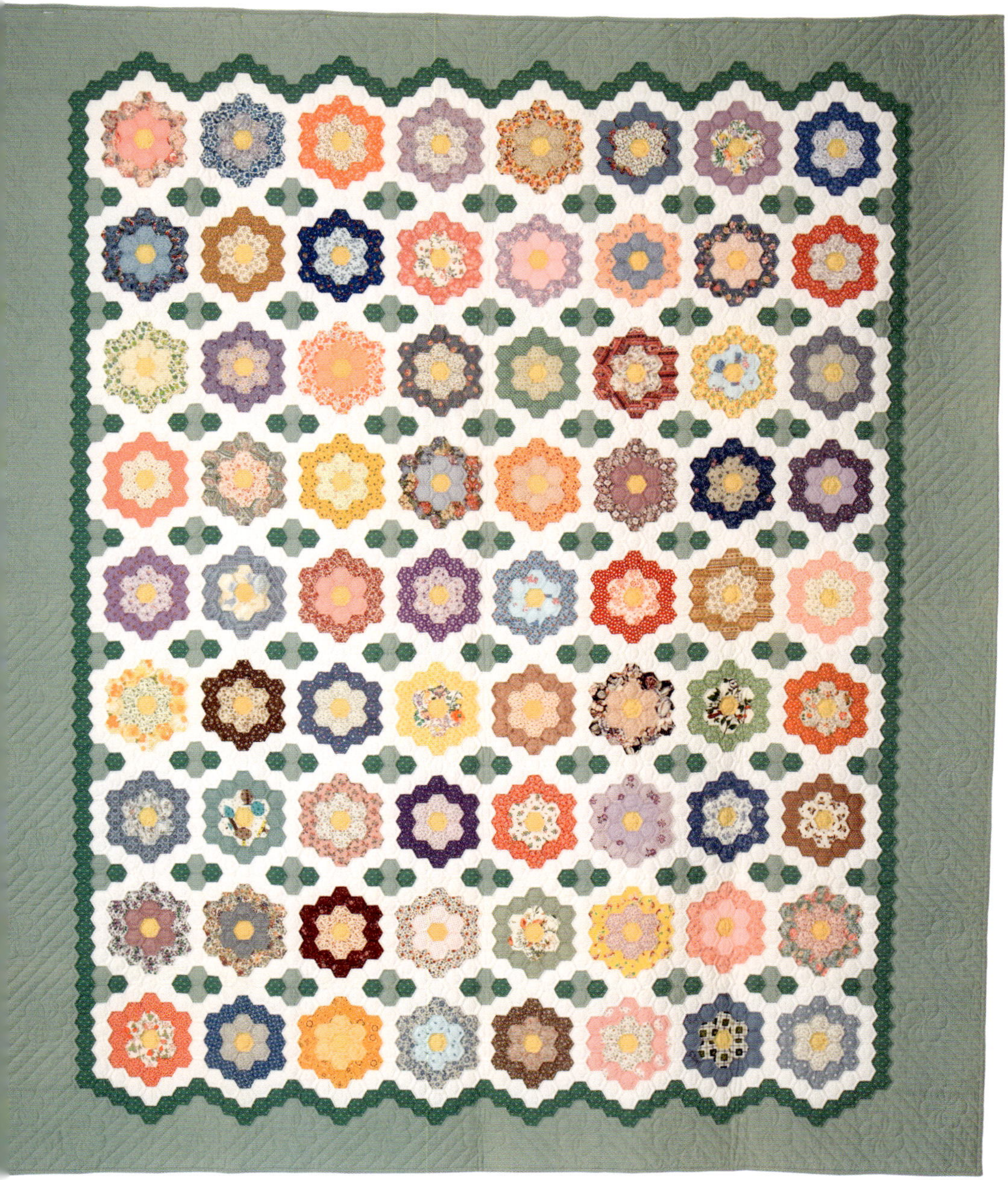

Quilt #78. "Flower Garden" made in the early 1990s; it is 80.5 inches wide by 92.5 inches long. A quilt similar to this was shown at an early Mississippi Quilt Association Gathering, and Martha went home and made one for herself. It is perhaps in a familiar pattern like this that Martha's exceptional talent and skills can be most appreciated. The horizontal rows of four green hexagons, suggesting the "leaves" of a flower garden, and the quilting of the solid green border are the details of a master quilter. Collection of the maker.

Quilt #90. "Hexagon Magic" or "Garden Mosaic" made in 1993; it is 72 inches wide by 85 inches long. A desire to work with hexagons is what led Martha to make this most interesting version of the familiar "Flower Garden" pattern. It took first place in the "Bed Size" category at the Gulf States Quilting Association show in 1993. Collection of the maker.

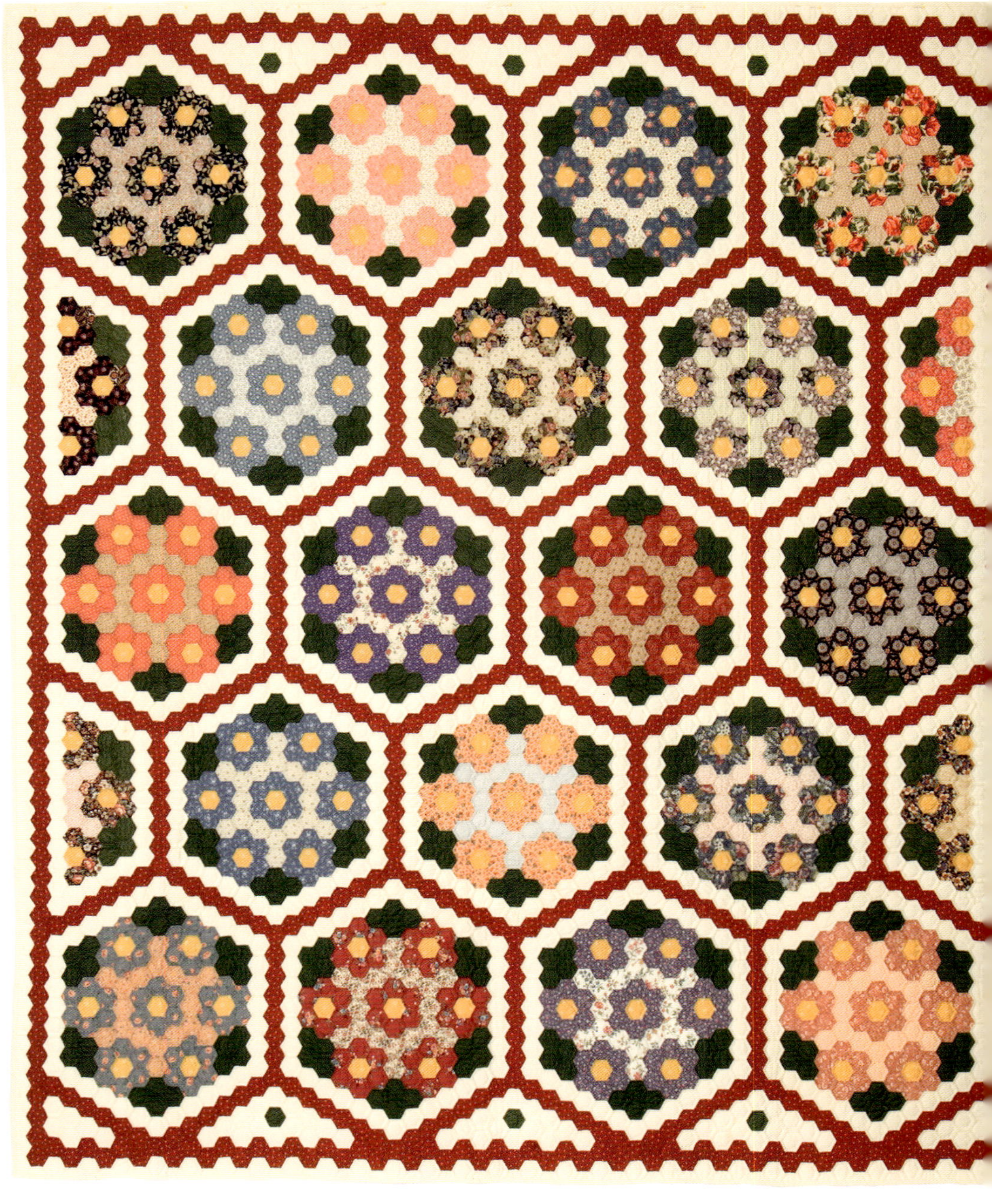

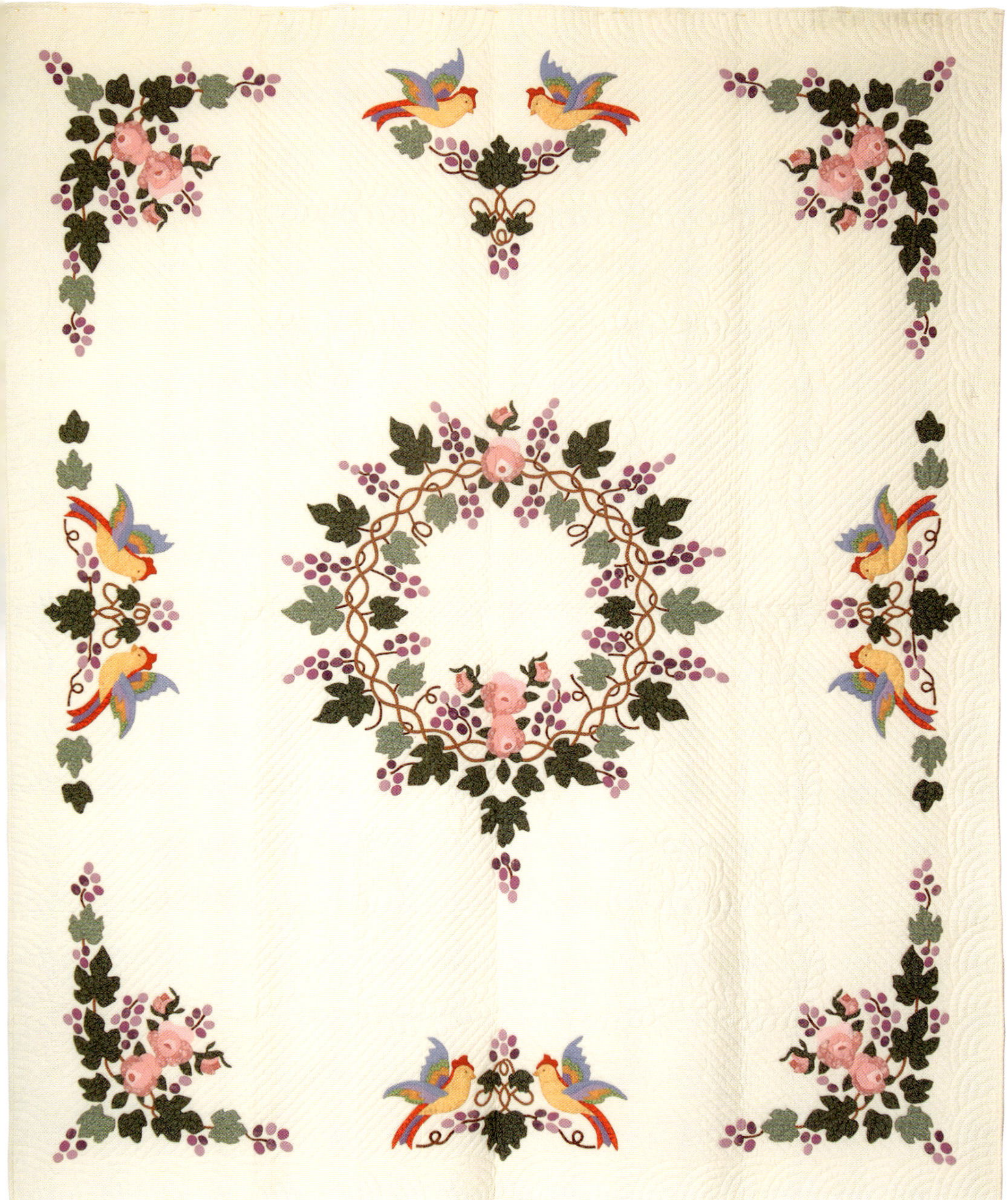

Quilt #104. "Birds and Blooms" made in the early 1990s; it is 79 inches wide by 93 inches long. This design was recognized as a spectacular piece when it came to the public eye around 1920. At least two finished quilts of this pattern, besides Martha's, are known to exist, but one omits the appliqué of the center wreath, executing the intricacies of grapevine and roses in quilting stitches alone. Martha drew her pattern for the quilt following a tiny photograph, but even so, she was able to capture many of the details such as the varied sizes, shapes, and colors of the grapes. Collection of the maker.

Quilt #117. "Sunburst" made in 1993; it is 72 inches wide by 85 inches long. This quilt took "Best of Show" at the Gulf States Quilting Association Show in 1993 and tied for first place in the category of "Mixed Techniques" at the same show. It was featured in *Mississippi* magazine in the September/October 1995 issue and was published in both *Quilting Today* and *Traditional Quiltworks*. Collection of the maker.

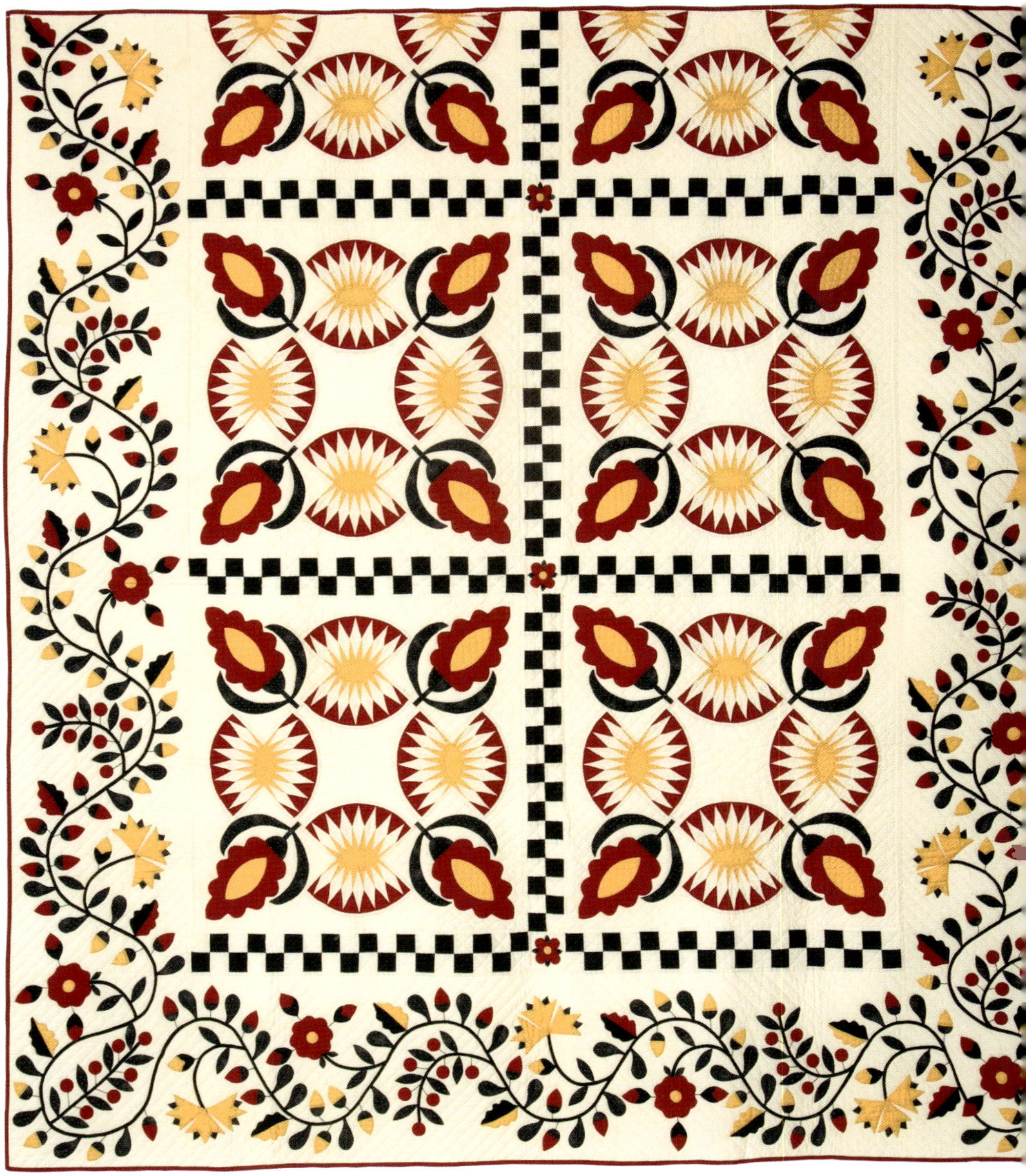

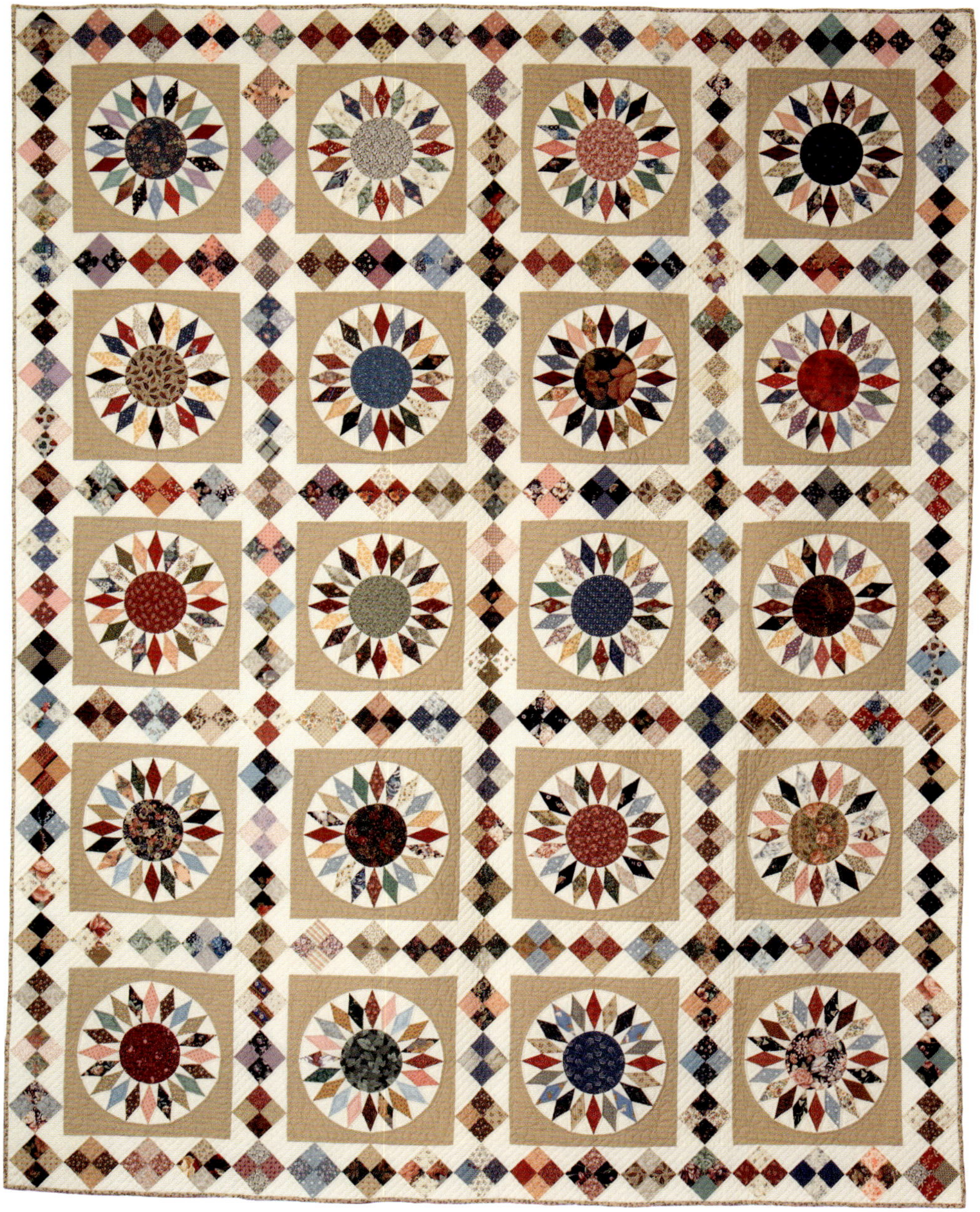

Quilt #83. "Sunburst and Four-Patch" made in 1994; it is 84 inches wide by 103 inches long. When this quilt was exhibited at the American Quilter's Society show in Paducah, noted quilt historian Mary Barton (of Iowa) wrote to Martha saying that when she first saw it, she had thought it was a quilt that she owned. Martha was thrilled because she knew of and greatly admired Barton's collection of antique quilts. In fact, it was Barton's quilt that had been photographed for *Lady's Circle Patchwork Quilts* and gave Martha the basic pattern. The "Four-Patch" borders were Martha's addition. The quilt has been published in the book *The Quilt: Beauty in Fabric and Thread*, by Marie Salazar (1997), and in *The American Quilter* (winter 1995). Collection of the maker.

Quilt #115. "Roses Aplenty" made in 1994; it is 83 inches wide by 86 inches long. A 19th-century quilt similar to this in a catalog from the Denver Art Museum gave Martha the idea for the four main blocks of this quilt, and the polyanthus roses Alan had carefully tended in the Skeltons' garden were the source for the luxuriant border. The quilt was exhibited at the American Quilter's Society 11th annual show in Paducah in the spring of 1995 and published in the winter 1995 edition of *The American Quilter* magazine. Collection of the maker.

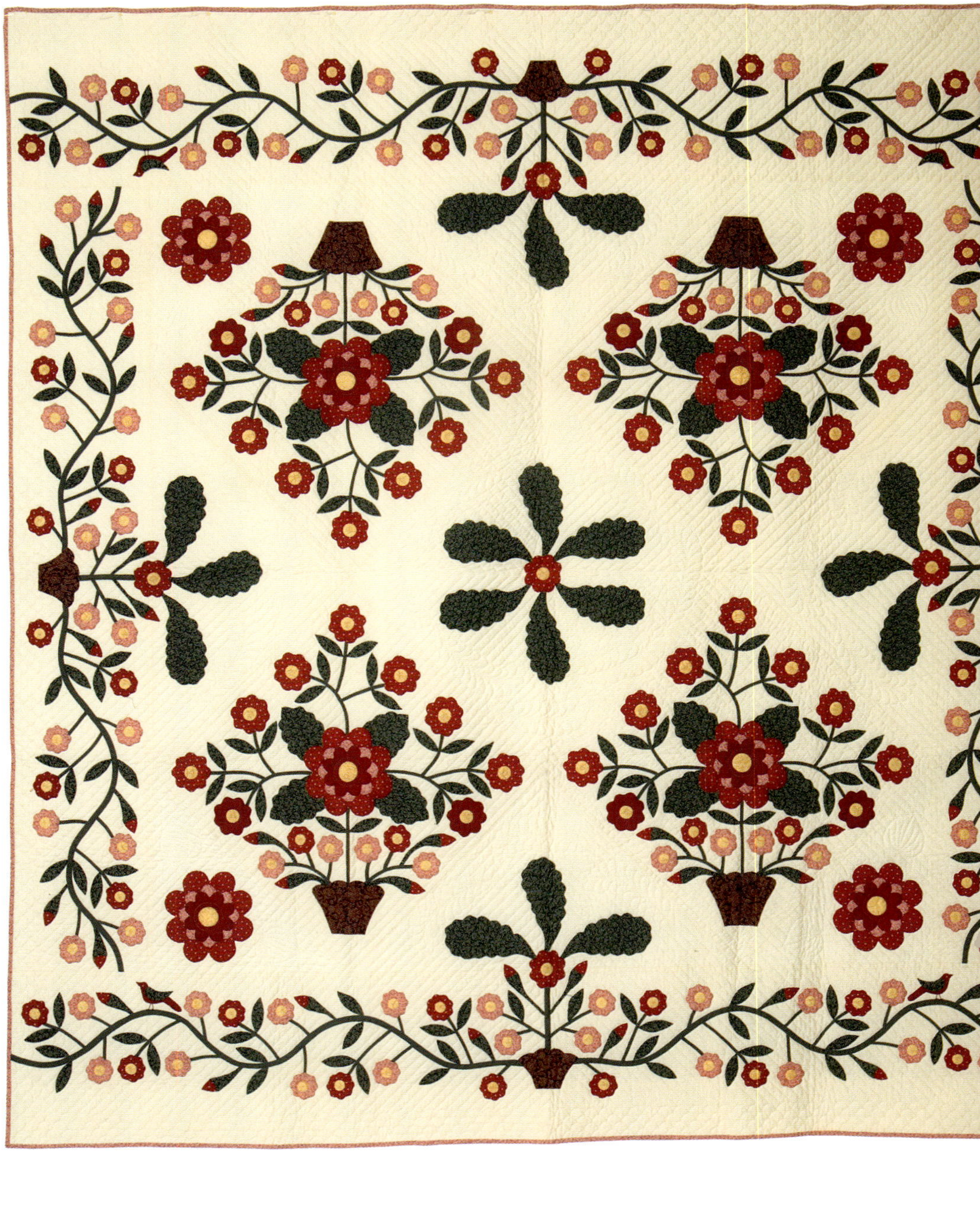

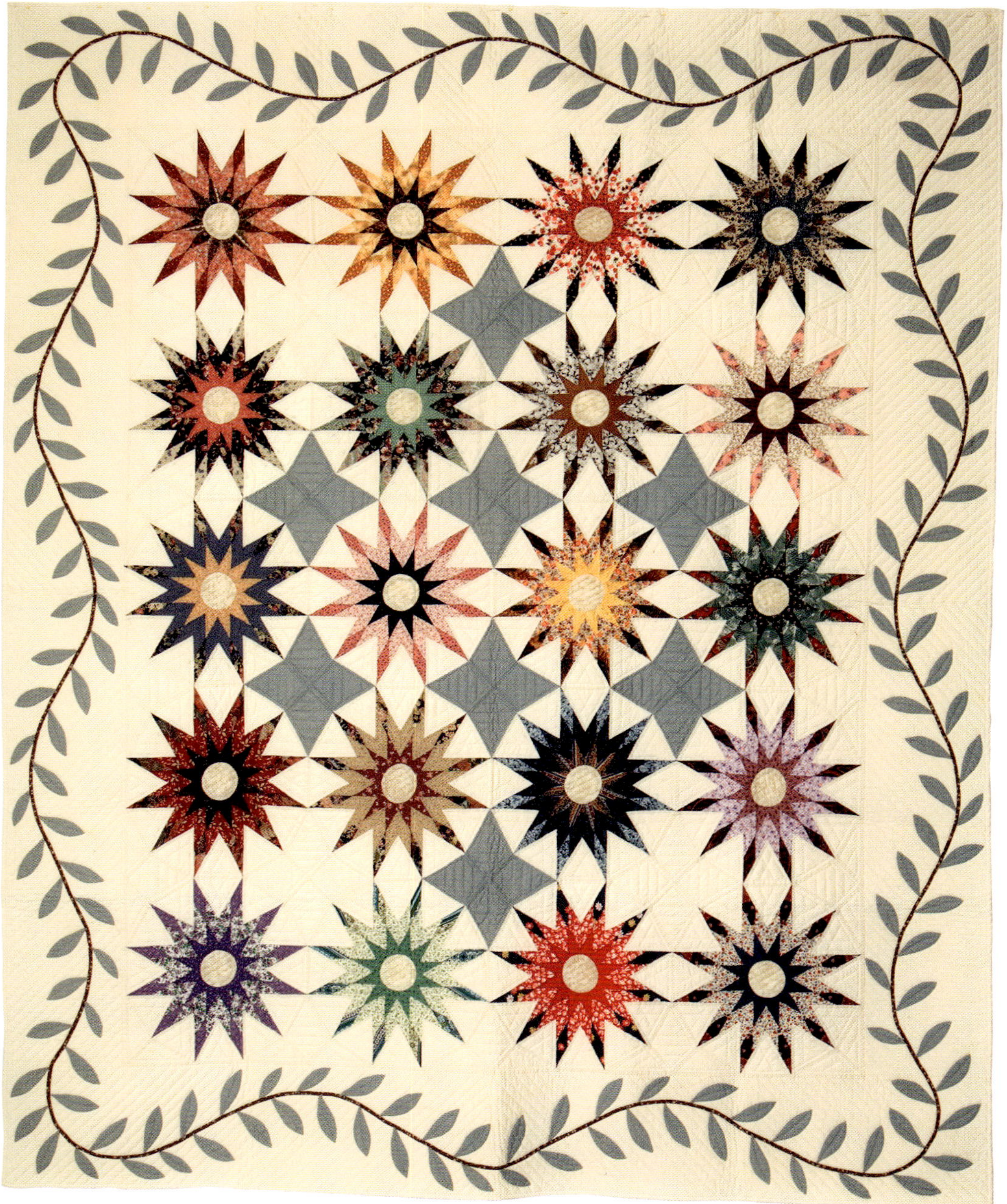

Quilt #89. "Moon and Stars"; made in 1995; it is 78.5 inches wide by 93 inches long. A block from the 1930s named "Man in the Moon" appeared in *Lady's Circle Patchwork Quilts*; Martha's version includes 8 four-point stars and a vine border that were not part of the original design. It was exhibited in the July 1995 Jackson Quilters' Show and was published in a calendar, "Quilt Art '95," as well as in *Mississippi Quilts*. Collection of the maker.

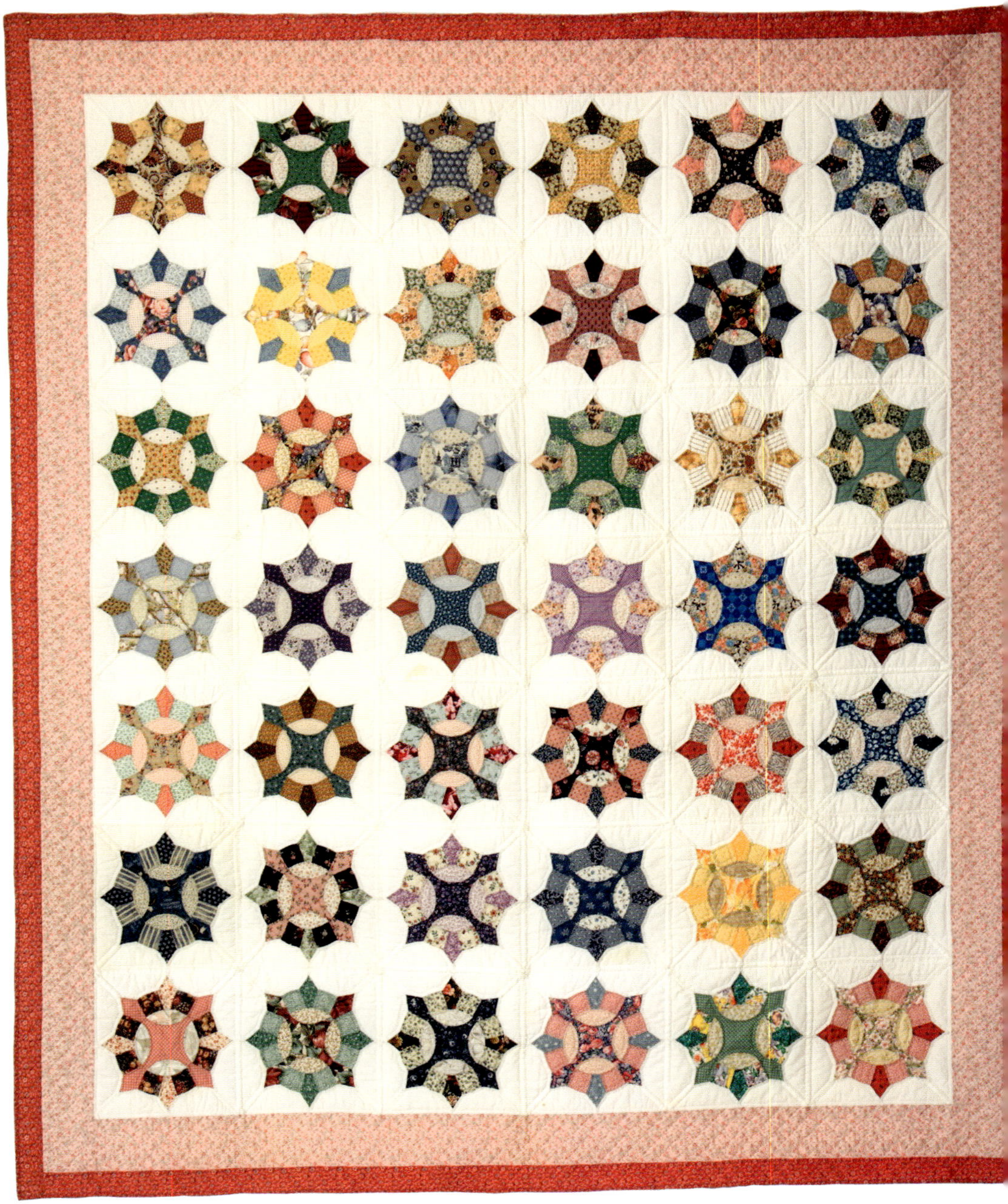

Quilt #130. "Caesar's Crown" made in the early 1990s; it is 77 inches wide by 88 inches long. Nancilu Burdick's second book about Talulah Bottoms, *Family Ties: Old Patterns from New Cloth*, included patterns, and that is where Martha obtained the one for "Caesar's Crown." (See "Glittering Stars" for the first Talulah Bottoms quilt that Martha duplicated.) Collection of the maker.

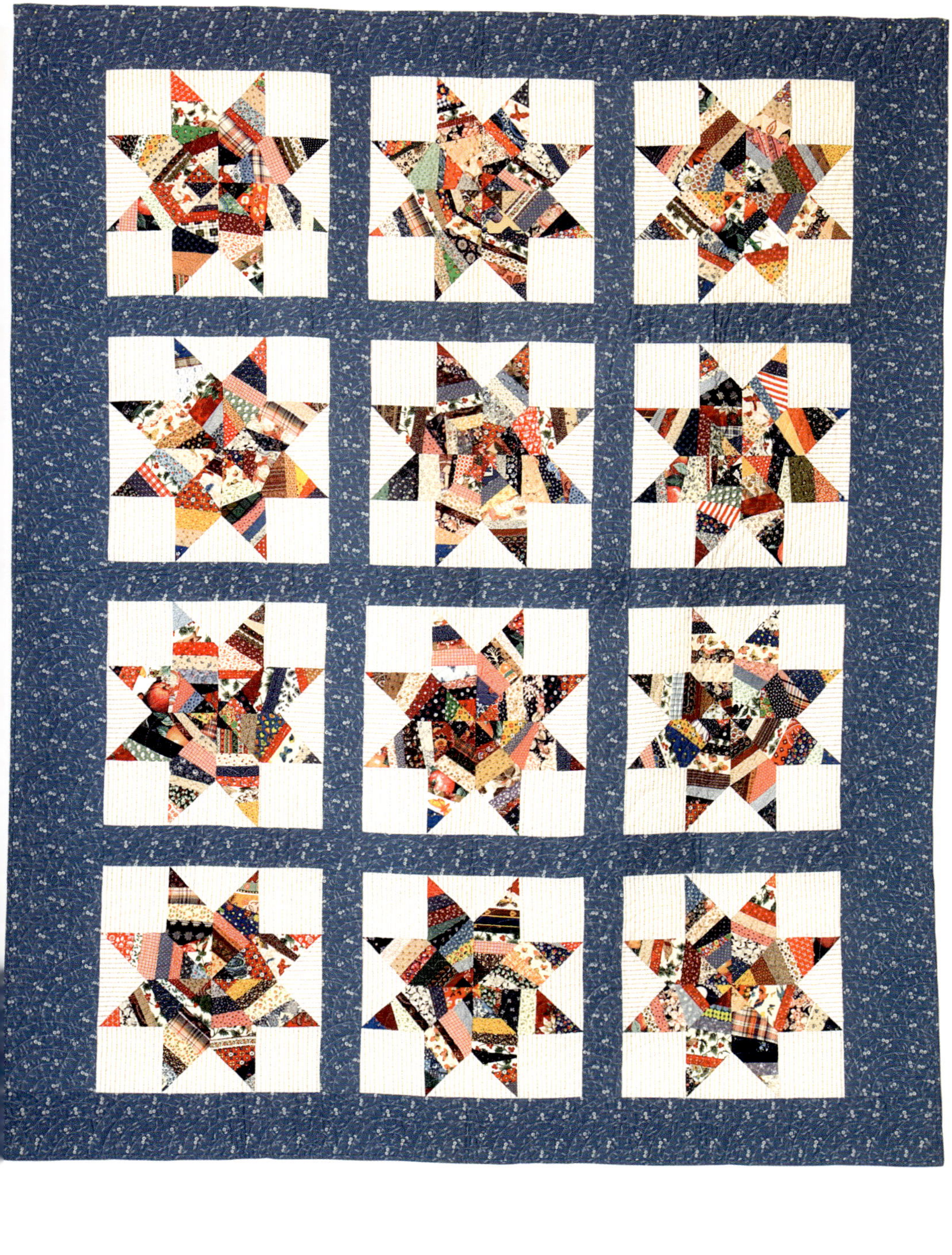

Quilt #141. "String Star" made post-1995; it is 69 inches wide by 83.5 inches long. From the very beginning of Mississippi Quilt Association's quilt documentation days, lots of string quilts showed up, especially string star designs. Martha soon wanted to make her own "String Star," which she took to an MQA Gathering and shared in the "Show and Tell" portion of the program. Collection of the maker.

Quilt #99. "Postage Stamp" made in 1997; it is 81 inches wide by 92 inches long. When it came to Martha's attention that the mother-in-law of her good friend and fellow Cotton Patcher Carole Schultz had made nine "Postage Stamp" quilts, Martha was inspired to develop an easier and faster method of working the pattern. Martha begins piecing at the center and adds rows of tiny squares round and round it, never breaking her thread! ("Easy" and "fast" are relative terms in this case. The squares that comprise each block are usually no larger than one inch on each side, and they all have to be cut ahead of time. This is a wonderful choice for a scrap quilt.) It was exhibited in a Vicksburg Quilters' show and in a Mississippi Quilt Association trunk show. Collection of the maker.

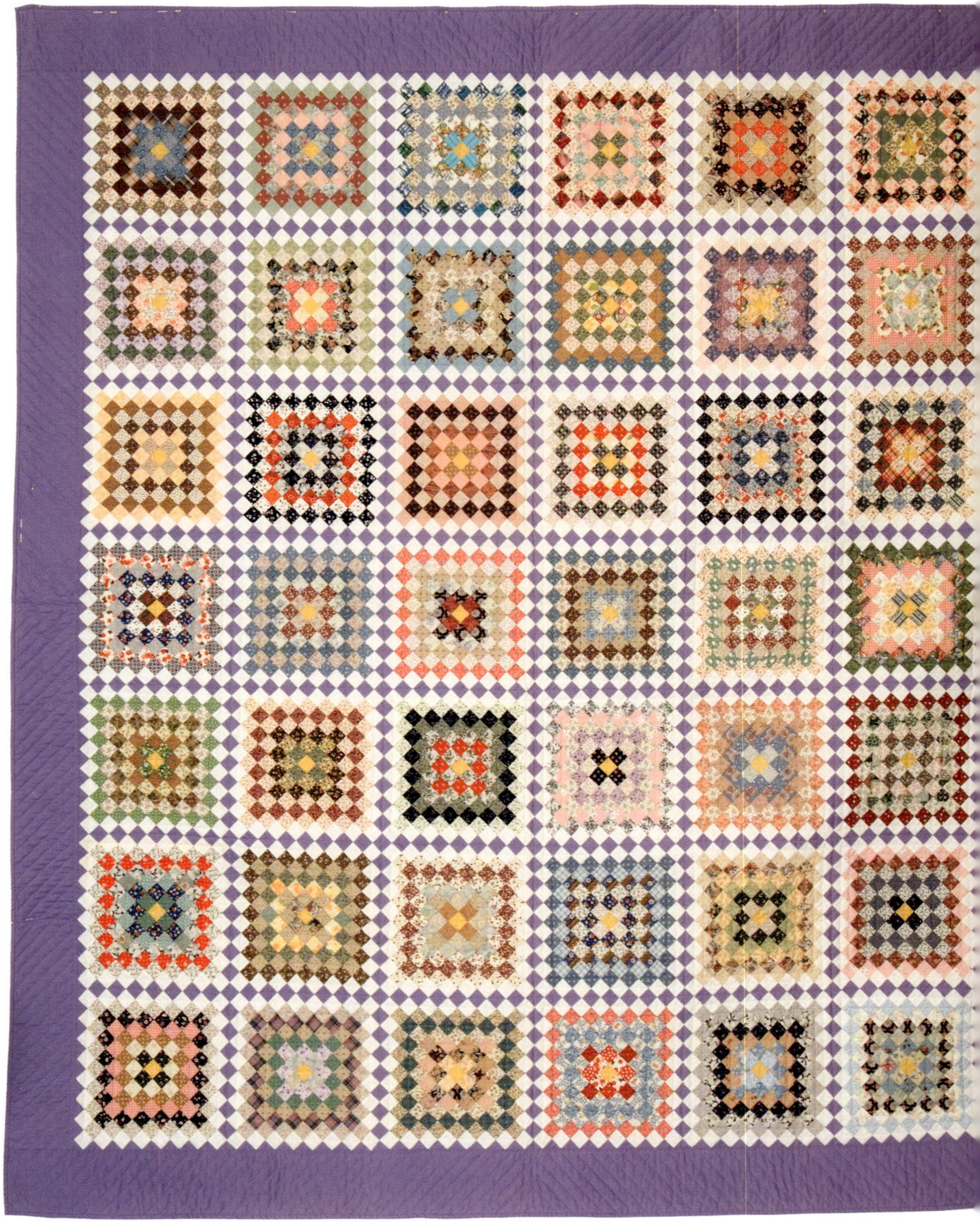

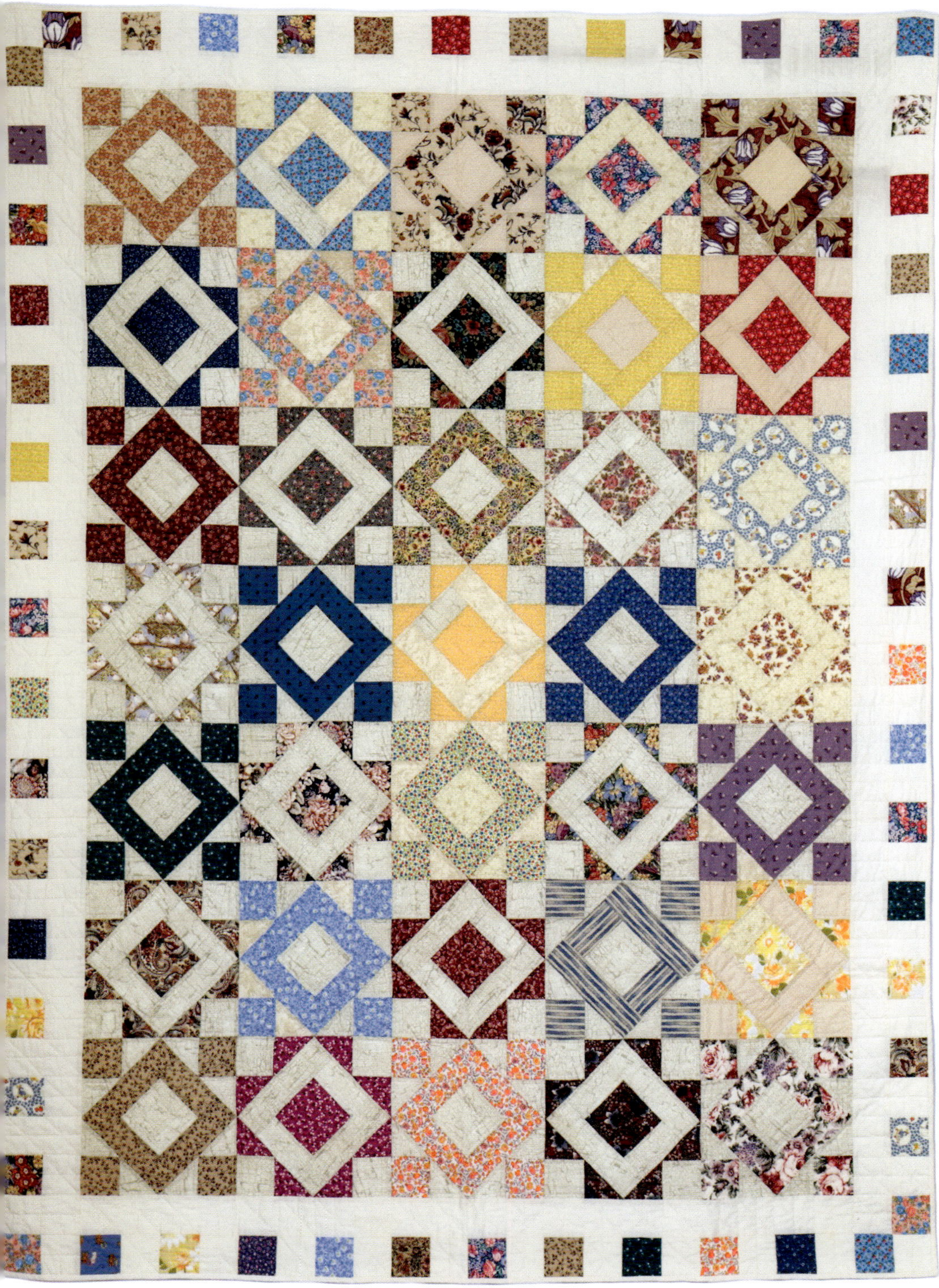

Quilt #134. "Toad in the Puddle" made in 1998; it is 60 inches wide by 79 inches long. This pattern appeared in *Vintage Quilting* magazine in the fall of 1997, and Martha saw it while on a retreat with the Quilting Friends at Lake Tiak O'Khata (near Louisville, Mississippi). Collection of the maker. Photograph by Brian Loden.

Quilt #132. "Wreaths and Papercuts" made in the late 1990s; it is 79.75 inches wide by 80 inches long. Two masters of the "Baltimore Album" style of appliqué influenced this quilt. Five of Jeana Kimball's floral wreaths, offered as a block-of-the-month program at Ann Root's quilt shop, and four of Elly Sienkiewicz's paper cuts were combined to make the field of the quilt, and Martha designed the border to have a light touch. Collection of the maker.

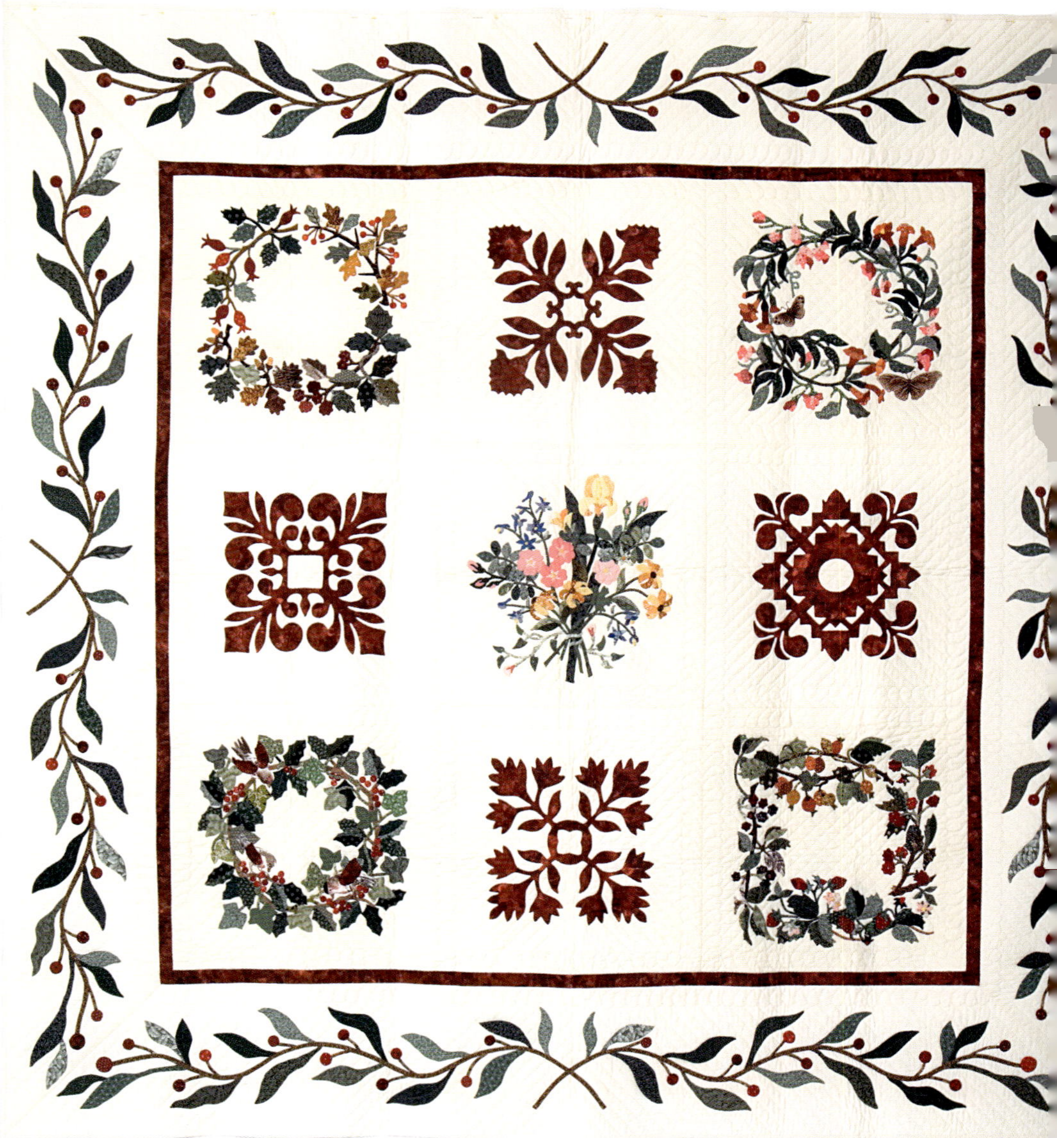

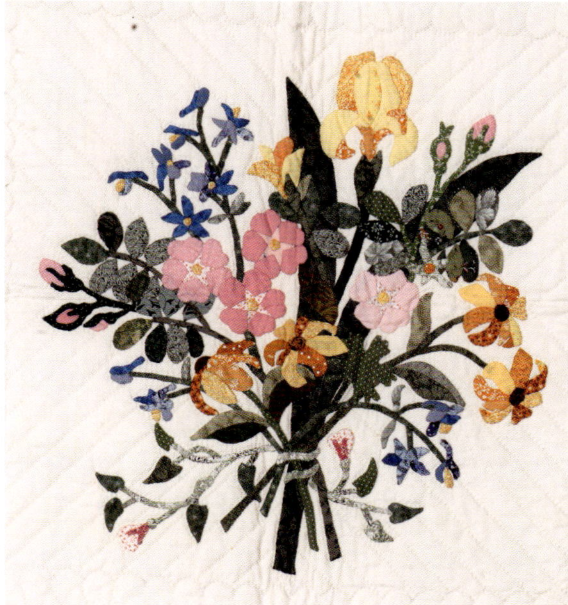

Quilt #132. "Wreaths and Papercuts" detail. Only in close-up does a bouquet of appliquéd flowers display the attention to detail that makes it look so lifelike.

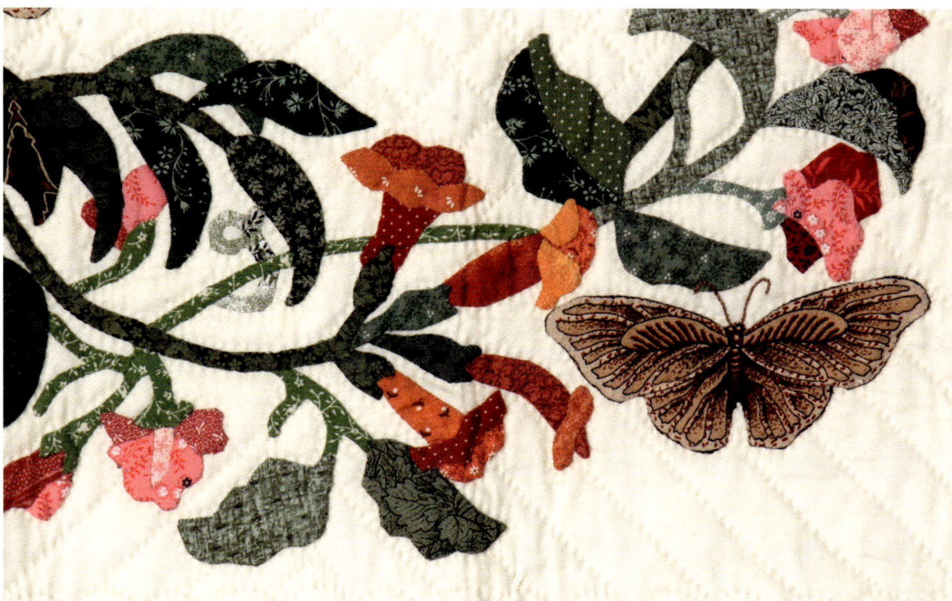

Quilt #132. "Wreaths and Papercuts" detail. Although the butterfly was cut in one piece from the fabric, the trumpet vine and sweet pea blossoms and the leaves were built up with a variety of fabrics.

Quilt #111. "Tomato Flower" made in the late 1990s; it is 85 inches wide by 85 inches long. The style of this block, a design that has many variations, captured Martha's attention when she saw it in a catalog of quilts from the Denver Art Museum. It is one of the last quilts Martha submitted to the American Quilter's Society for their annual contest and show in Paducah. Collection of the maker.

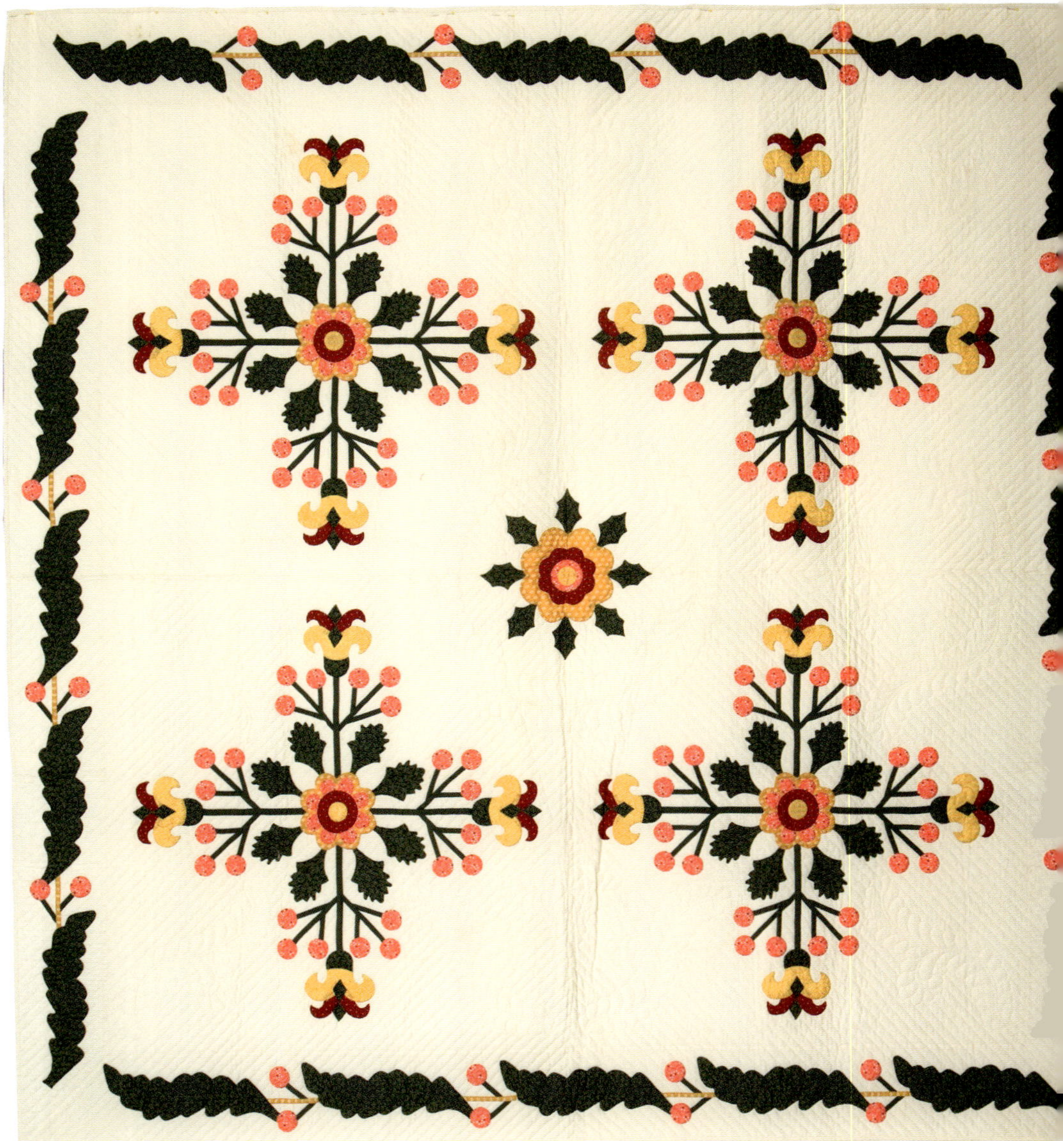

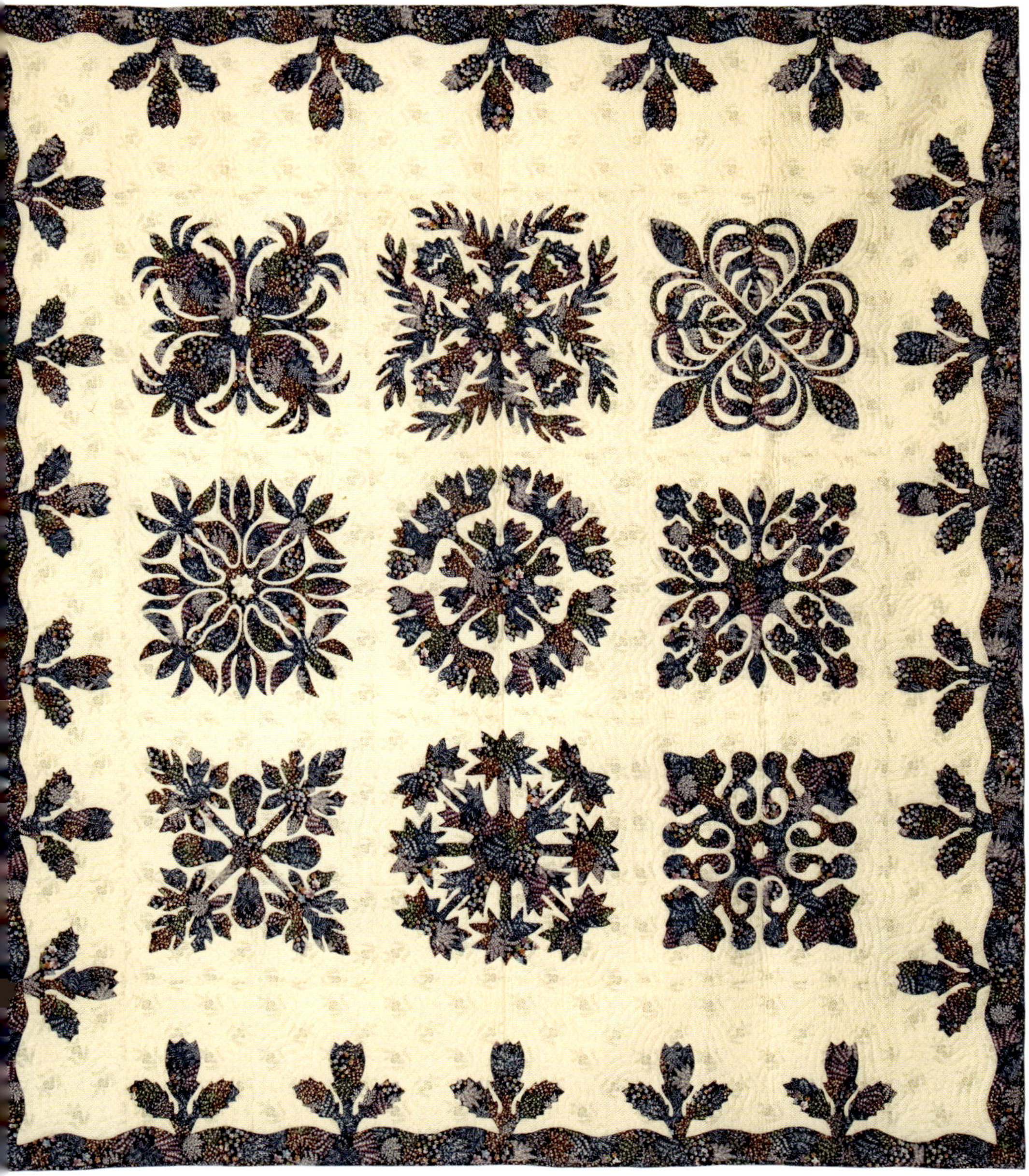

Quilt #84. "Hawaiian Sampler" made in the late 1990s; it is 88.5 inches wide by 94 inches long. After taking a Gulf States Quilting Association seminar on Tahitian appliqué, Martha searched and found these distinctive designs in *Quilter's Newsletter Magazine* and in a book on Hawaii. It was exhibited in the 2000 Vicksburg Quilters' Show and at the Gulf States Quilting Association Show. Collection of the maker.

Quilt #116. "Small Stars" made in the late 1990s; it is 78.5 inches wide by 93 inches long. Martha has a particular fondness for stars, and she thinks small diamonds are "fun to work with," so when she saw a quilt similar to this in *Star Quilts* by this author, she knew she wanted to make it. The "Streak o' Lightning" setting strips in navy (which were red in the inspiration quilt) make the little stars really pop! The quilt has been shown locally. Collection of the maker.

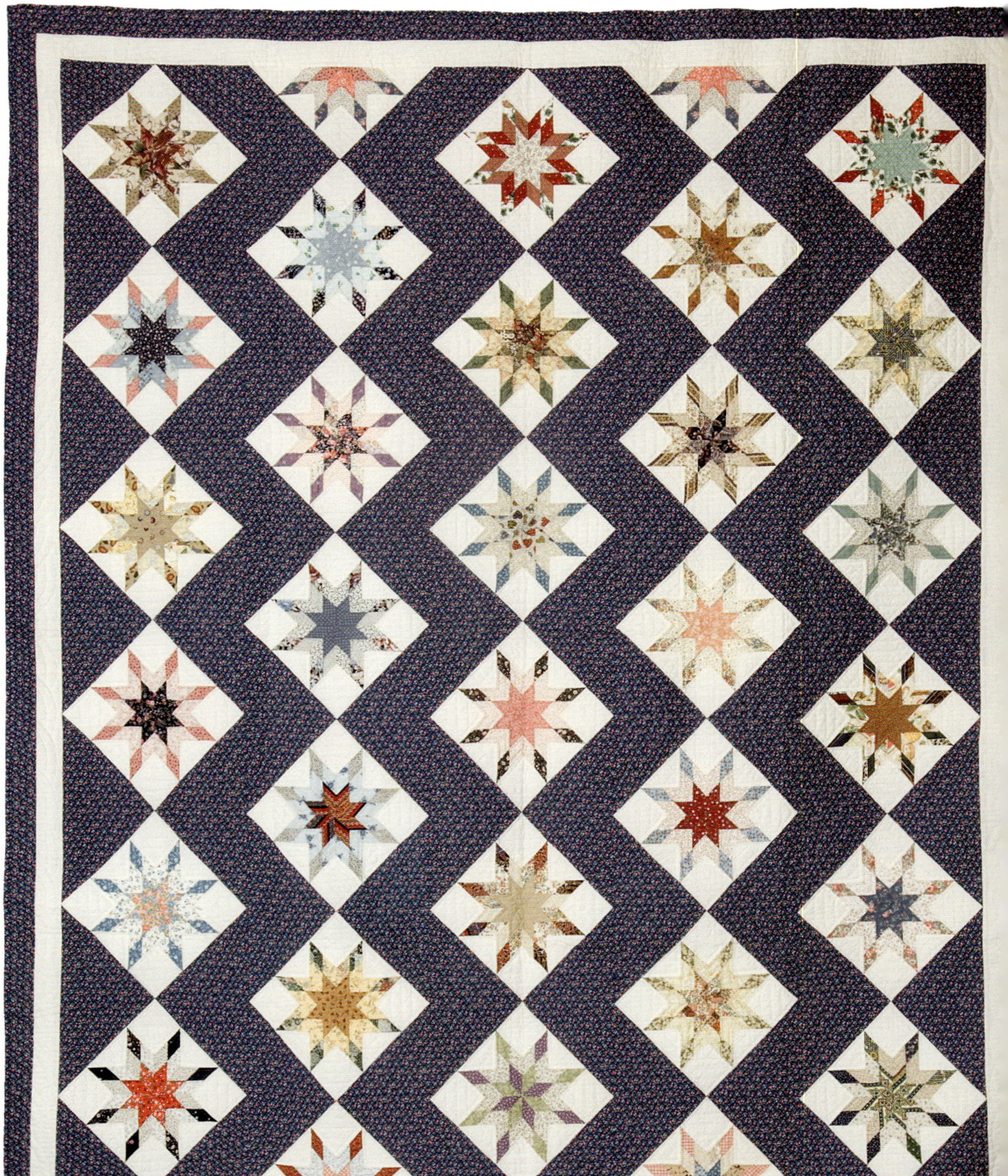

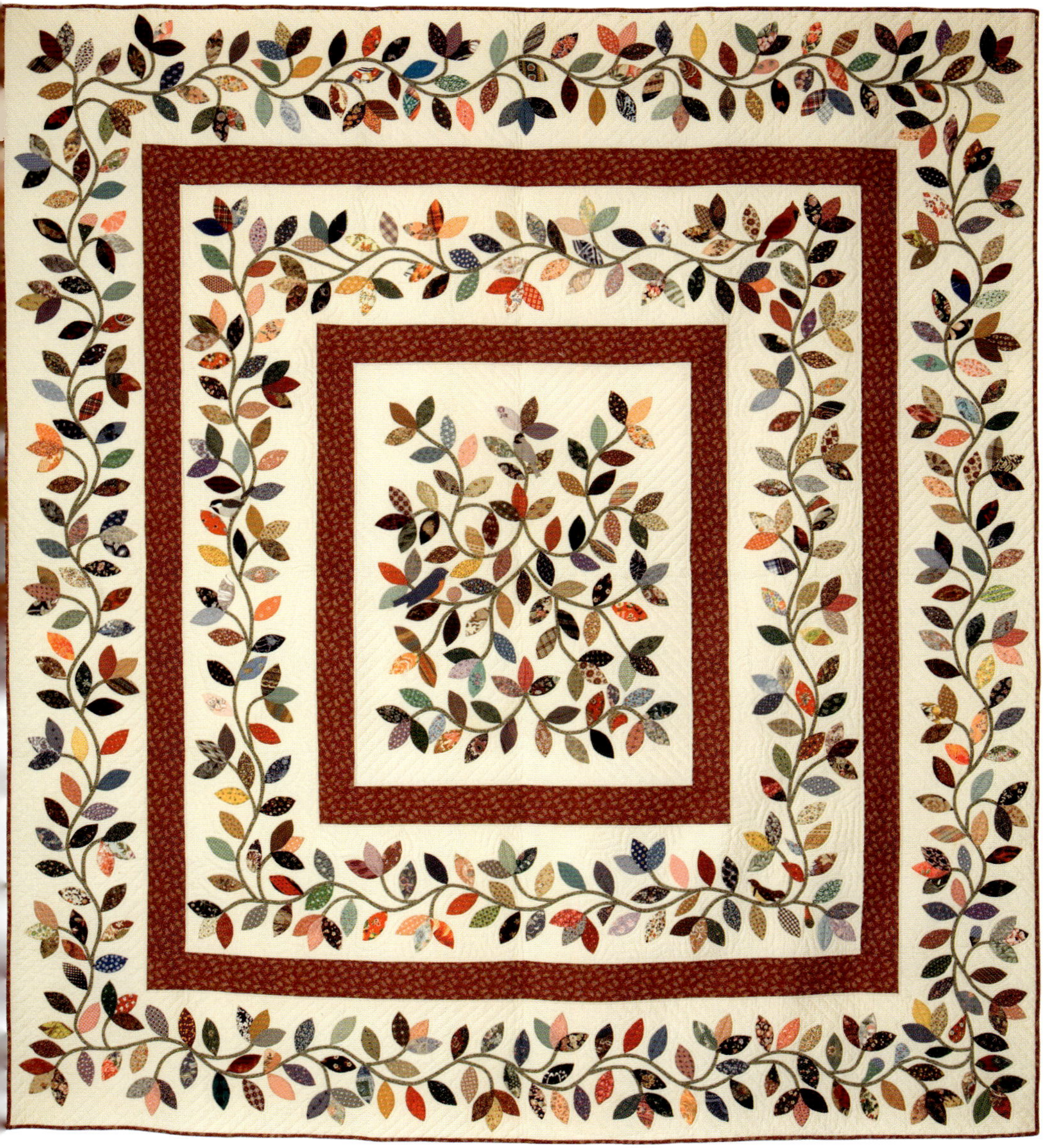

Quilt #103. "Autumn Leaves" made in the late 1990s; it is 80 inches wide by 88 inches long. When Martha's older sister, Virginia, got the pattern for a leaf quilt from a lady in Oklahoma, she knew just who would enjoy it. Her sister's love of trees and nature was part of family lore. Sure enough, Martha set right to work on a quilt, only she doubled the number of leaves, plus she hid five little birds in among them. She loves to coax children into seeing if they can find the birds. The quilt was exhibited in the 1993 American Quilter's Society show and contest and at "Quiltfest USA" in Louisville, Kentucky, was juried a regional winner in "Quilts Across America," and took second place overall at the Gulf States Quilting Association show in 1993. It took the "Judge's Choice" award plus second place for appliquéd quilts at the Pine Belt Quilter's Show that year. "Autumn Leaves" was published in *American Quilter*, winter 1995, and was featured on postcards sold as a fund-raiser for the Mississippi Quilt Association. Collection of the maker.

Quilt #92. "Feathered Star Medallion" made in the late 1990s; it is 72 inches wide by 83.5 inches long. Martha was thrilled when her friend Ollie Jean Lane gave her the "Feathered Star" block at the center of this quilt because it meant a lot to Martha to have something of Ollie Jean's work. She wanted a special setting, so she decided on a medallion arrangement. She pieced red stars, appliquéd green leaf-shaped squares, and pulled in some redwork she had stashed away. A simple border, suggested in a book by Ellie Seinkiewitz, provides the perfect frame. The quilt was exhibited in the Jackson Quilters' show and may have been in the American Quilter's Society annual quilt show. (Martha says we can't expect her to remember every show she's done!) Collection of the maker.

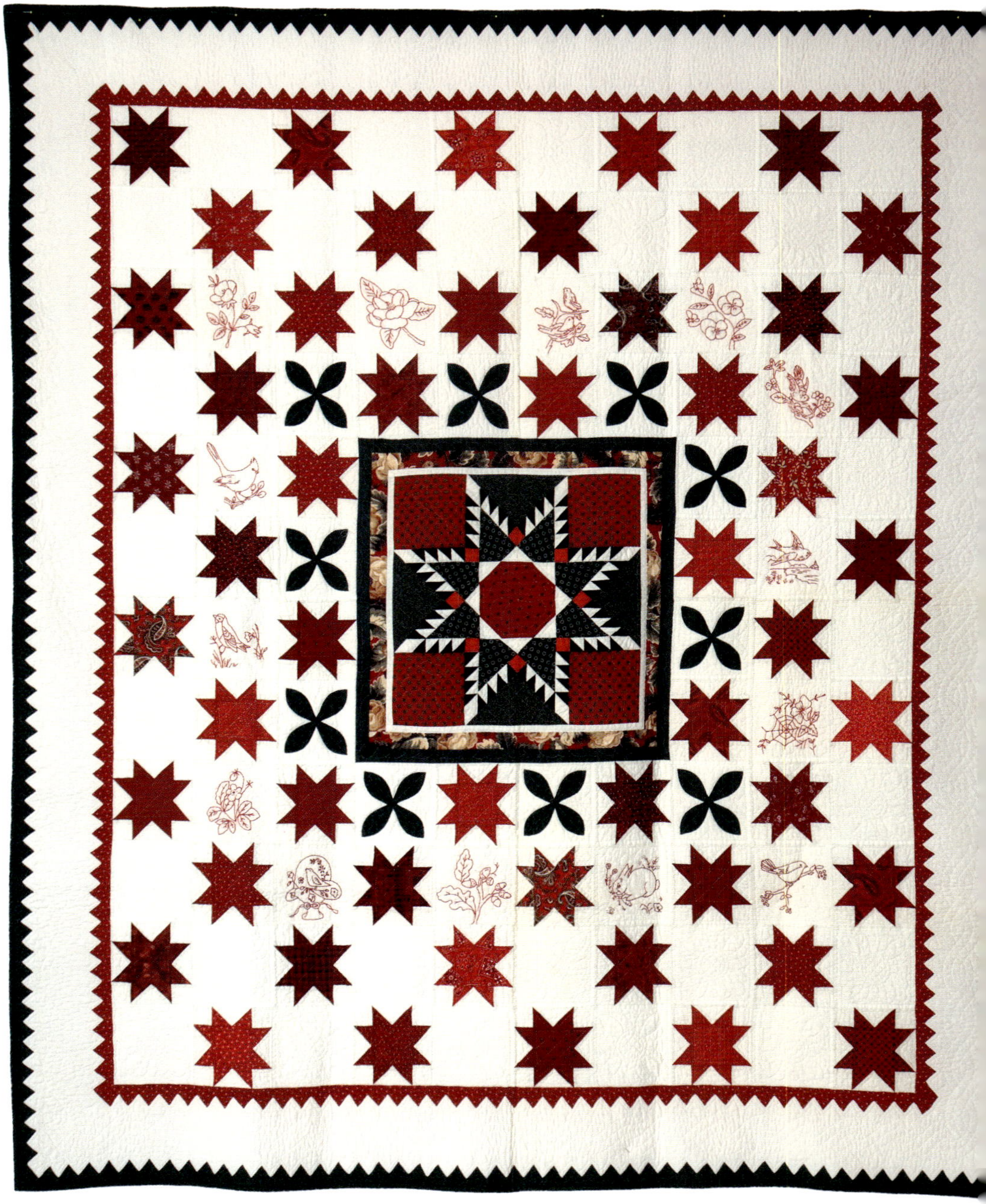

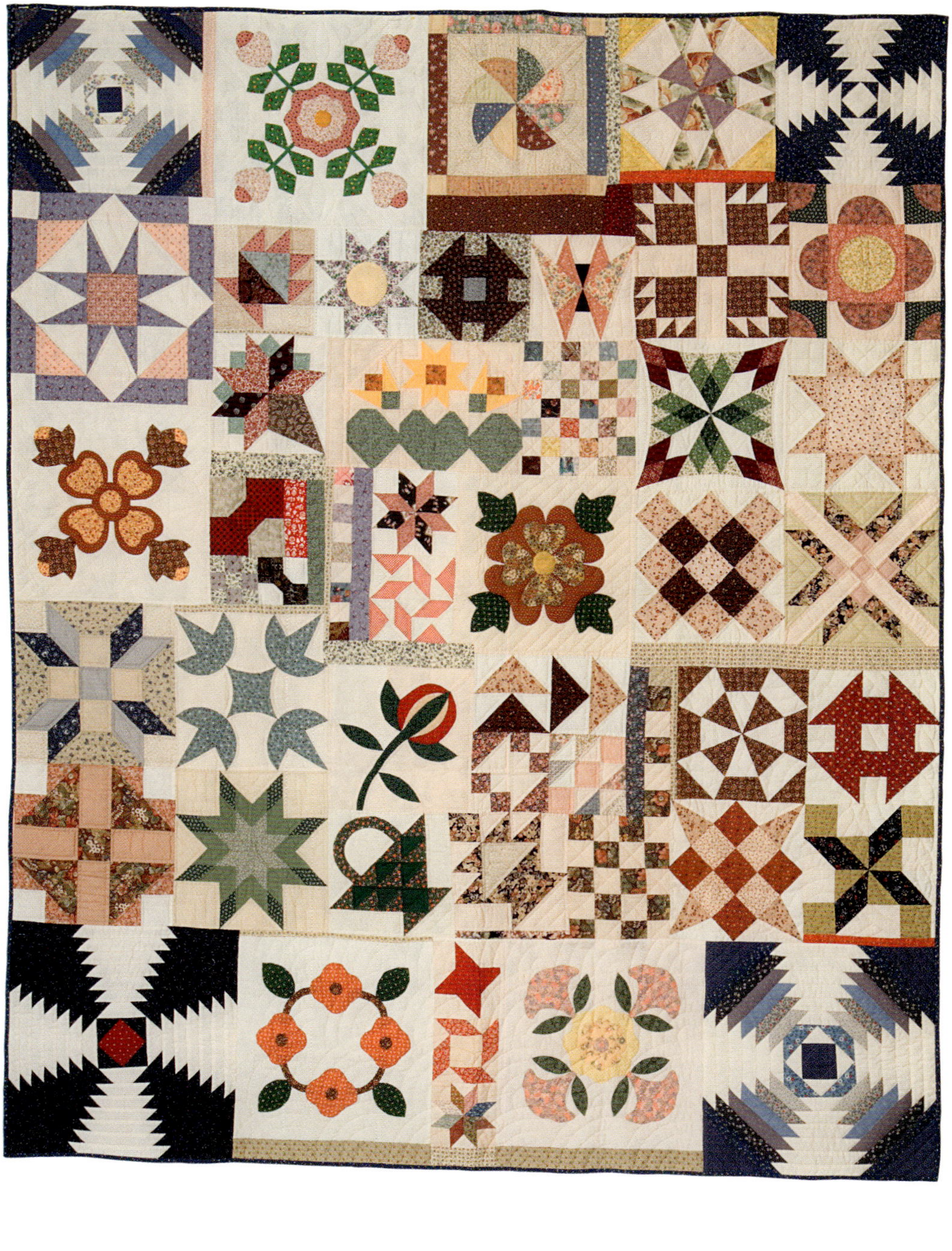

Quilt #136. "1990's Sampler" made from blocks used as class demonstration samples throughout the 1990s; it is 70 inches wide by 87 inches long. Martha recalls an old tradition of calling a quilt such as this a "pattern" quilt because quilters used to make sample blocks of different quilt patterns they were interested in, then sew them together. They would refer to the pattern quilt when they needed an idea for a new quilt. Collection of the maker.

Quilt #24. "Baltimore Album" made in the late 1990s or early 2000; it is 74 inches wide by 89 inches long. Having made two previously, Martha "just wanted to make another 'Baltimore Album' quilt." (See "Baltimore Album Quilt" and "Wreaths and Papercuts.") Although she used traditional white for the backgrounds of the blocks, she chose neutral with a bit of color for the rest of the background fabric. Collection of the maker.

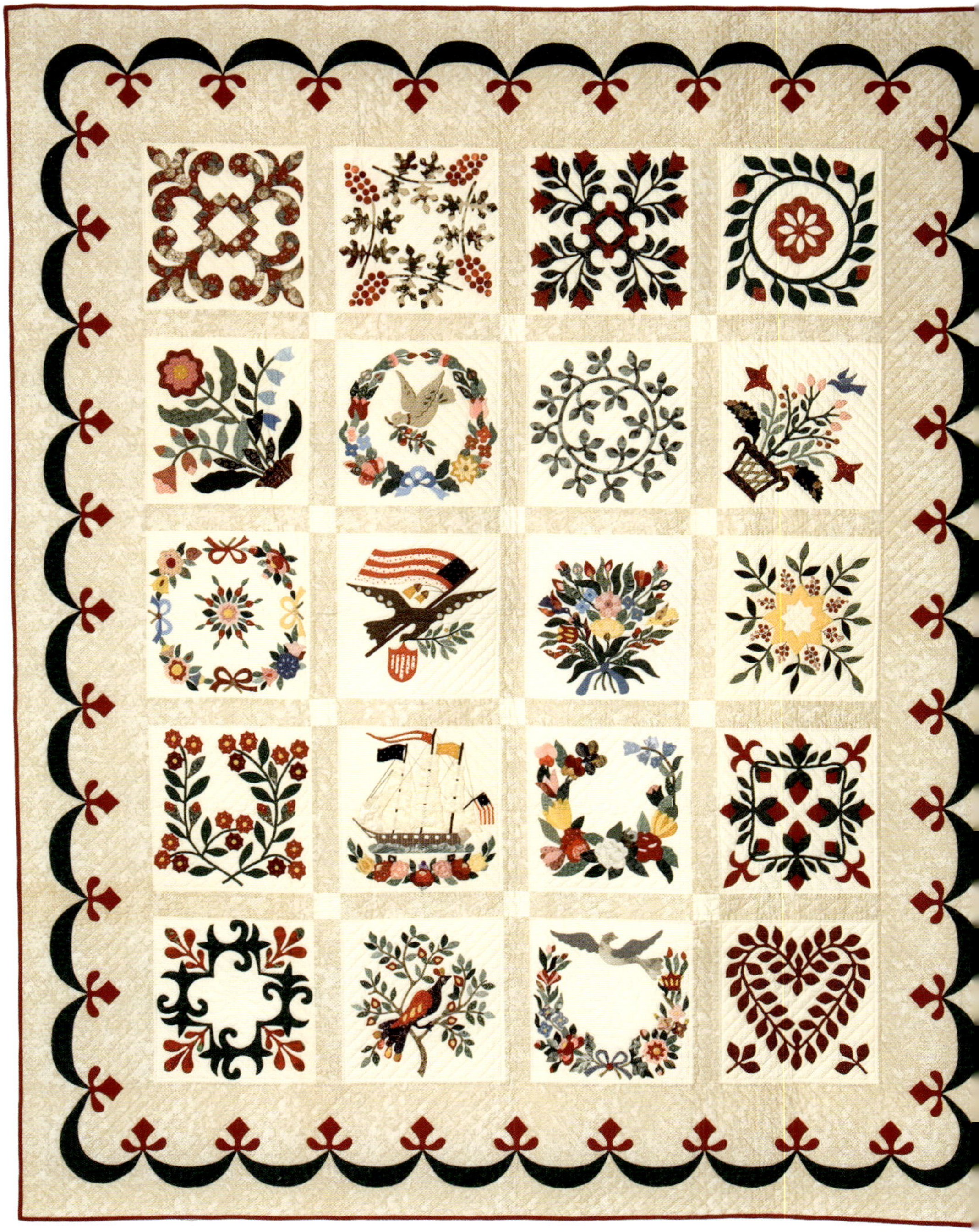

Additional Quilts Made between 1990 and 2000

"Blue Double Wedding Ring," late 1980s–early 1990s[10]

"December Song" wall hanging, 1990[11]

"Peekaboo" or "Pinwheel variation," early 1990s[12]

"Chicken Foot," 1990s[13]

"Aunt Ethel's Block," 1990s[14]

"Bear's Paw," 1998[15]

"Dove in the Window" wall hanging, early 1990s[16]

"Bride's Album" wall hanging, c. 1990s[17]

"Little Blocks Sampler," c. 1990s[18]

"Rose Dream," late 1990s[19]

"Checkerboard Paths," 1997–1998[20]

"Nine-Patch," late 1990s[21]

The Private Martha: At Home, 2000–2007

By the time you have viewed the photographs of the quilts in this book, examined the immaculate workmanship in all of them, weighed the possibility of ever making so many quilts yourself, *much less hand quilting them*, you may feel like you don't really have very much in common, as a quilter, with Martha Skelton. You would be wrong. As accomplished as she is, she still shares many traits with quilters like you and me.

First of all, just like most of us, she is an avid consumer of quilt books and magazines. She reacts with excitement and enthusiasm to a new book or a fresh issue of a magazine, especially if they deal with some aspect of the history and heritage of quilt making. Many of her ideas for the quilts she wants to make come while reading, especially in state documentation project books and others that concentrate on historic quilts. In fact, when asked to name those professionals in the quilt world whom she admires, those who have perhaps influenced her in some way or another, she mentions a now-retired magazine and book editor first. "I admired Carter Houck for her magazine [*Lady's Circle Patchwork Quilts*], because she put so many antique quilts in it, and those are what I love. Great old quilts always make me stretch myself a little bit."[1]

Next, hard as it is to believe, she doesn't have a regular quilting schedule. Martha still considers quilting something that she works in and around the other things in her life. She quilts, she says, "whenever I have five minutes of time. I can piece something, or cut out something. I always have something going—at least three or four projects—because, that way, you can make good use of your time. I have always lived on a schedule, ever since I was a little girl going to school, then to the university, and I had to squeeze in anything extra that I did. I learned to make the minutes count. That's why quilting has worked out for me. It doesn't call for you to get out a whole lot of stuff that makes a big mess, so you don't have to put it all away before you can do something else. You can stop in the middle of a seam, and you're okay. Quilting is a good thing to do for a person who's always busy—I've always been busy."[2]

She enjoys the back and forth of chatting with people about quilts. "I treasure the friends all over the state that I've made through quilting—with teaching, the state fair, the documentation efforts, the Craftsmen's Guild," she says. "Those friendships have been the most important benefit that quilting has brought to me."[3] Although she may not say so, those friendships reach beyond the borders of Mississippi; she regularly receives calls from all over the quilt world, which is now international.

Like most quilters, Martha believes that belonging to a quilting group is very important. She begins on a general note, but soon it is clear she is talking about her beloved Cotton Patchers. "I wish everyone who quilts had a group to go to. I think it just does so much for you and the strength you get from being with other people who are interested in the same thing. Also, sometimes circumstances in your life give you something hard to work through. While you may not tell your friends what your hard things are, at the same time just knowing that they care for you and they're glad to see you when you come through the door makes you feel better. You can kind of work on through your problems and be all right."[4]

As do most of us, she loves to obtain new quilt patterns, especially if it involves interacting with someone and gives her an opportunity for a good, long sit-down chat with someone about quilting. She loves to reminisce about the various circumstances in which she has obtained different patterns. She likes to stay abreast of

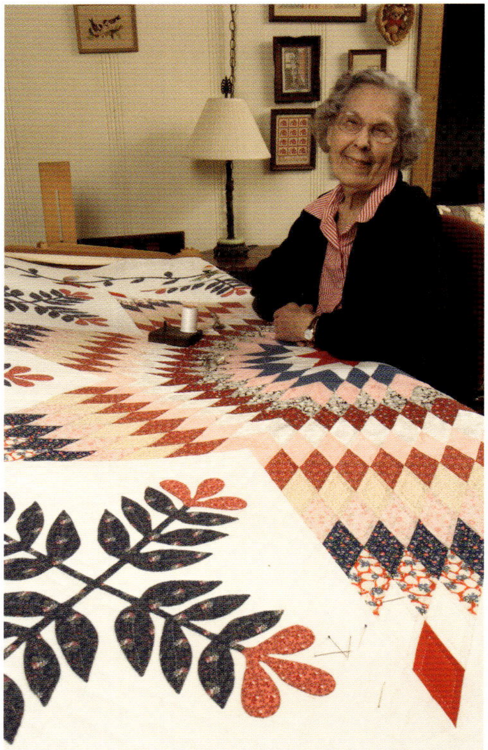

Over the years, Martha has established a practice of always having a quilt in the frame, as well as keeping one patchwork and one appliqué piece under construction. So, whatever she is in the mood for, she already has a project going and can just start stitching.

changes in the quilt world, even though she is considered a traditional quilter. "I'll try new things in order to keep up. I did it especially when I was teaching, so that I could help students who might be doing those new things."[5] She, like us, takes ideas for new quilts from several influences. Many times a picture she's seen in a publication causes her to think about making a particular quilt. Often she will see a quilt that she wants to copy (of course, hers never looks exactly like the original). Sometimes a particular person will influence the quilt, particularly if Martha is making it specifically for that individual, in which case she looks for design elements that will please the person. And, like many of us, she may hold an idea for a quilt in her mind for a good while before she gets around to working on it. "Sometimes I'll have it in the back of my mind. It may be two or three quilts back that I started thinking about the one I'm on now. It will work around and all at once I'll say, 'I can do that one now,' and I'll start it then."[6]

She is like almost any quilter in that the piece she is currently working on is the one about which she's most excited—more than any that she's already finished, even the prize winners and those sold to institutions. *Not* like most quilters is the habit she has of keeping three quilts going all the time: one in patchwork, one in appliqué, and one in the frame being quilted. This routine ensures a steady production of quilts, and it is a hedge against boredom. For example, if Martha finds herself tired of stitching down appliqué pieces, she can just move to her quilting frame and continue to get work done.

She, like all of us, looks up to certain quilt teachers. Her major heroines are Jinny Beyer and Elly Seinkiwicz. "I have great admiration for Jinny Beyer because of her skill in drafting patterns and her way of working with fabric. I know she's had a lot of influence on me. For appliqué, Elly Seinkiwicz has probably influenced me more than any one person because, first and foremost, she's a scholar, and that shows up in her work and in books."[7] The teachers that Martha so admires are probably appreciated most by students with some quilting experience. But what would she say to someone just starting out? "Find somebody local you can ask questions to when you get in a tight spot. Be willing to take it slow and easy so that you will grow and stretch yourself as you get better. Be accurate, stitch carefully, and use your fabrics well. Realize that the first quilts you make are not going to be perfect, but each one will be better than the one before. Practice helps more than anything. I think that's very important."[8]

Granted, there are differences between Martha and other quilters. Whereas most quilters have favorite techniques—they love to plan the layout of the quilt, then choose colors and swatch it, *or* they like to appliqué, *or* to piece, *or* to quilt—Martha loves every aspect of making the quilt. This is a woman who, back before rotary cutters, considered it fun to get together with her aunt and cut out quilt pieces with scissors and templates. "Aunt Ethel (from close to Tulsa) came to visit me in Mississippi many times. One time she came, and she stayed about three weeks. I had finished an appliquéd quilt that she thought was pretty. So I said, 'Aunt Ethel, if you want to make this, we'll cut out all your pieces.' That just tickled her to death. So we busied ourselves. I fixed Aunt Ethel up with my fabrics and pattern, and by the time she left we had her quilt all cut out."[9]

Martha says her attitude about quilting has stayed the same throughout the years. "I think I kept quilting because not only are you making something useful, you can express your creativity. I make quilts because I enjoy it so much. I enjoy handwork, and I enjoy the process of making a quilt from the start of thinking about what I'm going to make until I get through with the very last step. I'm really happy when I get to the binding, because that means it's finished and I can start another one. I still work very much the same way that I always did, although I use the newer things that we're so fortunate to have—like rotary cutters and rulers and good measuring tools. I have gotten several good compasses, so that if I want to draft a pattern that has curves or some funny pieces in it, I have the tools I need to work with.

"I've always felt that the fabric was important, so I continue to try to use the best material I can get. I still pre-wash everything. I know lots of people think that's not necessary. But they would if they've ever had a piece bleed. No matter how much you pay for a piece of fabric, it can fool you and bleed, and sometimes it's a real tragedy. You might even have to throw something in the trash. I don't want to have to do that, so I still wash everything. The other reason I pre-wash is that I make my quilts primarily to be used, so they're made to be washable.

"I'm not really interested in making pieces that hang up on the wall because they really don't give me the satisfaction that I get when I make a good quilt that I know someone will wrap up in some day and be nice and warm and comforted. I have a friend that I gave a quilt to who said it was just like having me come to see her when she would wrap up in that quilt, because I had made it and given it to her. She's been real sick, so I feel it's been a true comfort to her."[10]

Perhaps the greatest difference between master quilter Martha Skelton and most of the rest of us is that she finishes what she starts. "I am blessed with a personality trait of feeling that I have to finish a project. Whatever I'm working on is not useful if it's not finished."[11] There are many quilters who would come much closer to having a body of work the size of Martha's if they could just master that one vital work habit! This one thing is ultimately the secret to her success.

Martha rises to the challenge that each new quilt brings. "Whenever I start a quilt, I'm never really sure how it will end up. The greatest challenge I set for myself is looking to see if there's anything about the quilt that I can change or improve in some way. But it doesn't matter what the challenge is—it may be that I don't have quite enough material to make that quilt, so it becomes a challenge to make it anyway, because it pushes me."[12]

A close examination of a couple of quilts, "Wheel of Fortune" and "Mississippi

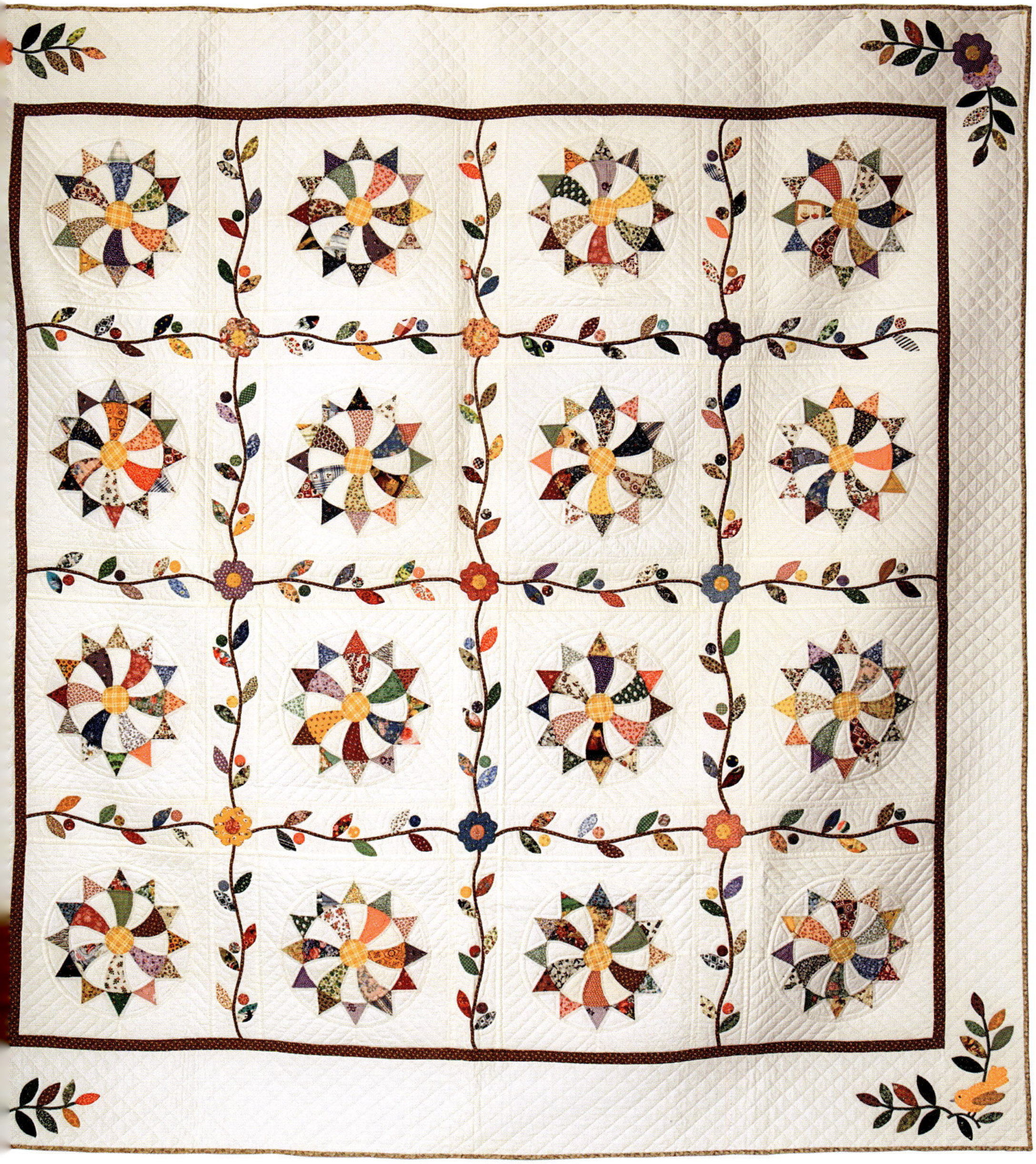

Quilt #91. "Wheel of Fortune" made in 2002; it is 84.5 inches wide by 86 inches long. The pattern for the patchwork block came from a book by Leisure Arts. The quilt tied for "Viewer's Choice" at the Vicksburg Quilters' show in 2002. Collection of the maker.

Quilt #91. "Wheel of Fortune" detail. The basic pieced block is not so simple to make as it may appear. The segments have curved sides, and the finished wheel is surrounded by a border pieced of triangles.

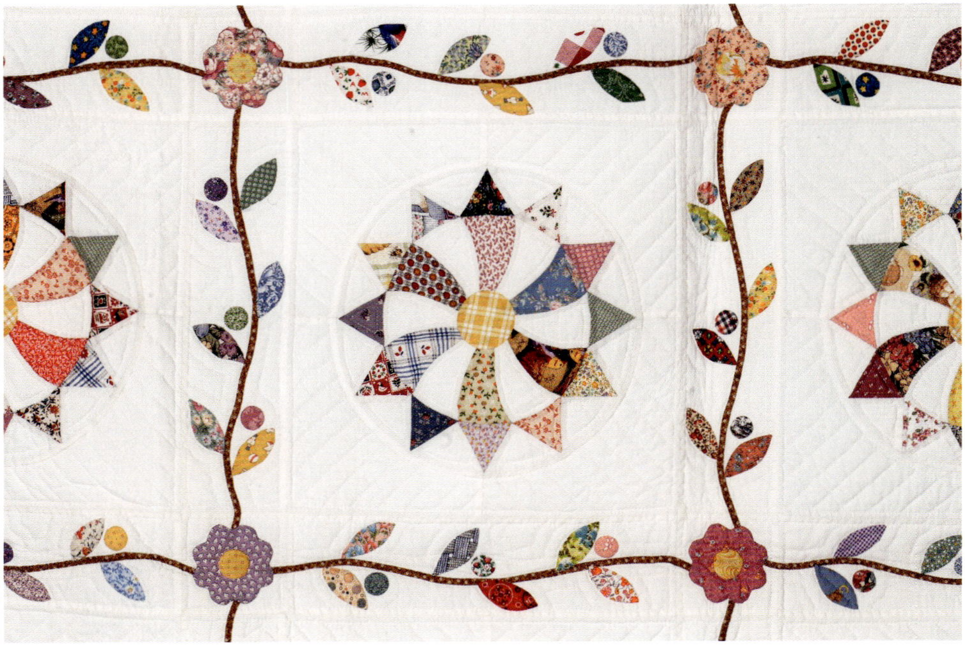

Quilt #91. "Wheel of Fortune" detail. Birds are basically a signature motif of Martha's, and when she designed the border for this quilt, she included two—one red and one yellow.

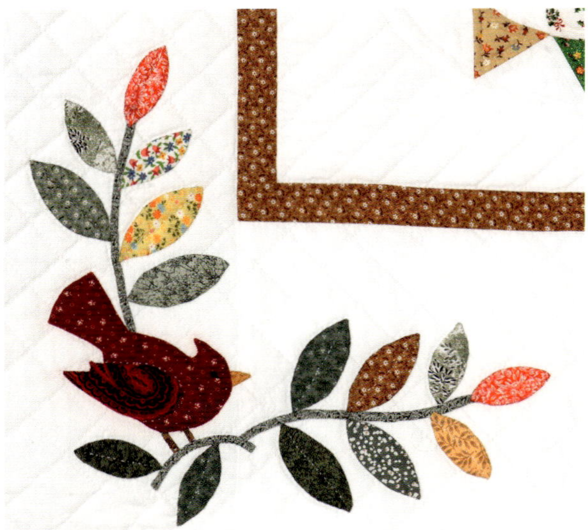

Hardwood," that Martha has done within the past five years may illuminate to some degree just how the challenges she sets for herself have led to her mastery of the many aspects of quilting. The first example, "Wheel of Fortune," is a pieced design Martha admired in a book. The example in the book was probably stitched in two, at most three, solid colors if it is typical of most "Wheel" quilts. The reason for the solid colors is that a wheel is a fairly difficult pattern for any quilter to piece, especially when it has curved segments set into a ring of triangles like this one, and most quilters think their work shows up better with plain fabrics rather than prints. So the first departure from tradition, or the "challenge" that Martha set up for herself, was to use fabrics from her scrap bag. She probably bought the white fabric for the background, but all the colored bits come from her stash.

After piecing the sixteen blocks of the design, she decided that she didn't want to set her blocks side by side, as they were in the photograph in the book. So she inserted a strip of white sashing between the blocks. This gave her a perfect spot to incorporate another design element, and she chose one very different in character from the precise geometry of wheel shape—a gently curving vine. The vines cross one another at each of the four corners of the blocks, and Martha decided to place a flower at those intersections. She also included some circles (to represent grapes or berries, maybe?) among the leaves of the vine. The final area of the quilt to be designed was the border. First, Martha framed the field of the quilt with a narrow inner border, deliberately dark, to provide a margin for the main border. In keeping with the delicate touch she used in the design of the sashing, Martha placed appliquéd motifs in only the four corners. The two lower motifs contain a bird perched in the leaves of a vine; the two upper ones incorporate a couple of the flowers used at the junctions of the vines in the sashing. Although the changes Martha made to the original source for her "Wheel of Fortune" seem fairly simple, she actually handled the challenges she set for herself with a great delicacy of touch. One might call them "refinements" of the design. They make the quilt uniquely Martha's.

Martha's scrap quilts like "Wheel of Fortune" are beguiling. There is something about them that is different from scrap quilts made by other people. It is not easy to pin down what that difference is, but Martha attributes it to two factors: she doesn't

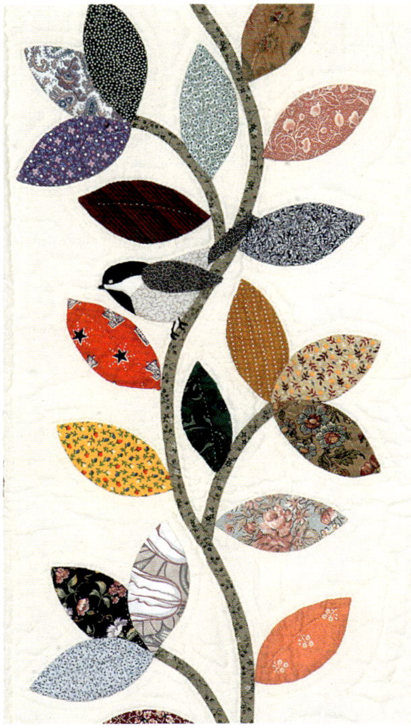

"Autumn Leaves" detail. Martha's uncanny color sense enables her to successfully use scraps. Although her birds are rendered in colors that resemble what nature would have specified, her leaves are of fanciful colors and motifs.

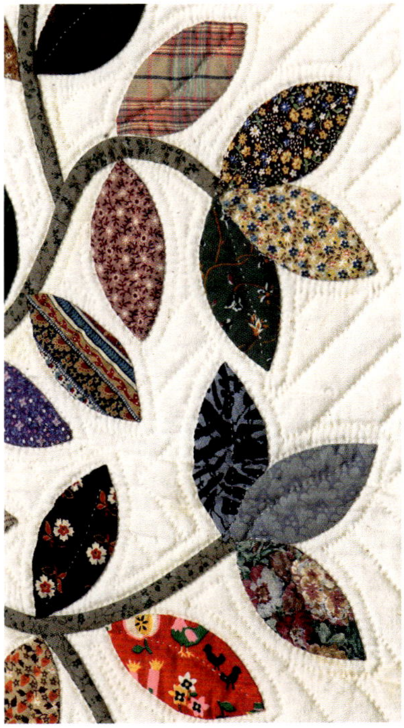

"Autumn Leaves" detail. Readers will undoubtedly occasionally spot a familiar fabric, perhaps one they have used themselves, in the hundreds that Martha uses in a quilt such as "Autumn Leaves."

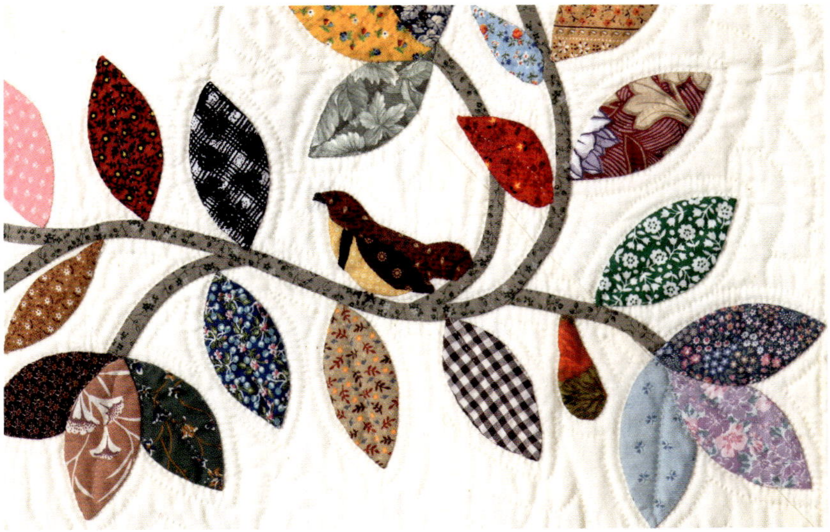

"Autumn Leaves" detail. Even the most unusual prints, which might not initially be considered appropriate for leaves, work wonderfully in Martha's skilled hands.

sort her scraps according to color, and she's got heaps of fabric left over from years of garment making. She vows that she is still using scraps from clothing she made forty or so years ago. "Some people sort all of their fabrics and have all their red fabric in one box and their blue fabric in another one and so on. Mine are all mixed up; I don't have them separated. That's one reason why I end up with more variety than I possibly would if I had them separated. I tried one time to sort out a whole lot of stuff according to color. It was a lot of dreadful work, and it didn't help my quilt making. Because I have so many different fabrics left over from sewing for the children and myself over so many years, I can always find a piece that will make the color fit in that particular spot. Then, when I'm quilting, I enjoy running across a piece I remember from a certain garment. Also, I love finding a piece that someone brought back from a certain place or from one of their quilts. I have a friend in the Cotton Patchers who is always bringing me little scraps from her sewing, and it's great to run up on one of those when I'm quilting the quilt."

The second quilt in this examination of the challenges Martha sets for herself is named "Mississippi Hardwood" and is one of her completely original designs. She made the design using a procedure described in the *Vicksburg Evening Post*, back on May 6, 1976: "A real perfectionist, Mrs. Skelton picked a magnolia blossom and looked at it as she worked to create her design." Martha thinks her love of drawing is one of the reasons, maybe even an unconscious one, that she has always quilted. Being able to draw makes it possible for her to interpret what she sees in her mind's eye.[13] There is no question that drawing is an invaluable skill for a quilt artist, especially when appliqué is the medium.

All of the leaves of this quilt came from Martha's beloved woodland hideaway, "The Farm." Gordon, Martha's son, who is as fond of "The Farm" as Martha, helped her collect leaves from the many types of trees that grow there. She drew her extremely realistic patterns while the leaves were still fresh. As she sketched, she discovered that the trees were often more precisely portrayed with a small branch or cluster rather than a single leaf. Finally, after getting the look of each individual tree right, she grouped the various specimens into loose groups of four. Then she

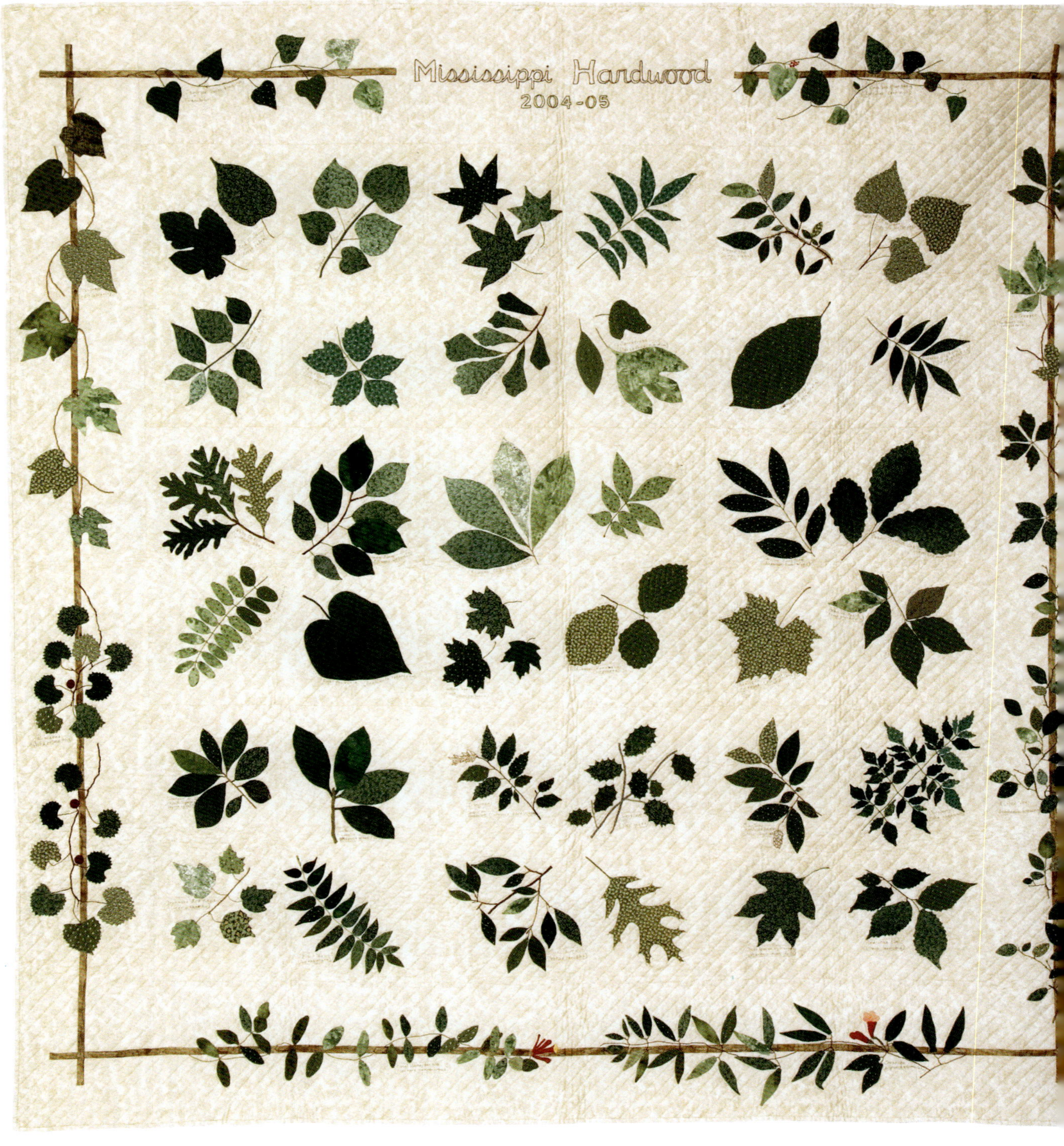
Mississippi Hardwood
2004-05

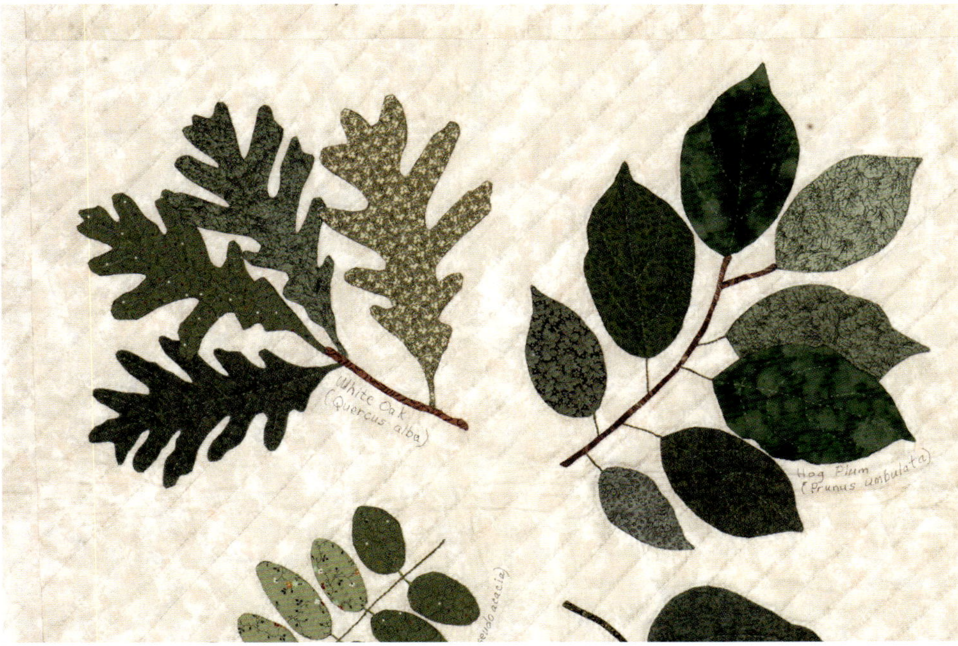

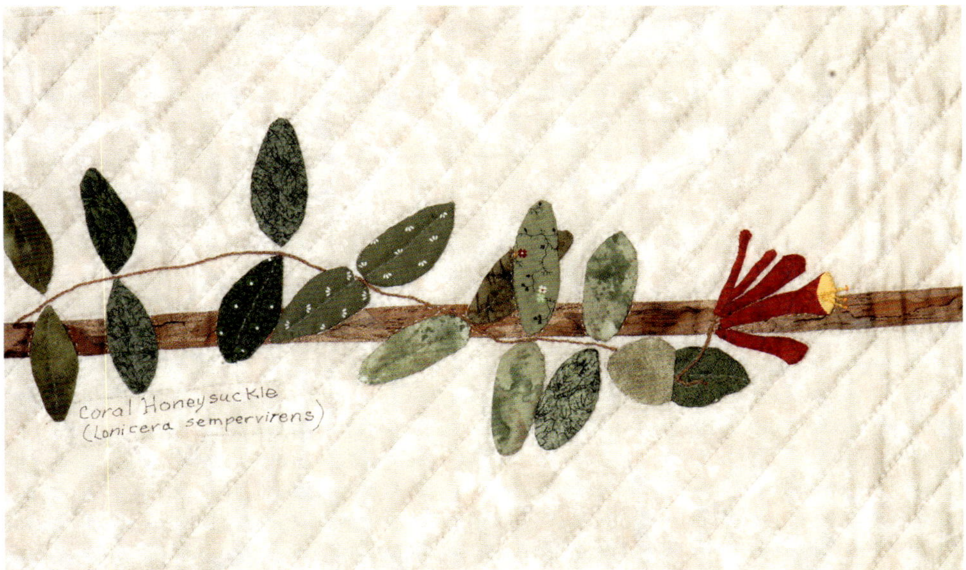

Quilt #70 (preceding page). "Mississippi Hardwood" made in 2004 and 2005; it is 84 inches wide by 84 inches long. The hardwood trees that grow over the acreage at "The Farm" supplied the leaf silhouettes for the design of this quilt; vines are used for the four borders. A mottled fabric for the background suggests depth. Collection of the maker.

Quilt #70. "Mississippi Hardwood" detail. Sometimes a spray, rather than a single leaf, made the most accurate representation of the tree. Each example is labeled with its scientific name.

Quilt #70. "Mississippi Hardwood" detail. As the idea for this quilt took root and developed, Martha began collecting all kinds of green fabrics.

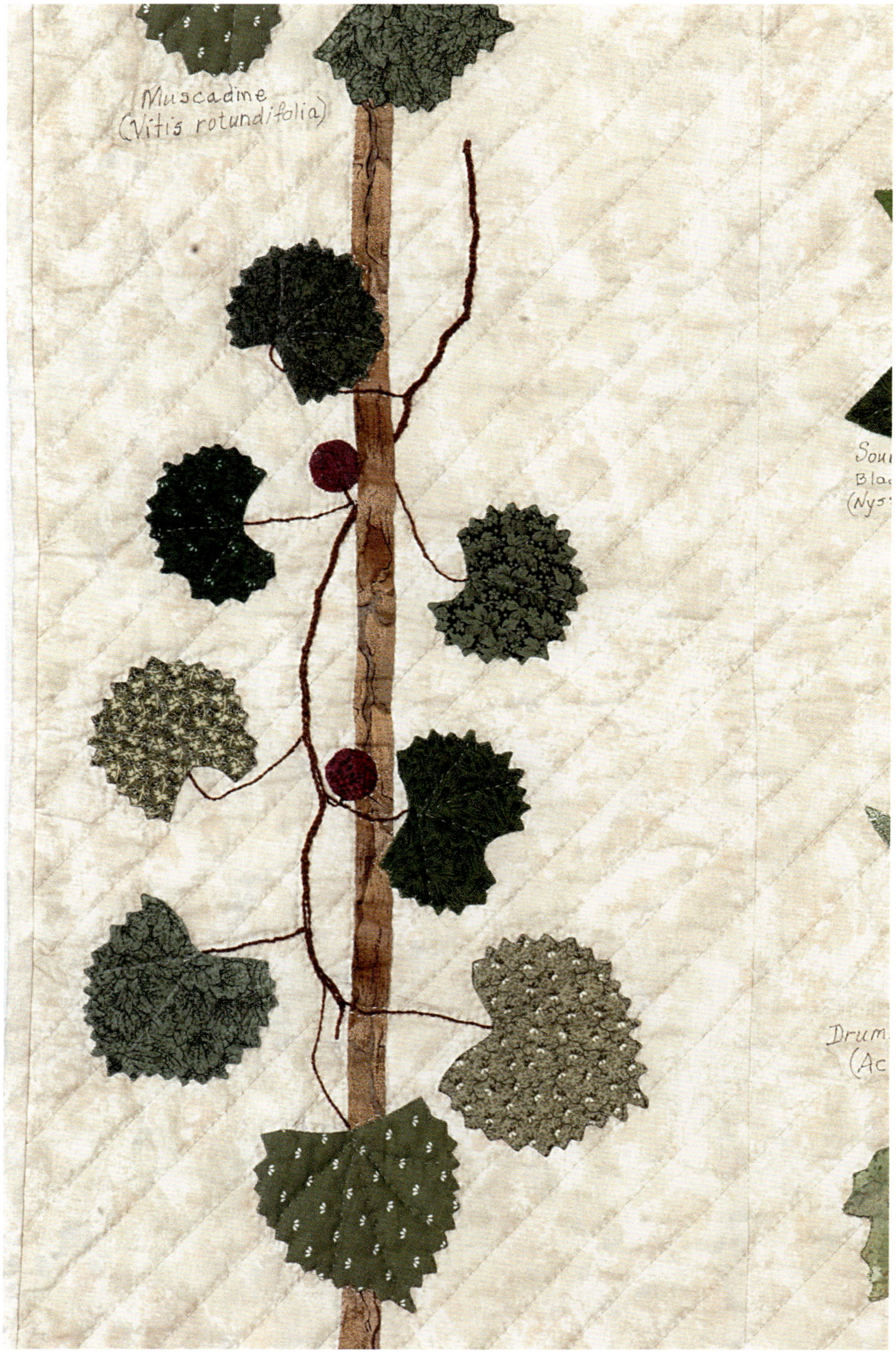

Quilt #70. "Mississippi Hardwood" detail. The details tell the story. These would not be grape leaves without the tiny scallops around the outer edges.

stitched it. Her mastery of the sewing techniques of appliqué and embroidery are imperative to the success of this quilt, and they make it almost photographic in its representation of subject matter. The challenge Martha established for herself lay in creating a piece completely from scratch that successfully invokes the atmosphere of a very special place; she can wrap herself in this quilt and feel as though she is actually at "The Farm."

Martha is jubilant that her daughter and granddaughter love quilting as much as she does. "That's one of the real joys of my life—the fact that Ann has taken such an interest in quilting and has become really a fine quilter. In turn, we were able to introduce Jennifer to quilting, so she has the technique and has done some quilts on her own. Ann has always done all sorts of hand sewing because I had encouraged her to learn to embroider and to do the different kinds of needlework. So, that has become a part of her life as it was part of mine.

"Ann's daughter, Jennifer, at two or three years, would stand and watch her mother quilt, even though she could barely see over the top of the frame. As she grew older, Jennifer went along with her mother to Ann's quilt guild meetings. She knew she had to sit quietly, so she began to take a little bit of sewing along. Eventually, she decided she wanted to piece some blocks, so I cut out some squares for a 'Nine Patch' and showed her how to mark the seam lines. She learned how to start and stop a hand-sewn seam. After Jennifer had a bunch of 'Nine Patch' blocks, Ann helped her set them together into a 'napping' quilt. Ann and I then showed her how to tie, or tack, the quilt (because we really didn't think she was up to actually quilting it) and finish the edges by bringing the front to the back. So, she finished her first little quilt by herself when she was four or five years old.

"A couple of years later, Jennifer came to spend some time with me. I asked her what she wanted to do while she was here, and she said she thought she wanted to make her cat a quilt. That worked out nicely because I had a day-long class at Brookhaven, and she could piece her squares while she was at the workshop with me. I looked around once during the workshop and she was busily showing somebody in the workshop how to do something. . . . When she had her blocks pieced,

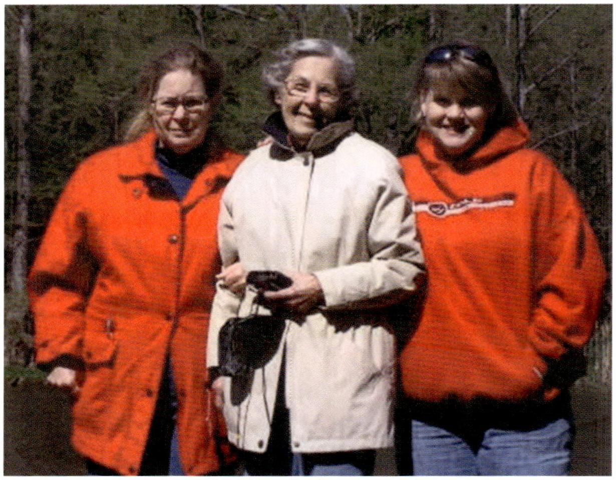

Martha Skelton (center) with daughter, Ann Hope (at left), and granddaughter, Jennifer Ann, on Easter Sunday 2007. Jennifer arranged the weekend getaway for the three at a state park in the Mississippi Delta. They stayed in a 1932 Civilian Conservation Corps cabin with a fireplace, and the agenda for the weekend included reading, quilting, napping, visiting, and walking in the woods. Martha loves all those things, and she enjoyed the time immensely. Jennifer is planning a similar retreat for next year.

we went to the store and got some lining for it, and she finished that little quilt with a lot of pleasure. Now, she quilts really nicely."[14]

A true highlight of Martha's life was the publication of a photographic essay more than twenty years ago, when Jennifer Ann was still a child. *Lady's Circle Patchwork Quilts* traveled to Mobile, Ann Hope's home at the time, to get the story about the three quilters: mother, daughter, and granddaughter. Featured in the July 1985 issue were Martha's "Indiana Wreath," Ann Hope's "Blues in the Night" (a sampler quilt), and Jennifer Ann's small, strippy "Shoo Fly."

To this writer, and probably to many other people, Martha's insistence that her fabulous quilts are supposed to be used, even to the point of being completely worn out, or "used up," as she says, is beyond understanding. In fact, the idea seems preposterous. That is because Martha's own regard for her work is so different from most quilters today. Maybe if they were not of such superior workmanship and beauty—maybe if they were all like the utility quilts she stitched up quickly in the early years of her marriage—we could better understand Martha's insistence that these are temporal, disposable objects. Certainly, her quilts meet, and no doubt surpass, her grandmother's requirement that she do "nice work," so it can't possibly be that Martha harbors a fear that her quilts are not "good enough" to keep. She admits to "picking her work apart," or criticizing it, but even she would have to confess that she really is a good quilter! (However, she probably would say that if she has become a better quilter over time, it is because she has gained so much experience.)

It all comes down to the fact that, in Martha's view, her quilts are utilitarian items. She does not think of herself as creating heirlooms to be put away, only brought out for viewing on special occasions. Her quilts are made to be used, and that is their greatest value. They may be beautiful, and Martha tries to make sure they are, both in appearance and technique; but, in her view of things, needlework is a natural part of daily life, something a family used to do to provide certain necessary items for the home. She was also taught that one must always do the best one can, and this belief is at the core of her genuine humility.

When Martha was reminded that, in 2004, the general membership of the American Quilter's Society named her one of twenty-four finalists for the title of All-American Quilter, her response was, "It was such a surprise—I couldn't believe it. I think that it might have been a fluke."[15] Upon being told that it was, indeed, not a fluke, but a big honor, Martha went on to say, "You can't imagine how it makes you feel. It's hard for me; it really is. I think that the nicest thing about it was that Mississippi does deserve to be along with everybody else, and any time we get a little credit, it helps all of us. I was glad that I could be one of the ones who was there [at the presentation ceremonies]. I didn't expect anything more than that, and I really hadn't even dreamed of being there. I was delighted when Jinny Beyer came in as number one. It was a very humbling thing to have happen, I'll tell you."[16]

Martha Skelton is one of the rarest of humans: a person who has excelled at something for no reason other than she likes doing it so much. She loves to quilt. As Martha is fortunate to have found her calling early in her life, so are we lucky to be beneficiaries of that calling. Not only can we look at her beautiful quilts, admire and study them, but we can take her example as encouragement to follow our own path, wherever it may lead us. Hers has been an honest journey, motivated by nothing more than her zeal for quilting. "I've not done any of it for the glory. Nor to make money. I somehow just didn't really want to be one of those people who puts all that pressure on themselves; I wanted to enjoy my quilting."[17]

And she does.

Quilt #102. "Second Hawaiian Quilt" made about 2000; it is 82 inches wide by 89 inches long. While perusing a Japanese quilting magazine, Martha came upon a story on Hawaiian quilts that included lots of photos. She chose a small motif and enlarged it to fit in the center of the top; her first Hawaiian quilt contained nine motifs. Another change Martha made was choosing a medium-toned floral fabric for the appliqués so that the contrast between motif and background was not so stark as in traditional Hawaiian quilts. The quilt has been exhibited locally at the Vicksburg Quilters' Show and at the Cotton Patchers' Show. Collection of the maker. Photograph by Brian Loden.

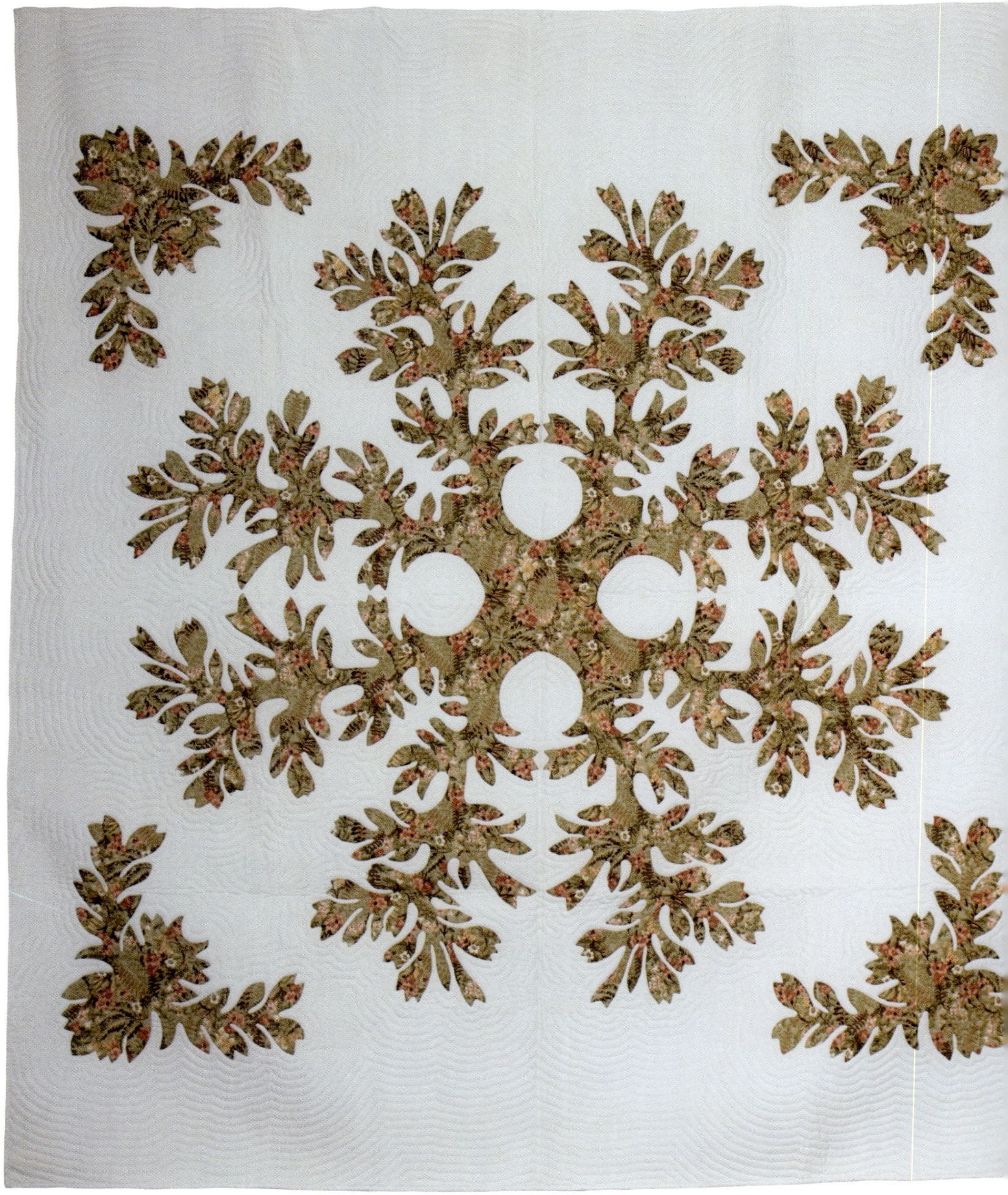

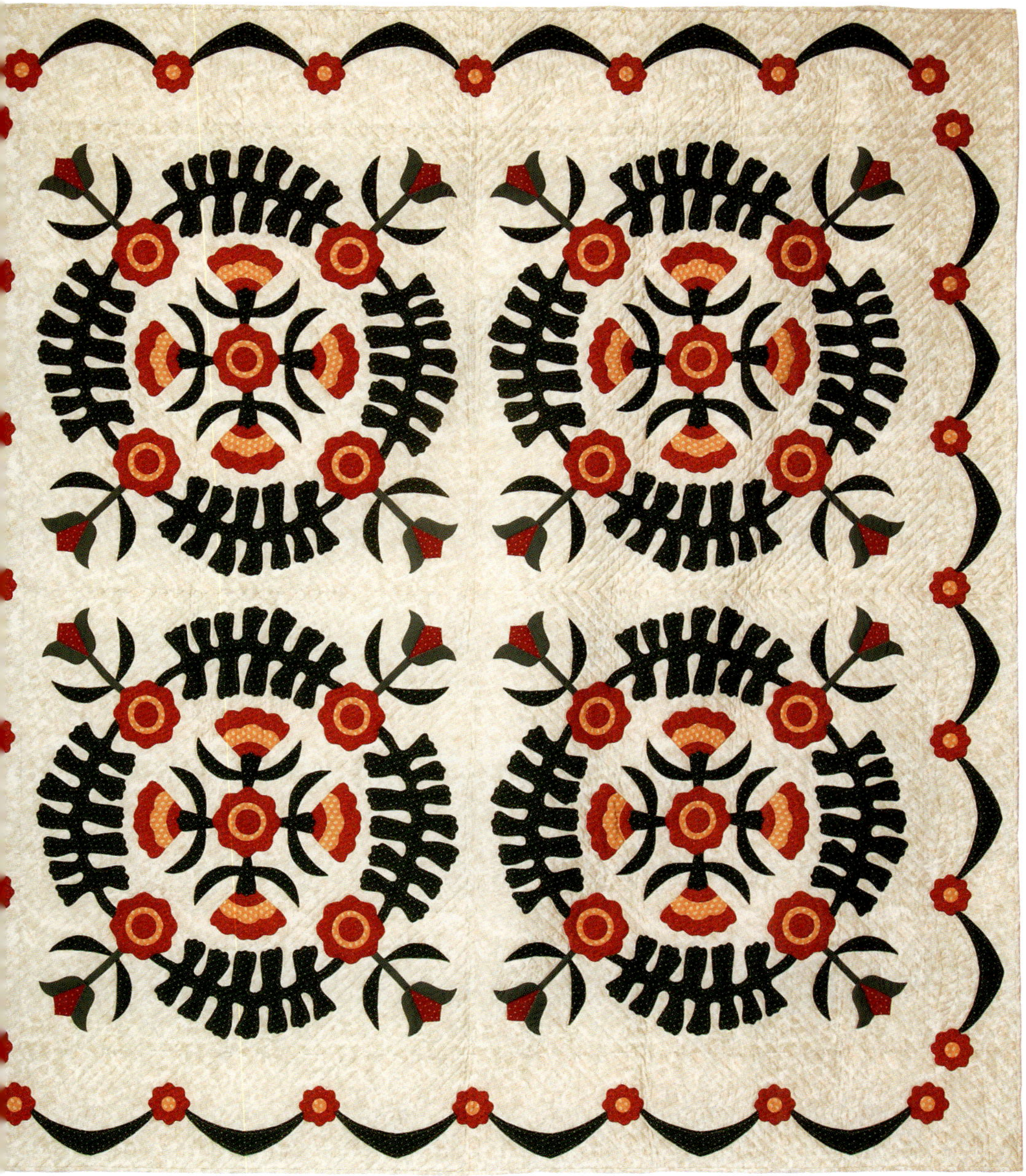

Quilt #72. "Coxcombs and Tulips" made in 2000 and 2001; it is 83 inches wide by 88 inches long. While working as an analyst for the Mississippi Quilt Association Heritage Quilt Search, Martha was so taken with the original antique quilt of this design that she asked permission from the owner to trace the pattern right there on the spot. The owner was delighted to share the pattern and was even more delighted to view her antique quilt next to Martha's duplicate at the 14th Annual Paducah Rotary Club Antique Quilt Show in April 2002. Collection of the maker.

Quilt #118. "Tulips and Butterflies," circa 2000, is 75.5 inches wide and 89 inches long. A similar antique quilt was brought to the Mississippi Quilt Association's documentation quilt search in Philadelphia, Mississippi. Martha followed the color scheme of the old quilt. She combined a butterfly pattern she had and the tulip pattern. She decided this old-fashioned pattern was just the right one to display the many prints and colors from her scrap bag. Collection of maker. Photograph by Brian Loden.

Quilt #53 (following page). "Joseph's Coat," circa 2000–2006, is 67.5 inches wide by 88 inches long. The Woodville Homemaker's Club made a quilt like this for their home economist (home demonstration agent). When Martha saw the quilt, she was intrigued with the pattern and just had to make one for herself. Collection of the maker.

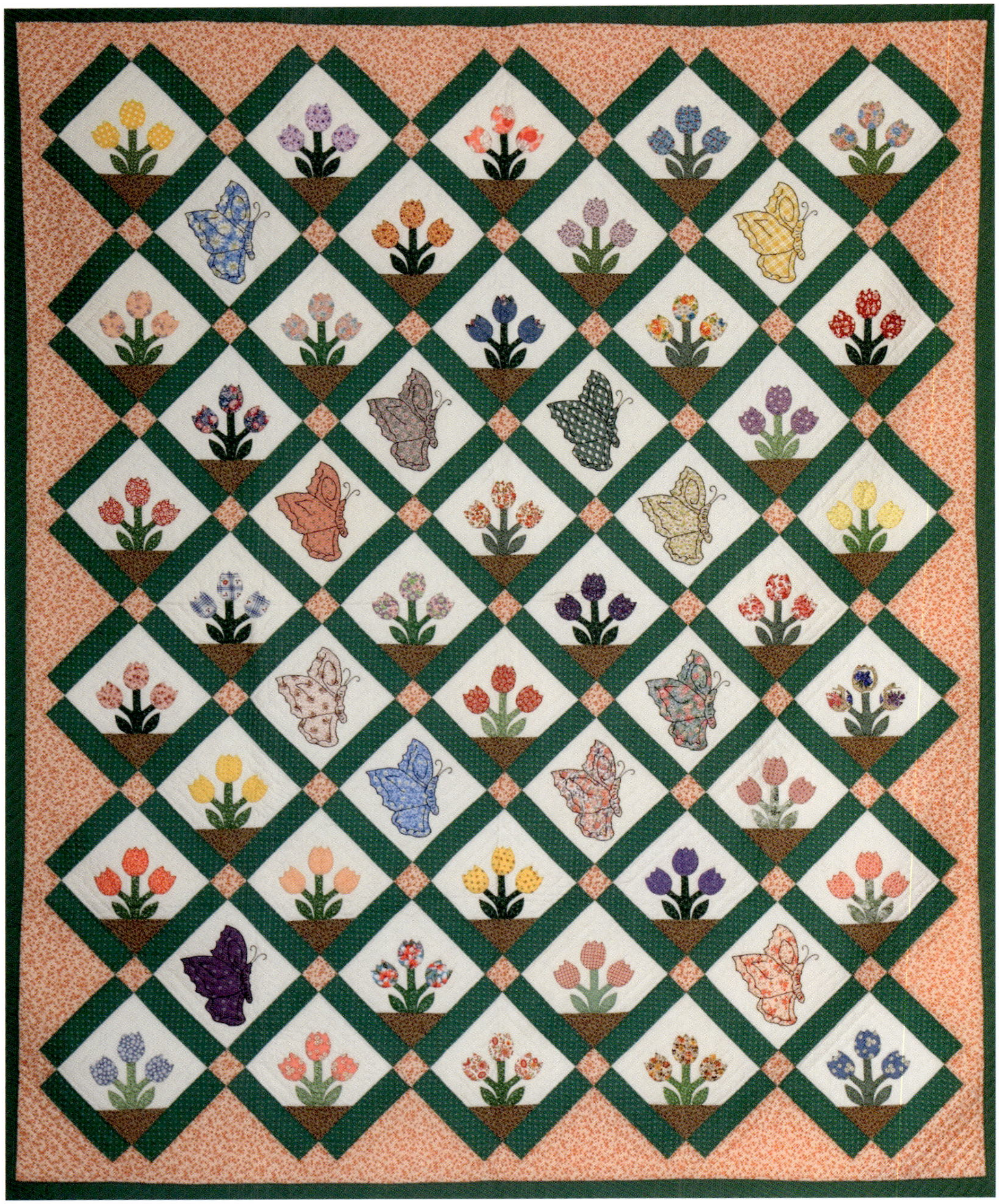

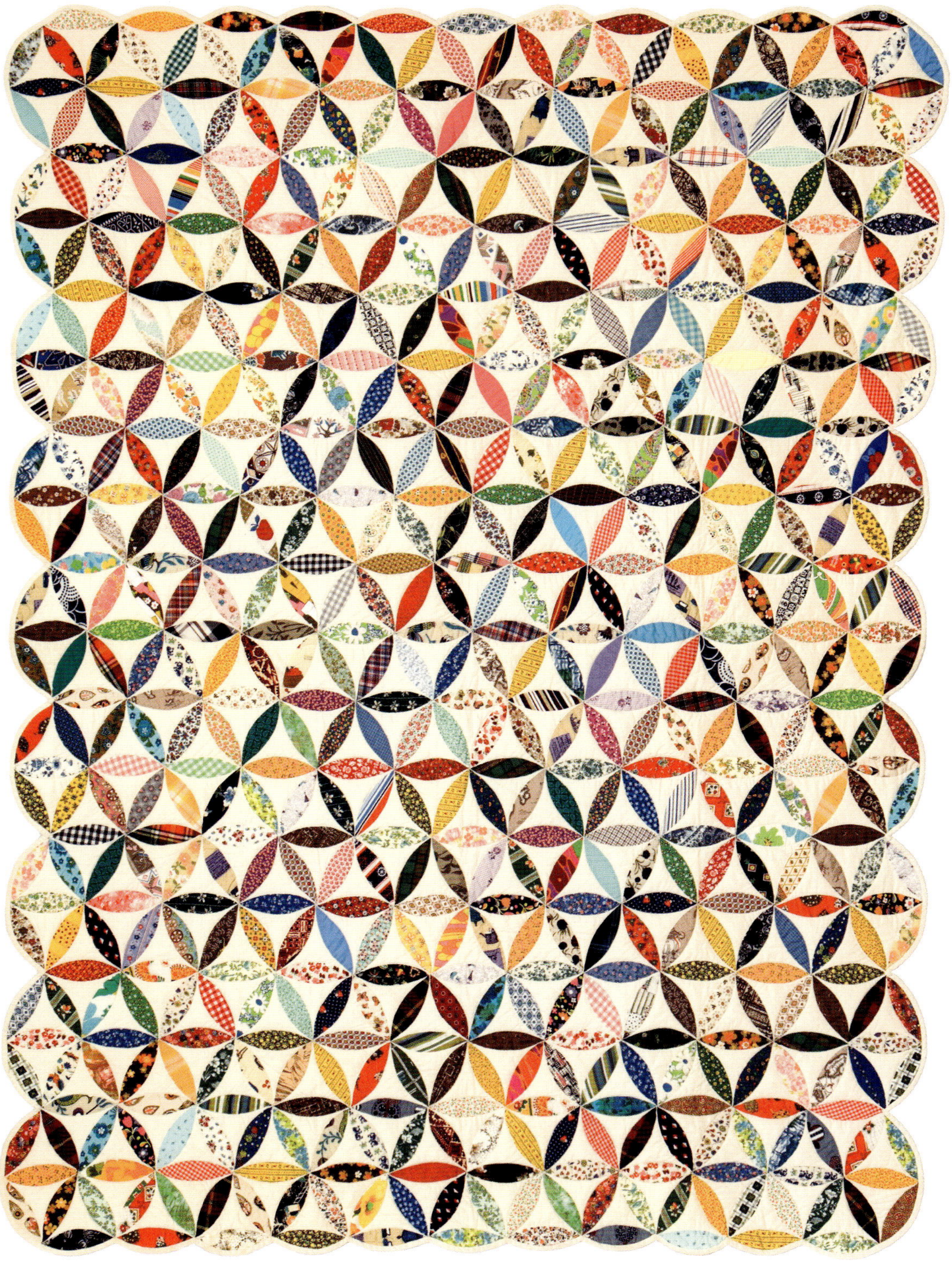

Quilt #126. "Floral Nine-Patch" made in 2003; it is 64.5 inches wide by 83 inches long. Florence Peto was a quilt historian, writer, lecturer, and an excellent quilt maker. She directed many of America's most famous quilts to the museums in which they are now housed. In 1951, after seeing a drawing in *Women's Day* magazine, Mrs. Peto made a "Floral Nine-Patch" that has been widely published and which motivated Martha to make her version. All Martha's flower appliqués are different from Mrs. Peto's, plus Martha substituted 4 bird and 4 butterfly blocks for 8 floral ones. Although Martha's borders and other details are also slightly different from Mrs. Peto's, the juxtaposition of pieced "Nine-Patch" blocks against appliquéd floral ones is memorable in both quilts. Martha's quilt has been locally exhibited. Collection of the maker.

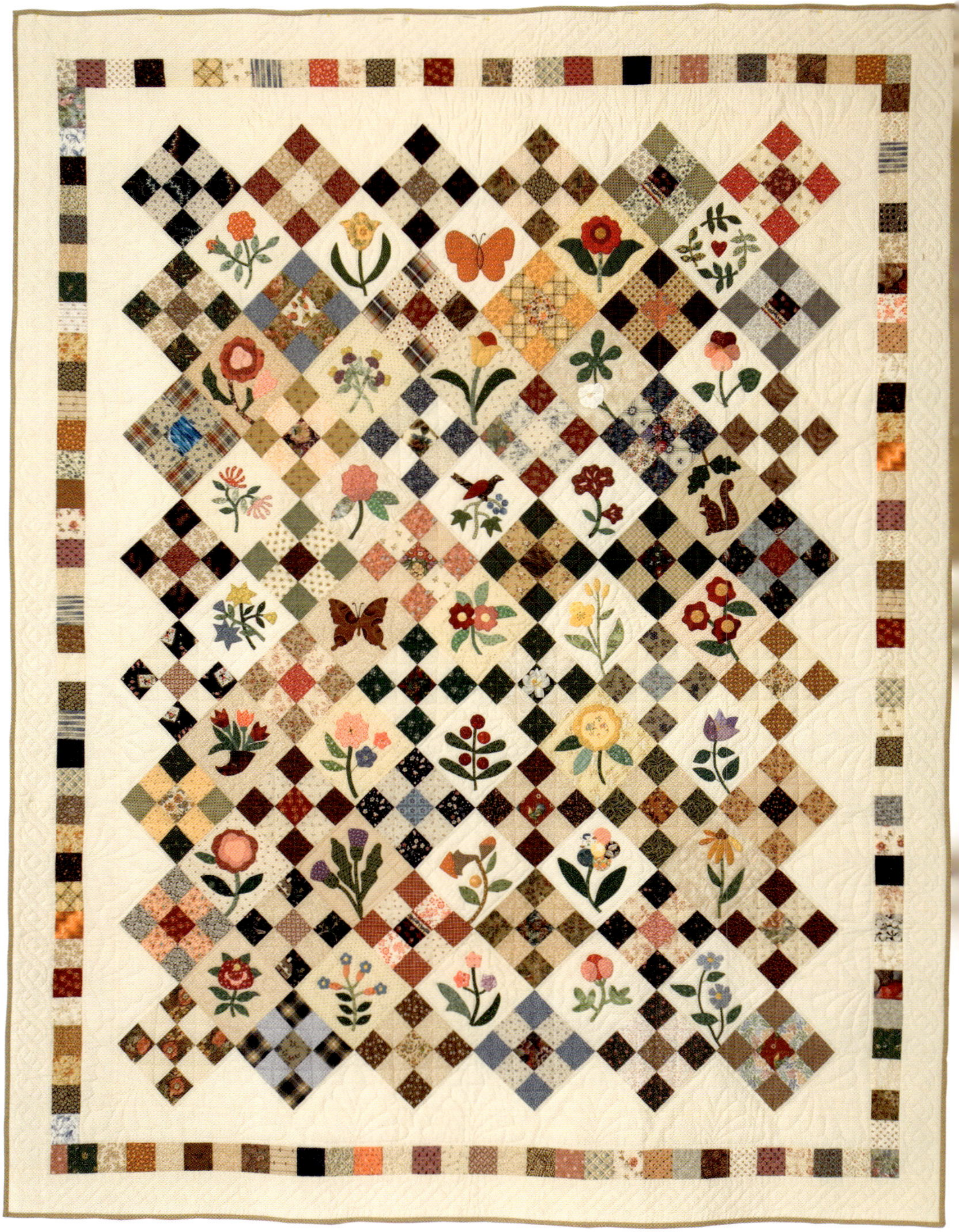

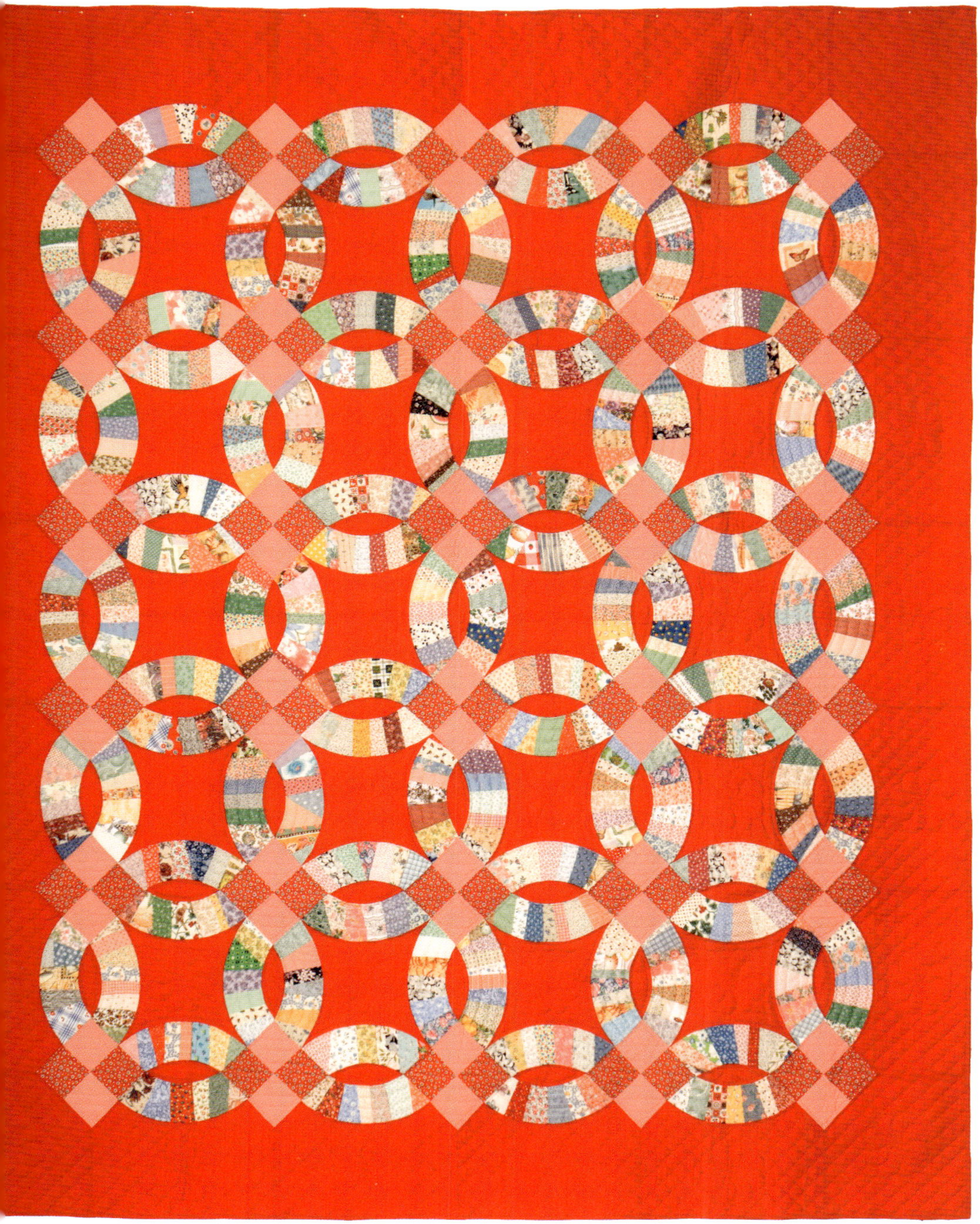

Quilt #137. "Double Wedding Ring" made in 2004; it is 78 inches wide by 92 inches long. When she spotted this design on a red background in a new book by Bobbie Aug and Sharon Newman (*String Quilts with Style*, 1999), Martha was moved to make another quilt by this pattern; the second quilt she ever pieced was a "Double Wedding Ring." Collection of the maker.

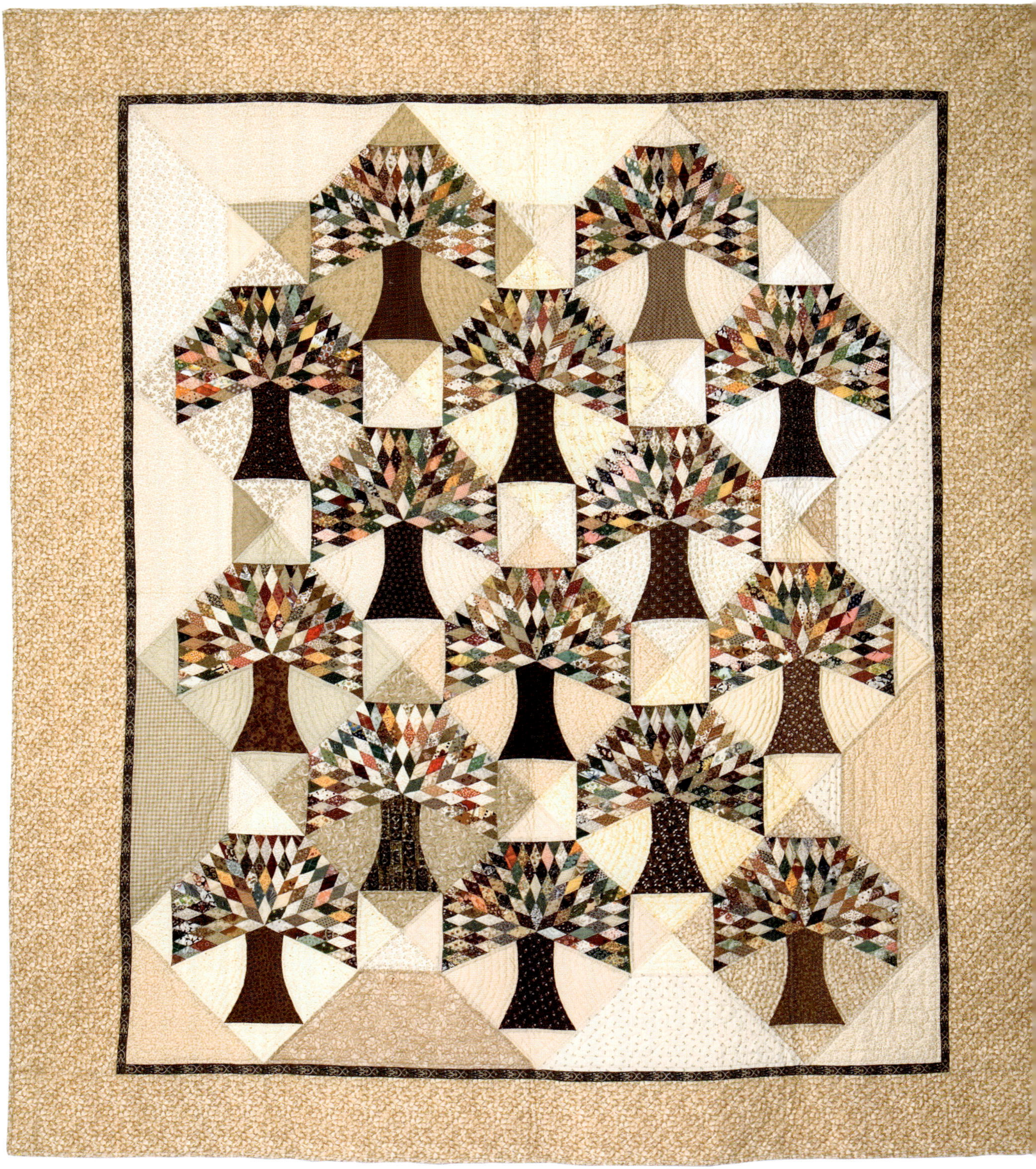

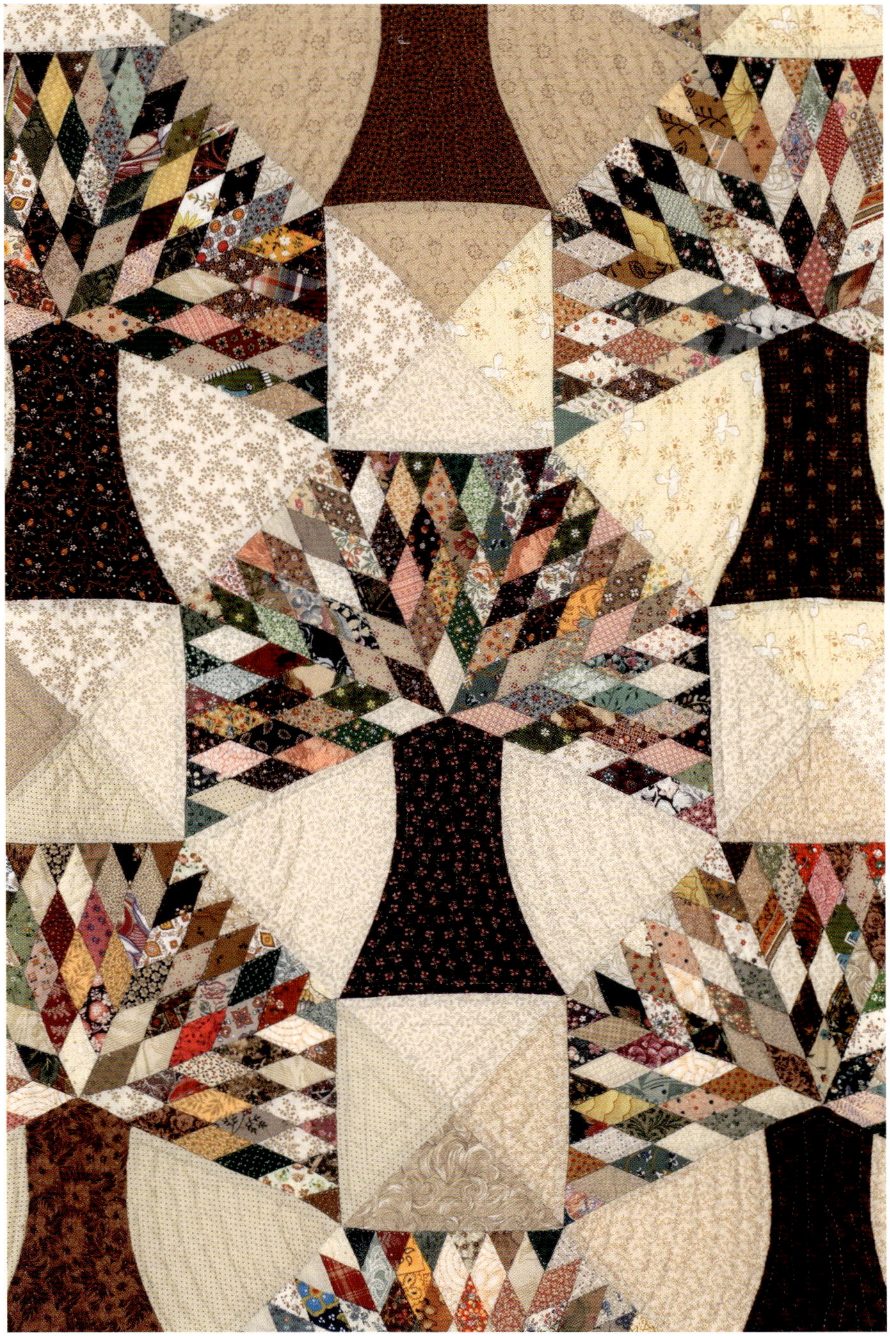

Quilt #93 (preceding page). "Live Oak Trees" made in 2004; it is 75 inches wide by 82.5 inches long. This design popped into Martha's consciousness from three different sources practically simultaneously: the Maryland quilt documentation book (*Maryland, a Middle Temperament: 1634–1980*, by Robert Brugger, 1988), *Lady's Circle Patchwork Quilts*, and *Ladies Art Catalog* all had versions. Collection of the maker.

Quilt #93. "Live Oak Trees" detail. Martha remembered an old live oak tree pattern from the Maryland documentation book. She combined it with another tree quilt pattern from *Lady's Circle Patchwork Quilts* for her own version.

Quilt #94. "Stars and Cross" made in 2004; it is 78 inches wide and 93 inches long. Martha had made lots of small stars; after much thought and trial and error, she decided to put them together with an old setting from an antique quilt. The stars are all two-toned and 3.5 inches in size. She had a very small amount of green in her scrap bag and chose it for the crosses. When she completed the quilt, there were only inches of the green to spare. Collection of maker. Photograph by Brian Loden.

Quilt #74 (following page). "Spider Lily and Snowflake" made in 2005; it is 86 inches wide by 86 inches long. A quilt similar to this in a magazine attracted Martha's and Ann's attention, and they decided they loved it. Martha remembered that *A Garden of Quilts* contained a comparable design, complete with patterns for the two different blocks that alternate to make the field of the quilt. Naturally, Martha made her own modifications, primarily to the "Snowflake" block, to which she added a center shape like that of the "Spider Lily" block. The slashed areas are reverse appliqué. Collection of the maker.

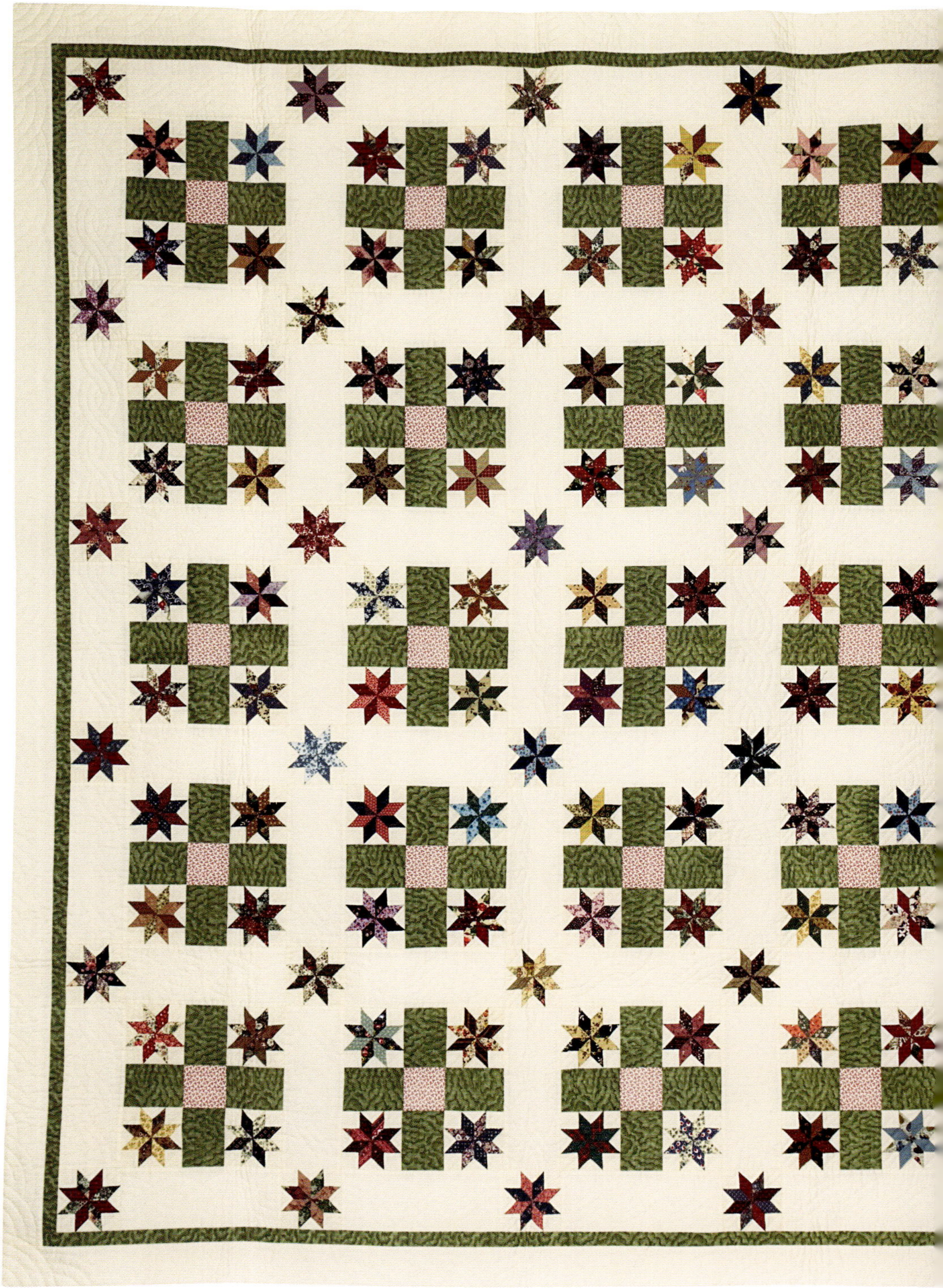

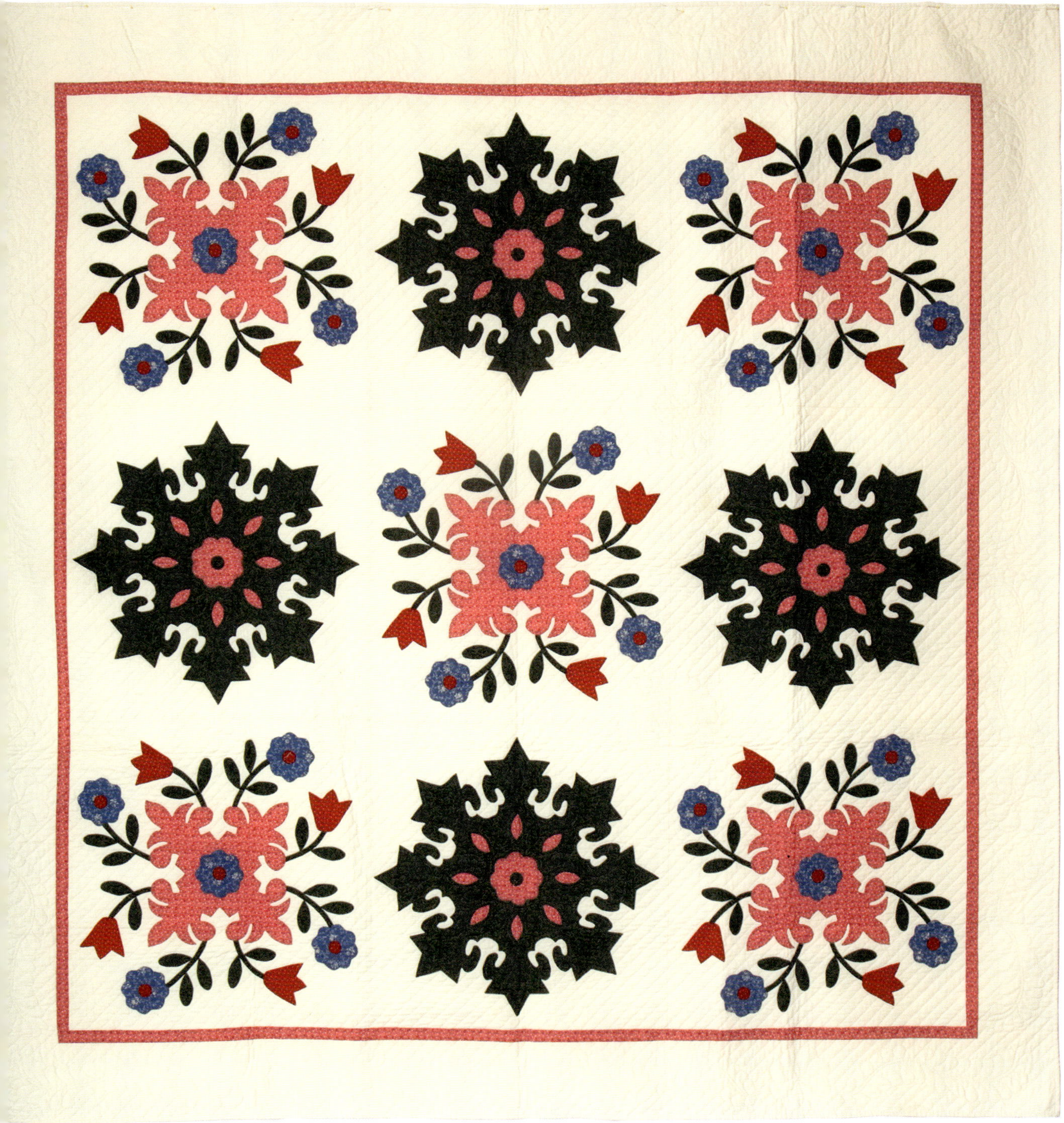

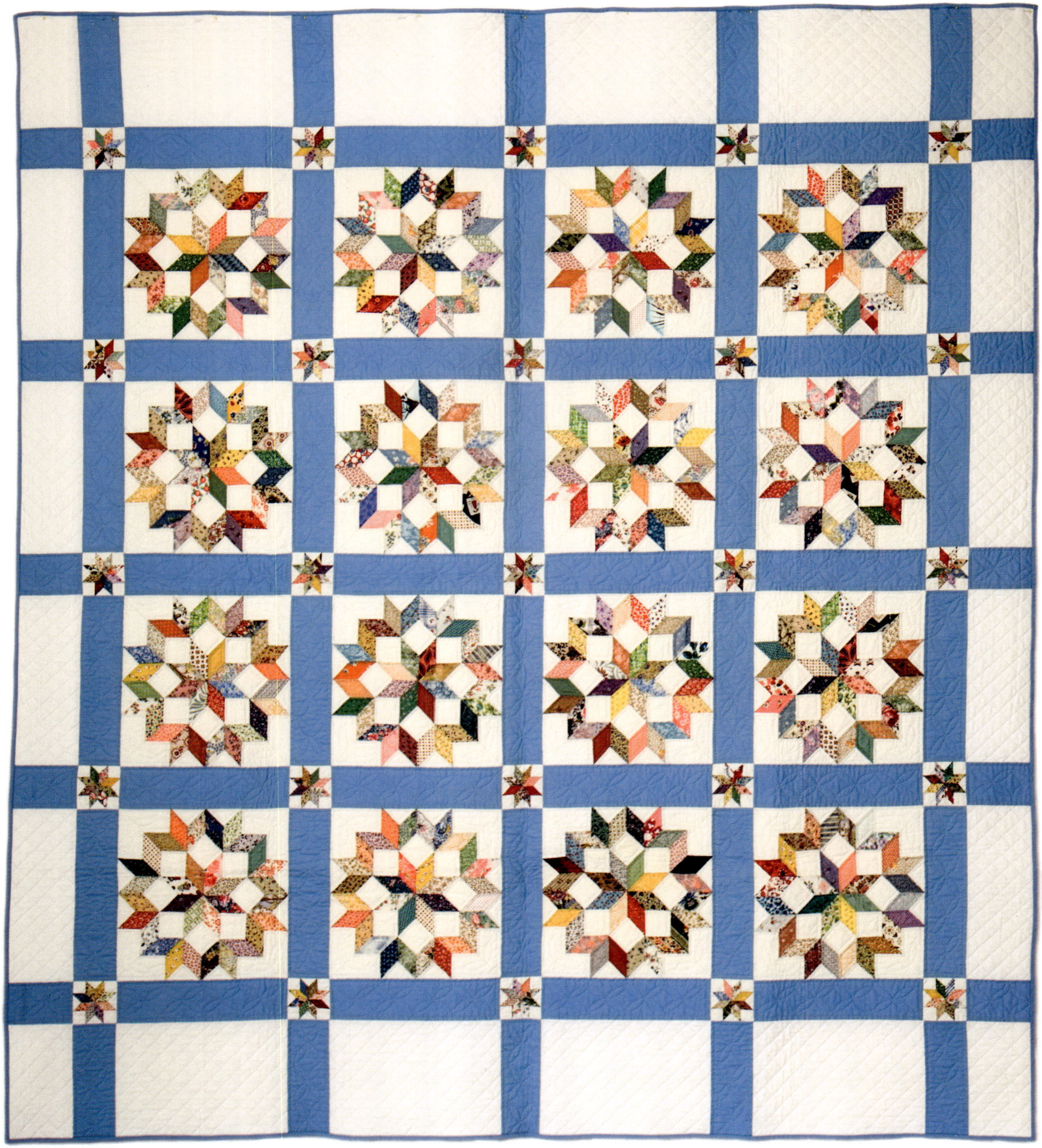

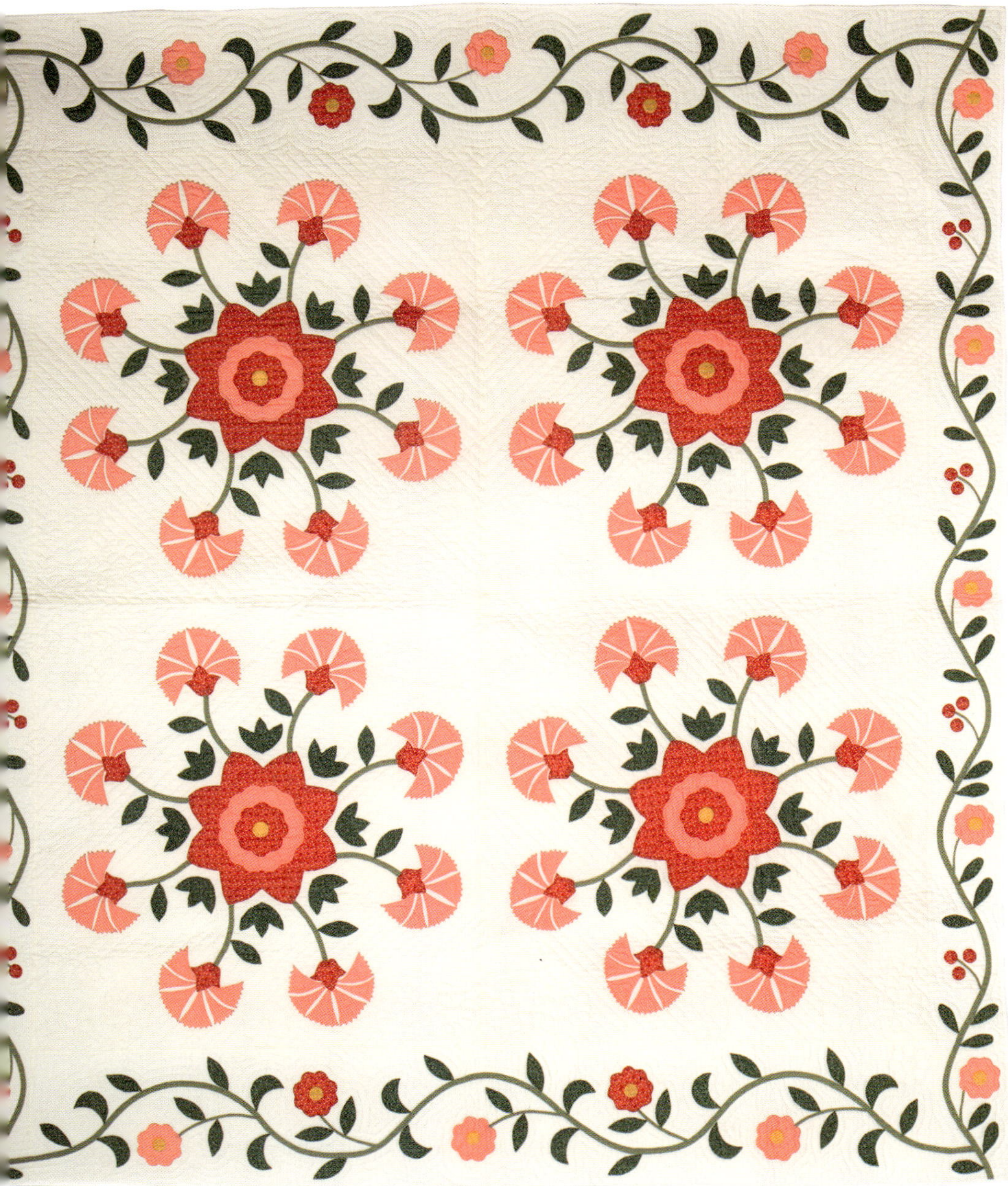

Quilt #162 (preceding page). "Dutch Rose" made in 2006; it is 76.75 inches wide by 86 inches long. An unusual aspect of this quilt is the way Martha finished it off, with unpatterned partial squares instead of a traditional border. The tiny eight-point stars in the cornerstones are a lovely detail. Collection of the maker.

Quilt #163. "Four-Block Carnations" made in 2006; it is 81.75 inches wide by 91.75 inches long. Martha has always been interested in four-block quilts and has made several, including "Rose of Sharon" in 1963. The blocks are generally quite large when only four of them are used to make the top; on some antique quilts, they are as big as 36 inches square; they are almost that large on this piece. Notice the two different border styles. Collection of the maker.

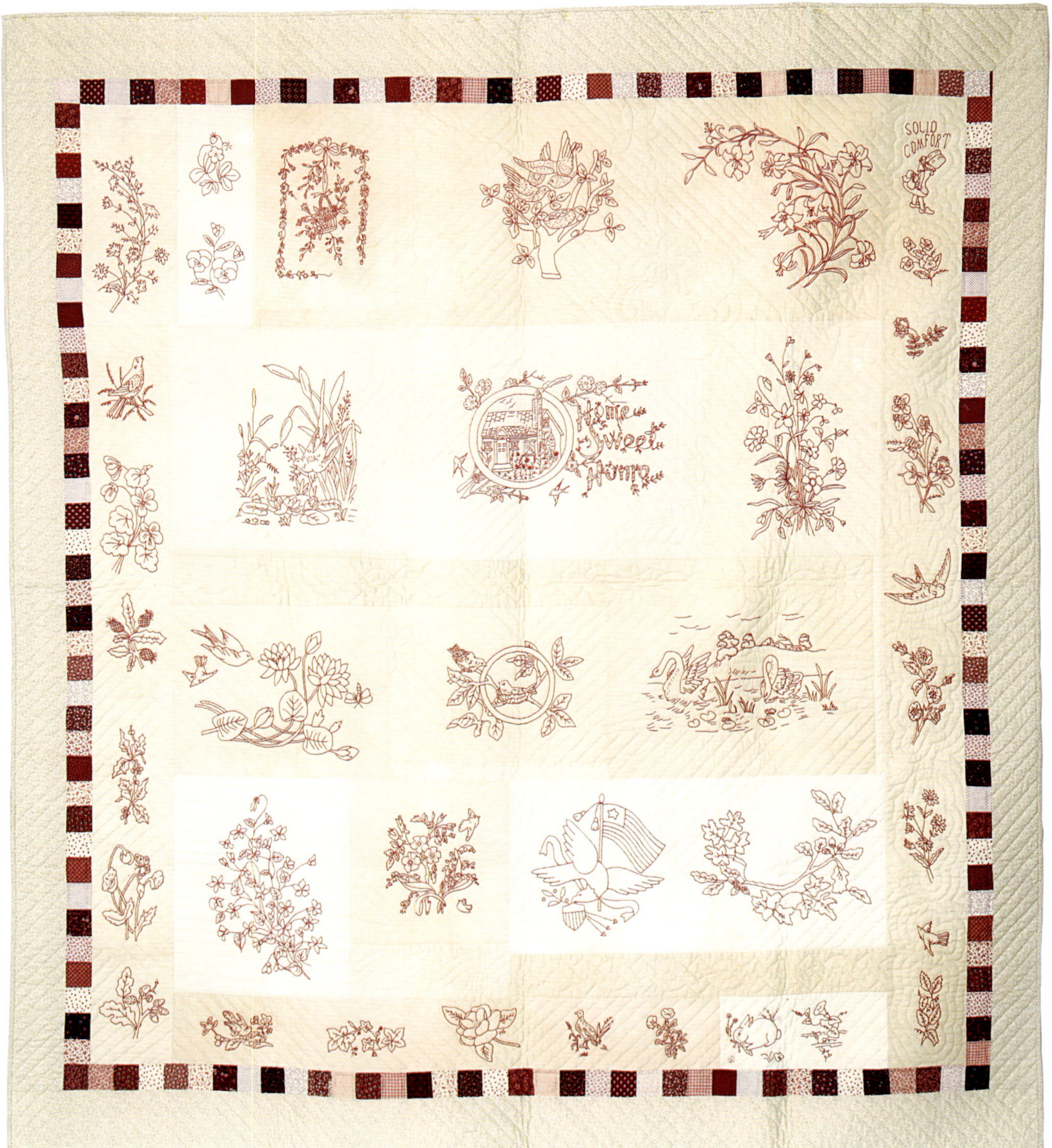
SOLID COMFORT
Home Sweet Home

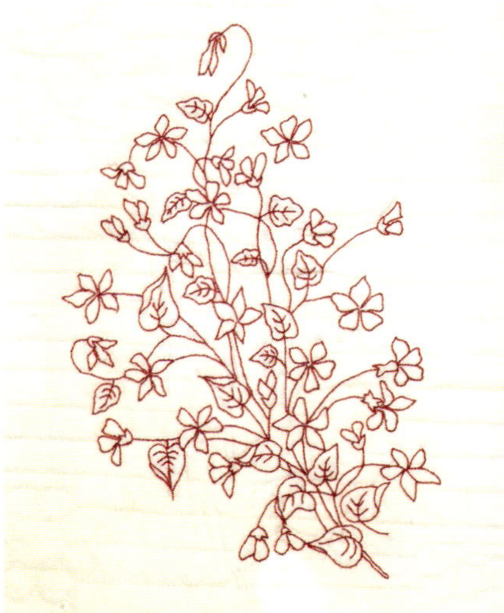

Quilt #164 (preceding page). "Redwork Sampling" made in 2006; it is 79 inches wide by 88 inches long. Everyone in the Cotton Patchers Quilt Guild got interested at the same time in doing redwork embroidery. Martha was attracted to it because she liked the idea of working with a single color. She used whatever fabric she had on hand for the background as she embroidered the different motifs, and that is why it varies from pure white to deep cream. Collection of the maker.

Quilt #164. "Redwork Sampling" detail. Violets blanket much of the South in the springtime, and that is surely why Martha chose this motif for her exquisite embroidery.

Quilt #164. "Redwork Sampling" detail. Another panel illustrates additional favorite themes of our quilter's life. Notice that the home is set in a flourishing garden and that there are several birds.

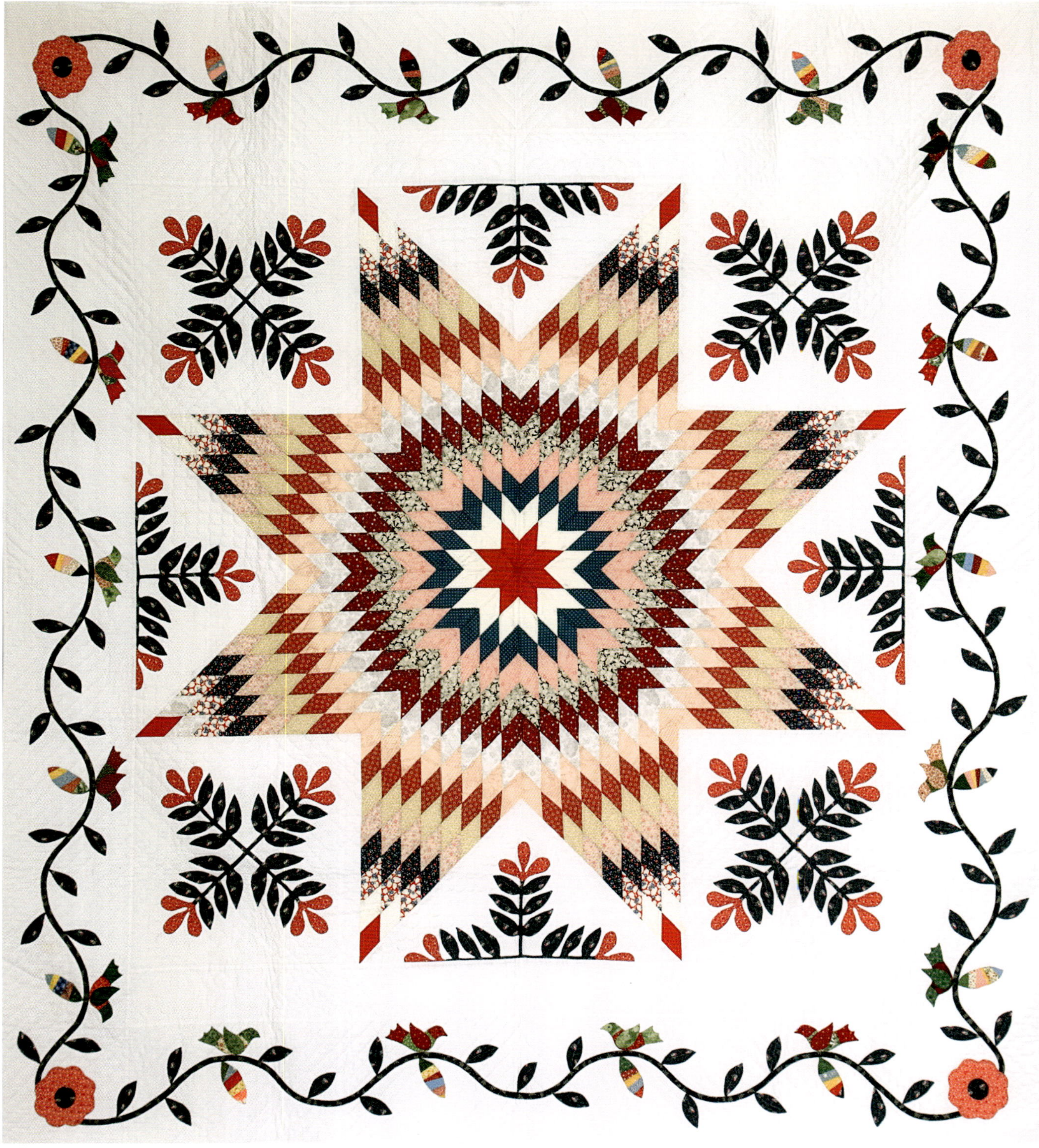

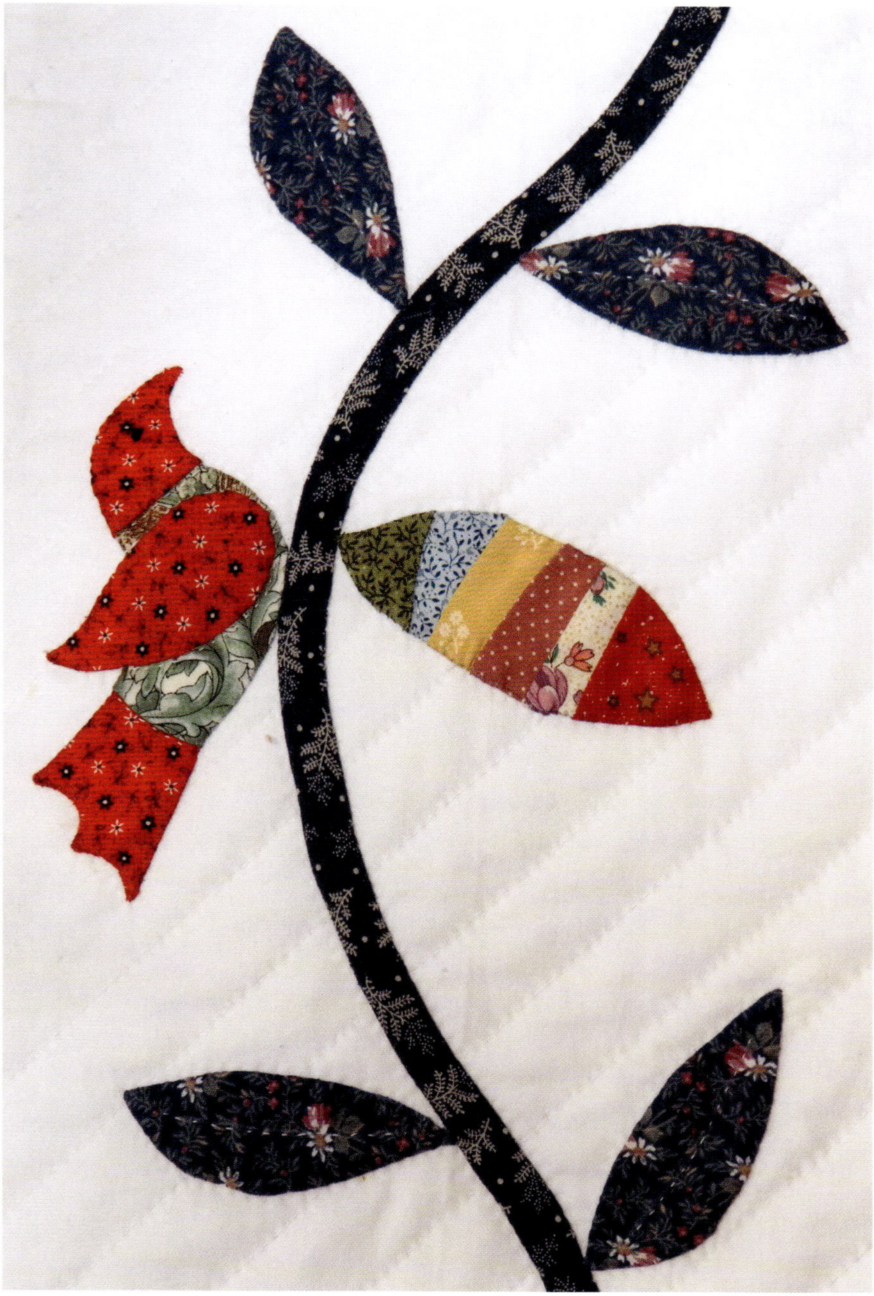

Quilt #165 (preceding page). "Bethlehem Star" made in April 2007; it is 82.5 inches wide by 88 inches long. Martha finished the quilt just as the photography for this book was taking place, so this quilt is "fresh out of the frame," as Cay Jones says. In recent years, the method most frequently employed for piecing a star design like this has been to make each of the eight points, then join them into twos, then fours, then finally through the center to make the whole. Martha didn't do this one that way; instead, she pieced from the center out, adding diamonds in rounds. She was working with scraps from her stash, and she said it was easier this way to judge how far a specific piece would go. Collection of the maker. Photograph by Brian Loden.

Quilt #165. "Bethlehem Star" detail. A string-pieced leaf is a new design element; it came about after Martha studied photographs of the work of Susan McCord, a 19th-century farm wife who had nine children and used fabrics from her scrap bag to piece her quilts; many of her masterpieces show string-pieced leaves similar to this one. Photograph by Brian Loden.

DONOR LIST

Platinum*
Pat and Barbara Cashman
Mississippi Quilt Association

Gold**
Martha Skelton

Silver***
Cay Jones
Diane Jordan, DJ's Creations
Southern Cultural Heritage Center
Carol Vickers

Bronze****
Mimi Alef
Back Forty Quilting
Gail Bird
Brandon Quilt Guild
B. J. Crawford
Delores Cronin
Ann and Troy Deemer
Elvia Edwards
Jo-Ann Evans
Faux Pas Quilt Guild, Clinton
Penny Sanford Fikes
Martha Ginn
Bobbie and Terry Gray
Nancy Henson
Mary Holman
Barbara Hutchinson
Jackson Quilters
Joe and Betty Jeffers
Joan Knight
Lakesiders Quilt Guild, Clinton
Betty Lewis
Diann Loper
Louisville Quilt Guild
Ella Lucas
Mary Nell Magee
Margaret and Ken Miller
Mississippi Band of Choctaw Indians
Alta Morehead
Oxford Piecemakers Quilt Guild
Cindy Pannier
Piecemakers Quilt Guild, Brookhaven
Pine Belt Quilters, Hattiesburg
Quilters by Heart's Desire, Brandon
Cynthia Reaves
Chaille Reed
Diane Rhyne
Irene Rogers
Scrappy Quilt Guild, Ackerman
Peggy and David Segrest
Ann Simcox
Gordon and Janet Skelton
Diantha Stafford
Stitch-n-Frame
Winston and Rosemary Taylor

Polly Thomasson
University Press of Mississippi
Vicksburg Cotton Patches Guild
Vicksburg Quilters Guild
Wanda Wallace
Shirley Wiltshire
Broach Winsley
Trish Wright

Patron***

Ameristar Casino
Mrs. W. W. Aydellott
Bay Oaks Quilt Guild, Diamondhead
Bayou Pierre Quilt Guild, Hermanville
Barbara Beasley
Rebecca Boswell
Bettye G. Buckley
Rose Cohen
Les Lee and Joe Crim
Nancy Critz
Hilda Crowe
Polly Duggan
B. Allan Dunaway
Dr. and Mrs. Paul Dyken
Grace Feller
Jennifer Fentress
Dr. Donald Hall
Ellen Hall
Horizon Casino
Linda Jabour
Yvonne James
Paula Jones
Carolyn Fisackerly Justice
Irma Kendall
Leslie Kiger
Nancy Knight
Ollie Jean Lane
Cline and Betty Mansur
Dr. and Mrs. Chester Masterson
Wynema McGrew
Sue Mitchell
Barbara Newman
Clara Oakes
Ocean Waves Quilt Guild, Long Beach
Pine Creek Golf Club, Purvis
Dr. and Mrs. Robert Sadler
Sand Stitchers Quilt Guild, Ocean Springs
Suzanne Schutt
Lou Speed
Gayle Wallace
Sara Ward
Annie Williams

Levels of Donations:

*Platinum: $5000 and above
**Gold: $3,000–$5,000
***Silver: $1000–$3000
****Bronze: $100–$1000
*****Patron: $100

APPENDIX
Twenty-five Years of Quilt Shows and Exhibitions

1973 (July) Local television stations in Vicksburg and Tupelo: Martha Skelton explains and exhibits quilts and quilted pillows.
(August) Roosevelt State Park: exhibit of Martha Skelton's quilted pillows.
(September) Valley Department Store, Vicksburg: one-woman show of Martha Skelton's quilts.

1974 (June) Jackson Stitchery Guild exhibit at Old Capitol Museum features quilts by Martha Skelton.
(July) Eighth Annual Festival of American Folklife in Washington, D.C., sponsored by the Smithsonian Institution, features quilts and demonstrations by Martha Skelton.

1980 Cotton Patchers Quilt Guild, Vicksburg: one-woman show of twenty-eight of Martha Skelton's quilts.

1983 Vicksburg Quilter's Show: "Oaks and Roses" by Martha Skelton.
Lone Star Quilt Festival (now International Quilt Festival), Houston: exhibit of quilts in the permanent collection of Mountain Mist, "Hollyhocks" by Martha Skelton.

1984 Vicksburg Quilter's Show.
Museum of the City of Mobile Quilt Show.

1985 Gulf States Quilting Association and Pine Belt Quilters Guild Show, Hattiesburg, "Heart of Quilting."

1986 Cotton Patchers Quilt Guild, Vicksburg, annual show, February 7–8: Exhibit of Martha Skelton's quilts.
Azalea City Quilt Guild, Mobile: exhibit at the Museum of the City of Mobile.

1987 Hinds Community College, Jackson: "Quilters 3" exhibit.
Pine Belt Quilters Guild Show, Hattiesburg: exhibit of ten Martha Skelton quilts.
American Quilter's Society show, Paducah, Kentucky: "New York Beauty" by Martha Skelton takes first place in its category of pieced quilts and is purchased for permanent collection of the Museum of the American Quilter's Society.

1988 American Quilter's Society show, Paducah, Kentucky: "Chips and Whetstones" by Martha Skelton takes second place in its category of pieced quilts and is purchased for permanent collection of the Museum of the American Quilter's Society.

1989 Museum of American Folk Art, New York City: "Me and My Dog Tip" by Martha Skelton is selected for inclusion in *Memories of Childhood*, an exhibit that traveled from New York to major cities in the United States, then to Japan.

River Oaks Square Arts and Crafts Center, Alexandria, Louisiana: "Martha Skelton, A Retrospective," sponsored by Rapides Regional Medical Center.

1992 Cotton Patchers Quilt Guild, Vicksburg.

Quilt Europa, The Hague, Netherlands: "Victorian Rose" by Martha Skelton.

1993 Quiltfest USA, Louisville, Kentucky: "Autumn Leaves" by Martha Skelton.

Pine Belt Quilters Guild show, Hattiesburg: "Sunburst" by Martha Skelton takes "Best of Show," "Autumn Leaves" by Martha Skelton takes "Judge's Choice" and first place.

Gulf States Quilting Association, New Orleans, "The Heart of Quilting" show: "Sunburst" by Martha Skelton takes a first place in its category and "Best of Show." "Autumn Leaves" takes second place. "Hexagon Mosaic" (aka "Garden Mosaic") takes first place in its category and wins for Martha Skelton the Lois King Award for best overall needle skills.

1994 (Spring) International Quilt Market and Festival, St. Louis: "Currants and Coxcomb" by Martha Skelton.

(Spring) European Quilt Market, Karlriche, Germany: "Currants and Coxcomb" by Martha Skelton.

(June) Mississippi Quilt Association, Christ United Methodist Church, Jackson: "Martha Skelton, Star Achiever."

(July 15–16) Cotton Patchers Quilt Guild, Vicksburg: one-woman show, "Martha Skelton and Her Quilts."

Mississippi Craftsmen's Guild's Twenty-ninth Anniversary statewide traveling show: "Little Baskets" by Martha Skelton.

1995 Jackson Quilters' show: "Roses Aplenty" and "Moon and Stars" by Martha Skelton.

American Quilter's Society show, Paducah, Kentucky: "Roses Aplenty" by Martha Skelton.

Cotton Patchers Quilt Guild, Vicksburg: "Grandmother's Flower Garden," "Album II," "Nine Patch," "Roses Aplenty," "Hollyhocks," "Moon and Stars," and "Little Trees" by Martha Skelton.

2000 Vicksburg Quilters Exhibit: "Hawaiian Quilt" and "Postage Stamp" by Martha Skelton.

2002 (April) Fourteenth Rotary Club Antique Quilt Show, Paducah, Kentucky: *Mississippi Antique Quilts*, "Coxcomb and Tulips: A Modern Duplication" by Martha Skelton.
Vicksburg Quilters Show: "Wheel of Fortune" by Martha Skelton wins "Viewer's Choice."
Southern Cultural Heritage Foundation, *Women in Art:* two quilts from Martha Skelton

2004 (June) Mississippi Quilt Association Spring Gathering, St. Matthews United Methodist Church, Madison, Mississippi: "Martha's Choice," a trunk show of Martha Skelton's favorite quilts.

2007 Vicksburg Quilters Show: Special exhibit of Martha Skelton's "Bethlehem Star," "Pink Carnations," and "Dutch Rose."

fabrics in each and made an even number of blocks in each to compose a full-size quilt of twelve blocks.

49. MSQC Quilt Documentation form #69, 1970s. Composed of different pieced and appliquéd blocks Martha had taught to various classes.

50. MSQC Quilt Documentation form #45, 1970s. Martha obtained the pattern for this beautiful lily design from a lady in Arkansas. It was published in *A Garden of Quilts* (1981), by this author, and has been displayed at the Mobile (Alabama) Museum of Art.

51. MSQC Quilt Documentation form #37, 1970s. Pieced of fabric scraps of many colors, the quilt probably caught Martha's eye in a magazine. It was exhibited at a Cotton Patchers' show.

52. MSQC Quilt Documentation form #122, 1970s. A collection of gingham scraps with coordinating prints inspired this pieced quilt.

53. MSQC Quilt Documentation form #129, 1970s. Pieced floral design in repeat blocks of gold, orange, and rust.

54. MSQC Quilt Documentation form #133, 1970s. Gold, yellow, and green appliqué of many different rose designs.

55. MSQC Quilt Documentation form #106, 1970s. Machine-pieced in cream, tan, pale yellow, and orange. "Just a fun thing to do," Martha commented.

56. MSQC Quilt Documentation form #156, 1970s. Exhibited in Craftman's Guild Show and at the Trade Mart in Jackson.

57. MSQC Quilt Documentation form #40, 1975. A grayed medium-blue provides the background for this quilt that was exhibited at the Mobile Museum of Art.

58. MSQC Quilt Documentation form #124, 1970s. Vertical strips of half-square triangles are separated by yellow strips in varying widths.

59. MSQC Quilt Documentation form #145, 1970s. Ann Hope stamped a cross-stitch pattern of the bird for her mother; Martha turned the finished piece into a wall hanging.

60. MSQC Quilt Documentation form #158, 1970s. Martha wanted to try curved piecing in this quilt that was shown at a Craftsman's Guild show as well as at the Museum of the City of Mobile.

61. MSQC Quilt Documentation form #88, 1970s. The only quilt of this type that Martha ever made was done so that she could show her students a combination of hand and machine work that was an improvement over handwork alone, as it resulted in a stronger quilt and a better look on the back. "Not her favorite quilt to make."

62. MSQC Quilt Documentation form #161, mid-1970s. Pattern for center block came from *Woman's Day* magazine.

63. MSQC Quilt Documentation form #64, 1977. Made to enter into *Good Housekeeping* magazine's contest. It is an original pattern, set into a medallion format with lots of quilting in a very open background.

64. MSQC Quilt Documentation form #4, 1975–1980. During one of Aunt Ethel's visits, she and Martha cut pieces so each of them could make a quilt like this. It was one of Martha's earliest appliqué quilts, and the pattern came from a friend who got it from *Progressive Farmer* magazine. Martha remembered Alan's fond indulgence toward his wife and her aunt pulling out their quilting fabrics and playing around in them, rather than participating in an activity that would have included him as well.

Martha in the 1980s: Teaching, Exhibiting, Competing

1. p. 27.

2. p. 28.

3. Letter dated August 14, 1973, from Ken Jones, Public Relations Officer, Mississippi Park Commission, to Mrs. Alan Skelton, Vicksburg, MS.

4. p. 29.

5. Letter dated March 6, 1978, from Jane Biggers, Director of Public Relations, Mississippi Park Commission, to Mrs. Martha B. Sketon, Vicksburg, MS.

6. *Vicksburg Evening Post*, July 20, 1976.

7. Letter dated March 16, 1973, from Dot Marie R. Evans, Extension Home Economist, Mississippi State University, to Mrs. A. G. Skelton, Vicksburg, MS.

8. p. 29.

9. Letter dated June 26, 1981, from Ina G. Kimbrough, District Leader, Home Economics Program, Cooperative Extension Service, Jackson, MS, to Mrs. Martha Skelton, Vicksburg, MS.

10. Letter dated April 10, 1980, from Guyla Gould, Resource Teacher, Vicksburg Middle School, Vicksburg, MS.

11. pp. 49–50.

12. From a column by Martha Skelton, entitled "Home Extension Quilting," that appeared in *Patchwork Quilts* magazine in July 1989.

13. Letter dated November 6, 1979, from Jim Buck Ross, Commissioner, Mississippi Department of Agriculture and Commerce, Jackson, MS, to Mrs. Martha Skelton, Vicksburg, MS.

14. p. 30.

15. p. 37.

16. p. 44.

17. Letter dated April 21, 1983, from William Winter, Governor, State of Mississippi, Jackson, MS, to Mrs. Martha B. Skelton, Vicksburg, MS. In 1981, the Winters had been the recipient of the Mississippi State Fair quilt, and Martha was on a first-name basis with the governor and his wife, Elise.

18. Article in the *Milwaukee Journal*, dated Sunday, July 17, 1983.

19. p. 45.

20. In 1933, Sears, Roebuck and Company sponsored the "Century of Progress" quilt contest to correspond with the World's Fair being held in Chicago that year. A total of 24,878 quilts were submitted; the prize money being offered was greater than the average family's annual income. See the bibliography for further reading.

21. p. 47.

22. pp. 46–47.

23. p. 48.

24. pp. 52–53.

25. p. 54.

26. Martha once received a letter addressed simply, "The Quilt Lady," Vicksburg, Mississippi.

27. MSQC Quilt Documentation form #148, 1980. Made as a teaching project for the Jackson Stitchery Guild.

28. MSQC Quilt Documentation form #123, 1980. Published in *A Garden of Quilts* (1981), by this author.

29. MSQC Quilt Documentation form #65, 1980. Made of blocks swapped with other members of Cotton Patchers. Ann Hope made the cat block, assembled, and quilted this quilt.

30. MSQC Quilt Documentation form #43, 1979/1984. Exhibited at Cotton Patchers' show.

31. MSQC Quilt Documentation form #149, 1982.

32. MSQC Quilt Documentation form #128, 1984. Made from blocks collected at a Cotton Patchers' swap.

33. MSQC Quilt Documentation form #62, early 1980s. All the members of Cotton Patchers were making a "Hole in the Barn Door" quilt.

34. MSQC Quilt Documentation form #63, early 1980s. This pattern from *Quilter's Newsletter Magazine* emphasized curves.

35. MSQC Quilt Documentation form #66, early 1980s. Another project undertaken by the Cotton Patchers. This was shown at the Cotton Patchers' show and perhaps at a Craftsmen's Guild show (Martha is not sure about the second show).

36. MSQC Quilt Documentation form #159, early 1980s. This old design was made popular again in the 1980s by Jinny Beyer; Martha made her small quilt as a teaching sample. It was shown at a Cotton Patchers' show and at a Craftsmen's Guild show.

37. MSQC Quilt Documentation form #50, early 1980s.

38. MSQC Quilt Documentation form #33, early 1980s. A teaching sample used to dem-

onstrate one-block piecing and use of color. The only fabric that was purchased new is the border fabric; every other fabric is from Martha's scrap bag. Exhibited at a Craftsmen's Guild show.

39. MSQC Quilt Documentation form #27, early 1980s. The center "Sunflower" block is the design that was used for one of the Mississippi State Fair quilts.

40. MSQC Quilt Documentation form #146, early 1980s. All guild members bought the same fabric but chose their patterns individually for making up their quilts. After their photo and this quilt appeared in *Lady's Circle Patchwork Quilts*, a woman from Colorado wrote to Martha asking for help in making the design as a wedding gift for a young couple. Martha, of course, helped the woman and received a note from the lady a year or so later, saying how thrilled the couple had been with their gift.

41. MSQC Quilt Documentation form #22, early 1980s. Nancy Page was the fictitious name of a designer for a newspaper syndicate in the 1930s. Martha had looked forward to making the design in 1930s fabrics she took from her own scrap bag.

42. MSQC Quilt Documentation form #140, 1980s. The pattern for this design featuring circles made of many sharply pointed triangles came from *Lady's Circle Patchwork Quilts;* Martha's individual touch was the choice of pink in the elongated ovals that appear as the scrappy circles overlap. The pink helps to hold the design together.

43. MSQC Quilt Documentation form #49, 1980s. The twenty pieced blocks of this quilt were inspired by an antique quilt in a magazine, as was the brown color scheme. Martha deviated from the antique quilt in the addition of the border.

44. MSQC Quilt Documentation form #48, 1980s. After teaching a class on this design, Martha assembled the blocks she had made during demonstrations.

45. MSQC Quilt Documentation form #41, 1980s. Martha adapted this design from an antique quilt pictured in *Lady's Circle Patchwork Quilts*; she added the border of red hearts to all four sides.

46. MSQC Quilt Documentation form #76, 1980s. Martha's daughter, Ann, challenged her mother to try her hand at a miniature quilt. This twelve-block quilt measures only eight inches wide and ten inches long; Martha says she enjoyed working with the little pieces.

47. MSQC Quilt Documentation form #20, 1980s. A quilt like this made by Martha's grandmother had gone to one of Martha's cousins, so Martha made her own. The pattern is from the Nancy Page Quilt Club, the name given a syndicated feature from designer Florence LaGanke, who ran this as a series quilt, offering one block a week. This quilt, originally named "Garden Bouquet," ran in the *Nashville Banner* from February through July of 1932. Martha's grandmother had found her pattern in the *Denver Post.*

48. MSQC Quilt Documentation form #61, 1980s. When she was invited to teach a class

on "Mariner's Compass" at Ann Root's quilt shop in Clinton, MS, and also at the Jackson Stitchery Guild, Martha made a class sample. In addition to illustrating the many pieced points of "Mariner's Compass," it shows how one large block can be turned into a wall hanging with the addition of supporting motifs (in this case, appliquéd dogwood blossoms and an interesting pieced border).

49. MSQC Quilt Documentation form #14, 1980s. Named for a lovely flower, this quilt was published in 1981's *A Garden of Quilts* by this author.

50. MSQC Quilt Documentation form #157, 1984. This interesting scrap quilt contains a "snowball" shape and sashing pieced of small squares.

51. MSQC Quilt Documentation form #114, late 1980s. The pieced "Flying Swallows" blocks are from fabric left over from a dress Martha had made to wear to bicentennial events; the design for the appliquéd smilax vine that meanders between the blocks came from an actual vine in her yard. The quilt was published in *Lady's Circle Patchwork Quilts* in July of 1989.

52. MSQC Quilt Documentation form #97, late 1980s. Inspired by a quilt she saw in a book (*Legacy: The Story of Talula Gilbert Bottons and Her Quilts*, by Nancilu B. Burdick [Nashville: Rutledge Hill Press, 1988]) about Alabama quilter Talula Bottoms, Martha drafted a pattern to make it.

53. MSQC Quilt Documentation form #66, late 1988. A home decorating magazine showed a similar quilt on its cover, and Martha was filled with enthusiasm for making one like it. This quilt was in the "ice storm" article that came about when Carter Houck and other staff from *Lady's Circle Patchwork Quilts* visited Martha to do a story on Vicksburg and its quilters. A freak ice storm extinguished electricity all over town, so Martha had to tour her guests through her own home, as well as the historic houses they wanted to see, with flashlights and candles. In addition to appearing in the July 1989 edition of the magazine, the quilt was also included in a specialty publication, *Lady's Circle Patchwork Quilts Editor's Choice*, in 1990.

A Statewide Organization: More Quilts than Ever in the 1990s

1. pp. 60–61.

2. p. 68. See Mary Elizabeth Johnson, *Mississippi Quilts* (Jackson: University Press of Mississippi, 2001).

3. The Mobile quilt-sharing day took place in early summer 1984, and approximately two hundred quilts were documented. No book of Alabama quilts was published at that time, although an essay on textiles comprised a chapter of *Made in Alabama*, a survey of the decorative arts of the state, presented by the Birmingham Museum of Arts in 1995.

4. pp. 67–68.

5. p. 66.

6. Article in the *Hattiesburg American*, March 20, 1997, and a press release dated March 10, 1997, from The Studio, home office of documentary filmmakers Diana and Stephen Young.

7. pp. 71–72.

8. The *Enterprise Tocsin*, Indianola, MS, Thursday, February 12, 1998.

9. p. 65.

10. MSQC Quilt Documentation form #142, late 1980s–early 1990s. Martha's students were asking for help with the pattern, so Martha made this one, with small rings, to refresh herself on how to make it.

11. MSQC Quilt Documentation form #147, 1990. A white silhouette of oak branches and a robin appliquéd onto a pieced one-patch background in four solid colors is accompanied by the inscription, "I heard a bird sing in December."

12. MSQC Quilt Documentation form #86, early 1990s. Made as a demonstration piece for schoolchildren who were learning machine piecing.

13. MSQC Quilt Documentation form #135, 1990s. Martha made this quilt just because she liked the pattern. The design of the quilt is actually carried by the sashing, which is pieced, and twenty white squares are produced. Martha quilted different leaf and wreath designs into the squares.

14. MSQC Quilt Documentation form #143, 1990s. No, this is not named after Martha's Aunt Ethel. It is from a block that fellow Cotton Patcher Carol Schultz had. Martha took a picture of it, then drafted her own pattern.

15. MSQC Quilt Documentation form #5, May 1998. The top was pieced so the quilt could be in the frame at the Greenville Folklife Festival.

16. MSQC Quilt Documentation form #144, early 1990s. Martha loves the Laura Engels Wilder books, and this quilt was mentioned as the one Laura made when she fell in love with Almanzo.

17. MSQC Quilt Documentation form #77, probably the 1990s. This was made from a pattern Martha bought.

18. MSQC Quilt Documentation form #54, probably the 1990s. All the blocks in this quilt were used in classes that Martha taught. She points out that the window of the "House" block is cut from a fabric printed with people, so that they appear to be looking out the window. The children she taught thought that was funny.

19. MSQC Quilt Documentation form #105, the late 1990s. Martha dug through her scrap bag to find the fabrics that "just seemed to suit" this old pattern. They appear to be mostly from the 1930s. The quilt was published in the March 1990 issue of *Quilt World* magazine.

20. MSQC Quilt Documentation form #113, 1997–1998. A black-and-white photograph

of this quilt appeared in Carter Houck's *Treasury of American Quilts: Including Complete Patterns and Instructions for Making Your Own Quilts.*

21. MSQC Quilt Documentation form #120, late 1990s. This quilt was pieced much earlier, of old fabrics. The "Nine-Patch" blocks are set on point.

The Private Martha: At Home, 2000–2007

1. p. 79.
2. p. 78.
3. Author interview with Martha Skelton, Vicksburg, February 8, 2007.
4. p. 77.
5. Author interview with Martha Skelton, Vicksburg, February 8, 2007.
6. p. 78.
7. p. 79.
8. p. 79.
9. p. 38.
10. Author interview with Martha Skelton, Vicksburg, February 8, 2007; also p. 76 of transcript.
11. Author interview with Martha Skelton, Vicksburg, February 8, 2007
12. pp. 77–78.
13. p. 77.
14. p. 51.
15. p. 75.
16. p. 75.
17. p. 49.
18. MSQC Quilt Documentation Project form #85, late 1999-early 2000. Martha saw a quilt like this in *Lady's Circle Patchwork Quilts*, made a few different pinwheels and decided she wanted to make a whole quilt with them.
19. MSQC Quilt Documentation form #98, 2000. The book *Dear Jane* by Brenda Papadakis presented the patterns for a sampler quilt, made in 1863 by Jane Stickle, that contained 169 blocks. For a few years, it seemed like everybody in America was making a "Dear Jane" quilt. "Dear Jane" clubs and chat rooms sprang up. It was a huge phenomenon in the quilt world. Martha did not use all the patterns in the book for her quilt, and she designed a slightly different border.
20. MSQC Quilt Documentation form #82, early 2000. *Lady's Circle Patchwork Quilts* devoted an issue to West Virginia quilts, and there was a quilt like this featured in the article. Because Martha was born in West Virginia, she decided to make her own version of

the quilt. (Mountain Mist® later bought the quilt from Martha for their permanent collection.)

21. MSQC Quilt Documentation form #96, early 2000s. Although Martha had once made a baby quilt of this design, she had never made a full-size quilt. She kept the blocks small in this larger quilt.

22. MSQC Quilt Documentation form #127, 2003. The pieces for this quilt were cut for some time before Martha stitched it up. It is a wonderful scrap quilt with a floral print for the border.

23. MSQC Quilt Documentation form #71, 2004–2005. Martha ordered the patterns for this quilt from the Daughters of the American Revolution Museum in Washington, D.C. It is made in the Baltimore Album style.

24. MSQC Quilt Documentation form #109, 2005. The challenge in this quilt, based on one of Carter Houck's personal collection that was photographed for *Lady's Circle Patchwork Quilts*, was the small (1½-inch) squares. A second challenge was stretching a small amount of pink fabric to make corner blocks where the "chains" crossed.

BIBLIOGRAPHY

Books and Calendars

American Quilter's Society editors. *MAQS: The Permanent Collection—QUILTS*, Vol. 1. Paducah, KY: American Quilter's Society, 1991. Martha Skelton's "New York Beauty" is featured on page 49.

———. *MAQS: The Permanent Collection—QUILTS*, Vol. 2. Paducah, KY: American Quilter's Society, 1995. Martha Skelton's "Chips and Whetstones" quilt is featured on page 17.

———. *MAQS: The Permanent Collection—QUILTS*, Vol. 8. Paducah, KY: American Quilter's Society, 2001. Martha Skelton's work is featured on pages 32, 53, and 119, with "New York Beauty" and "Chips and Whetstones."

———. *MAQS Quilts: The Founders Collection.* Paducah, KY: American Quilter's Society, 2001. Martha Skelton's quilt "Chips and Whetstones" is featured on page 23 and "New York Beauty" on page 119.

———. *Perpetual Calendar.* Paducah, KY: American Quilter's Society, 2005. Martha Skelton's "New York Beauty" is the featured quilt for December.

Burdick, Nancilu. *Family Ties: Old Quilt Patterns from New Cloth.* Nashville, TN: Rutledge Hill Press, 1993.

———. *Legacy: The Story of Talula Gilbert Bottoms and Her Quilts.* Nashville, TN: Rutledge Hill Press, 1988. (Re-issued in paperback in 1993.)

Cory, Pepper. *Mastering Quilt Marking.* Lafayette, CA: C & T Publishing, 1999. Martha Skelton's work is featured on page 73.

Faoro, Victoria, ed. *Award-Winning Quilts and Their Makers*, Vol. 1. Paducah, KY: American Quilter's Society, 1991. Martha Skelton is featured on pages 162–163.

———. *Award-Winning Quilts and Their Makers*, Vol. 2. Paducah, KY: American Quilter's Society, 1992. Martha Skelton is featured on pages 20–21.

Freeman, Roland. *A Communion of the Spirits: African-American Quilters, Preservers, and Their Stories.* Nashville, TN: Rutledge Hill Press, 1996.

Houck, Carter. *Treasury of American Quilts: Including Complete Patterns and Instructions for Making Your Own Quilts.* New York: Cyril I. Nelson, 1995.

Johnson, Mary Elizabeth. *A Garden of Quilts*. Birmingham, AL: Oxmoor House, 1984. Martha Skelton's quilts, "Bleeding Heart," "Centennial Lily," "Johnny Jump-Up," "Colorado Remembrance," "Clematis," and "Mississippi Springtime," appear on pages 37, 45, 59, 78–79, 80–81, 86–88, 95, 100–101, and 134–135.

———. *Mississippi Quilts*. Jackson: University Press of Mississippi, 2001. A write-up of Martha Skelton appears on pages 184–189.

———. *Star Quilts*. New York: Clarkson N. Potter, 1992. (Re-issued in paperback by Quilt Digest Press in 1997.)

Kiracofe, Roderick, and Mary Elizabeth Johnson. *The American Quilt: Cloth to Comfort, 1750–1950*. New York: Clarkson N. Potter, 1993. (Re-issued in paperback by Clarkson N. Potter in 2003.)

Levie, Eleanor. *American Quilt Making, 1970–2000*. Paducah, KY: American Quilter's Society, 2004. Martha Skelton's work appears on pages 100–101.

Quilt Art '89. *Engagement Calendar*. Paducah, KY: American Quilter's Society, 1988. Martha Skelton's "Flower Reel" is the featured quilt for May.

Quilt Art '97. *Engagement Calendar*. Paducah, KY: American Quilter's Society, 1995. Martha Skelton's "Moon and Stars," is the featured quilt for January.

Salazar, Marie. *The Quilt: Beauty in Fabric and Thread*. New York: Friedman/Fairfax, 1997. Martha Skelton's quilts "Sunburst" and "Four-Patch" appear on pages 37 and 24.

Shaw, Robert. *Quilts, a Living Tradition*. New York: Hugh Lauter Levin Associates, 1995. Martha Skelton's work appears on pages 105, 128, and 129. The featured quilt is "Fishermen Three: Wynken, Blynken, and Nod."

Waldvogel, Merikay. *Soft Covers for Hard Times: Quiltmaking and the Great Depression*. Nashville, TN: Rutledge Hill Press, 1990.

Waldvogel, Merikay, and Barbara Brackman. *Patchwork Souvenirs of the 1933 World's Fair: The Sears National Contest and Chicago's Century of Progress Exposition*. Nashville, TN: Rutledge Hill Press, 1993.

Magazines

American Quilter 3, no. 3 (fall 1987); 4, no. 2 (summer 1990); 11, no. 4 (winter 1995); 20, no. 1 (spring 2004). Published by the American Quilter's Society, Paducah, KY.

Country Living, September 1991. Published by the Good Housekeeping Corporation, New York, NY.

Lady's Circle Patchwork Magazine, various issues, including July 1985 and July 1989.

Lady's Circle Patchwork Magazine Editor's Choice 2 (1990).

Traditional Quilter, March 1995, Issue 37, p.47.